Saving *our* Adolescents

Supporting today's adolescents through the bumpy ride to adulthood

Best wishes

Maggie Dent

Maggie Dent
quietly improving lives

Publisher: Pennington Publications

P.O. Box 312 Murwillumbah, NSW 2484

Website: www.maggiedent.com

First Published 2010

Second Reprint 2011

Title: Saving Our Adolescence: Supporting today's adolescents through the bumpy ride to adulthood

Author: Dent, Maggie

Date of Publication: March 2010

ISBN: 978-0-9758456-5-3

Layout and Design: Katharine Middleton

Dedication

This book is dedicated to those parents, families and friends who have lost an adolescent through accident, illness, suicide or as a result of crime.

This is especially dedicated to my dear friend and graphic designer, Katharine Middleton who lost her very best friend in a tragic accident before they had a chance to realise their shared dreams; however, not before they became the absolute best of friends.

Contents

Preface

This book is for parents, teachers and those who work with adolescents. My aim is to bring a deeper compassion, understanding and awareness of that very bumpy ride from childhood to adulthood called adolescence. This book is the culmination of over 30 years of studying, working and living with adolescents. A sense of urgency drives my work for many reasons.

Never have a generation of young people been more at risk than today. More than ever it seems they have less supports to help them navigate the rough waters of adolescence. Our modern world has created many additional risk factors and potential dangers for children. This has impacted on today's adolescents who, I believe, are less able and less equipped to manage the unique pressures and challenges of the new millennium.

Education is paramount. With more knowledge and awareness adults can better support adolescents in the bumpy ride to adulthood without our youth being scarred or killed. My wish is that young people will come to know the true value of 'lighthouses', or 'adult allies' who can offer the respectful, empowering support they need to grow towards autonomy and awareness.

Every adolescent is unique and every journey into adulthood is different; each is filled with experiences that challenge and shape them. The environment, including physical and emotional environments, is a huge determinant to the future health and well-being of adolescents.

The metaphor of a journey is very helpful when exploring adolescence and it's also an excellent metaphor when exploring life. I have been a huge admirer of Joseph Campbell's work over the years and his concept of a hero's journey. The metaphor of the bumpy ride down the road from childhood to adulthood allows for the wide variance in the journey that many adolescents experience. The parents who walk beside their children as they head towards adulthood can also benefit from the use of this metaphor. There is no one simple interpretation of what happens, what may be expected to happen or when things will happen. We need to avoid generalising, especially when in the company of adolescents. There is no magic pill that makes it easy!

It really is an unpredictable ride for every individual through this time of enormous change. Even children who have loving, caring parents can get lost on the bumpy road to adulthood. There are no guarantees and often, quite ironically, adversity can be a positive thing—when seen retrospectively. Every child is unique with different stories, gifts, talents and challenges. The same goes for parents. Many parents secretly dread the teenage years well before they arrive, and that's sometimes because they remember their own! I want to reassure you that adolescents can flourish as adults even if they struggle at times during their adolescent years.

Research shows that adolescence is a time of confusion, massive change, uncertainty and serious risk. It is also a time of enormous potential in the development of new skills, knowledge and abilities.

Many young people who seem attractive, intelligent and confident on the outside are torn apart on the inside by insecurity, anxiety and self-doubt.

Bainbridge, D., *Teenagers: A natural history*, (2009).

The aim of this book is to inform parents, teachers and carers about some of the latest knowledge around adolescent development. This may help parents to better understand some of those moments of angst and know how to support their children on the bumpy journey towards adulthood. Much like it was for Dorothy in the *Wizard of Oz*, it is a journey of self-discovery and growth that shapes an individual faster and more deeply than any other time in a person's life. Everyone wants their children to become a competent, happy and well-adjusted adult who is resilient to whatever life may bring.

From the day we arrive on the planet
And blinking, step into the sun
There's more to be seen than can ever be seen
More to do than can ever be done
Some of us fall by the wayside
And some of us soar to the stars
And some of us sail through our troubles
And some have to live with the scars

The Circle of Life, The Lion King

In over three decades of working with adolescents I have met some amazing young people who, despite enormous challenge and adversity, have not only survived their rocky ride to adulthood, but they have flourished and realised their enormous potential. So often they share what helped and so often it was something quite small from someone who cared about them, like a word of encouragement, a hug, a safe bed for a couple of weeks.

As a high school teacher I discovered that optimism, kindness and genuine caring were the discipline tools that worked best in my classroom. Then, as a parent of four active, individual sons I found that the same principles worked best in the home. Children and teenagers grow according to how much or how little love and nurturing they receive from the significant carers in their lives.

Dysfunctional families do a lot of damage to the hearts and souls of our kids, especially when emotional, physical and sexual abuse occurs. Every family is dysfunctional to a degree because we do not live in a perfect world. However, there is an enormous potential for reparation and healing during adolescence that we could take more advantage of as the potential for rapid change is only present during for a few years during adolescence.

My lads (now men) inform me often of how I 'mucked up', how they wanted to run away and how unfair I was at times—since they have finally grown a pre-frontal lobe they can do this with great mirth at my expense! They also shock me with their insights into why I did some things, like keep them broke and make them save to replace a broken surfboard instead of just buying a new one whenever they lost or broke one. This is a clear sign the adult brain has finally replaced the hormone-driven, confused, forgetful, often narcissistic and disorganised adolescent brain. So, if you are a despairing parent who thinks you have failed, hang in there, you may be surprised in the years to come. I continue to be surprised!

Finally, as a therapist I have worked with the cutters, the stabbers, the runaways, those failing school, those who have lost a loved one and those who have attempted suicide. I have also attended and conducted too many funerals for adolescents who found it all too hard, or made a poor decision that cost them their lives. With more support and empathy for adolescents more lives will be saved and our world will be a better place. I agree with David Bainbridge in his book, *Teenagers: A natural history* (2009):

> *Adolescence is the zenith of human achievement, even if the changes we undergo at puberty do not always seem so positive at the time.*

We need to review the ways we parent and teach today's adolescents because the context in which they live is massively different to how things were when we were young. Massive social, technological and global change means the journey to adulthood has more roadblocks, potholes, detours and driving hazards than before.

Much of the change that happens to adolescents is something they did not ask for, and often they don't even know it is happening. They easily notice physical changes in things that drop, get hairy or stick out, but it's the invisible changes that frequently derail adolescents. This book explores much of that and how we can walk beside our developing adolescents—not in front leading, not behind pushing and certainly not carrying. Walking beside them allows them to grow in autonomy while they seek an identity that fits them well. Adolescents can find their own unique voice and place where they belong with the right supports. The underlying theme of this book is:

> *We adults must support and then allow young people to become who they really are, living with the highest expression of that authenticity, somehow or other making our world a better place. We need to focus on the gifts and strengths that can come with this stage of life rather than live with dread, anxiety and negativity. And we need to step forward and be there for them, quietly guiding and caring. And we need to be there now and not waste a minute more.*

Acknowledgements

To my amazing team of talented people: Liz my exceptional PA, Katharine my graphic maestro, Carmen my publicist and proofer for this book, and Tiffany my editor—you are all invaluable in my life. Thank you all so much for everything you have done to help in the birthing of this book. I love and respect you all.

I also wish to acknowledge every adolescent who has shared their wounds and their joys with me over the last 30 years. Thank you. To those who have given me the honour of allowing me to be a 'lighthouse' for a short or long time, I thank you sincerely—you know who you are!

To Mr Rob Daniel my Year 9 Social Studies teacher who saw beyond my 'bitch' mask and showed he cared, and who showed me how to be an exceptional teacher. You changed my life and I am deeply grateful. To Peter de Cort and the team at the Australian Book Group thank you for your chats and continued support and encouragement.

And yet again, I thank Steve, my husband and product manager, driver, cook and Mr Fix-it. Also, to my four fabulous sons, Michael, Ben, Alex and James thank you for your continued support and unconditional love. And thanks to my four-legged daughter, Jess (my fox terrier) who was beside me resting her long nose on my foot as I wrote this book.

I couldn't have done this without you. I am so blessed and grateful to have so many beautiful people deeply connected to me as I journey through this life.

Introduction

As a young child I felt unloved and not very special. I felt lost in a large family and became very noisy and demanding in order to be noticed. I could not sit still and was always asking 'Why?' which drove my mum to distraction. If I had not had 4,000 acres of backyard and 10,000 sheep to annoy, as well as my siblings, I probably would have been diagnosed with ADHD and sedated.

I was curious and enquiring and still am today. My low sense of self created a desperate need for attention and I was happy as long as someone noticed me. I was often naughty both at home and at school, and I remember many trips to our Deputy Principal while in primary school. And if that wasn't enough, I would sleepwalk at night. My Dad found me in strange places both inside and outside the house. My sister Sue would often be woken by the sound of me climbing out the window to go sleepwalking (usually to the orchard or the shearing shed).

Another way I gained attention was through illness and accidents. I had severe tonsillitis often as a child and ended up in hospital occasionally, suffering huge injections of penicillin into my (then) little bum. Most injuries though were the usual cuts and bruises that farm kids seem to acquire, usually involving daredevil antics with our bikes or our 'wars' in the bush.

Of course, when I was a child I wasn't aware I had a low self-esteem. I also wasn't aware that the behaviours I just mentioned are very typical of children who feel unloved and 'not special'. However, I was aware of feeling that I was the only one in the family, possibly the world, who felt this way.

I covered my poor sense of self as I moved into high school, although I was far better at pretending by this stage. I was a capable student and a competent basketball and netball player, so there were times when I felt OK about what I could do. Yet, I still hated myself. I was head girl at junior high and achieved an excellent examination result—hardly the outward signs of someone with low self-esteem. I graduated to a senior high school and continued to be an excellent student, becoming a prefect and successfully completing my Leaving Examinations (now called Tertiary Admittance Examinations in Western Australia).

On the outside everything looked fine, but on the inside I was still deeply lonely and very negative towards myself. I can remember feeling really ugly and unhappy that genetics had presented me with a very generous bum. I had such a distorted view of my bum and its ability to ruin my life on so many levels that I seldom went to social events as an adolescent. I kept people at a distance—even friends. I avoided places where alcohol would be present because of my negative childhood experiences. I chose not drink or smoke. To avoid the social scene I spent a lot of time on my own, but little did I realise how unhealthy that is for a teenager.

I moved on to university and continued my studies. The shift from the country caused me many problems. I was well out of my normal comfort zone and hated the city. This was compounded by my feelings of insecurity and fears of failing at university. In my first months in the city several events happened that challenged me. First, I was mugged on my way home from uni one afternoon and my bike and belongings were stolen. Then, someone broke into my room. Later, I was propositioned by a lesbian and I also witnessed students 'shooting up' at a social gathering. All of these things were intimidating for a kid from the bush and I didn't ever realise that I was actually struggling to maintain my 'I'm OK' mask.

I had experienced back problems for a few years and a doctor had prescribed Valium to help me manage the pain. Unfortunately, by the time I got to uni I couldn't sleep without two Valium at night. With my insecurity and heightened sense of fear while living in Perth and being at uni, it wasn't long before I needed three Valium to sleep. I felt so alone and disconnected, like I was skidding down a slope. I used the legal drug to self-medicate my emotional state and help me cope with living my quietly desperate life!

People who knew me at this time would probably be amazed I felt like this because I had plenty of friends and was never short of boyfriends. Indeed I was in a relationship with a teacher who was about nine years older than me! I was busy playing lots of basketball and working part-time. But all the while on the inside I was filled with self-loathing and self-hatred.

Then, at the tender age of 17, for the first time in my life I failed an essay. Suddenly I felt it was all too hard. My best mask had been my 'academically superior' one and it had cracked. I felt overwhelmed with the difficulty of life, the loneliness, struggle and despair of living the rest of my life as a complete failure.

I clearly remember sitting alone in my room and choosing that dying would have to be better than how I was feeling. I was filled with fear as I contemplated a long life with just more sadness, loneliness and disappointments. I took the bottle of Valium and poured every tablet into my hand, and without a thought for anyone who loved or cared about me, I shoved a handful into my mouth, desperately seeking relief from feeling such a failure. My action had been such a spontaneous one that I didn't have anything to wash the pills down with. Fortunately, one of the tablets crushed on my back tooth and it tasted so disgusting I vomited the rest out on the floor. I remember lying on the floor in a foetal position, sobbing and shaking in fear. I was completely alone.

No one came, but somewhere inside me, a part of my 'self' melted enough for another 'self', a wise and gentle part of me, to break through. I realised I wasn't meant to die. I knew I had to help myself and that I hadn't finished my purpose in life—it was too early for me to leave. I clearly remember lying on the floor with vomit, snot and tears, and a ray of sunshine came in through the window and gently warmed my sad, frightened body. I no longer felt alone.

It took me many years to really overcome my low sense of self, to really love and accept myself. I have had many wonderful teachers, mainly students and adolescents, who have shared their stories—many that were so much worse than mine. I have been blessed to have enjoyed teaching and being around young people in the formative years of adolescence. I am a lighthouse for many young people as I walk beside them on their bumpy road to adulthood. Not rescuing them, just walking beside them and shining some light on their sometimes dark journey and giving them hope. These were the things missing from my journey and they nearly had fatal consequences.

As I was working on this book I received an email from a student who was in a group of 240 14-year-olds I spoke with:

You recently spoke to my school and I want to thank you.

You have worked with adolescents. What can I do to feel less depressed or not depressed at all? I cry alot, i barely eat and i have lost my love of sport. It doesnt seem worth the time anymore. I hate how unhappy i am, constantly feeling no self worth.

I feel that i dont have friends and i am constantly bullied which doesnt help my situation.

PLEASE HELP ME !!!

Many adolescents who live in loving homes are struggling invisibly. They see themselves harshly when they compare themselves to today's media images of the 'It' people. And there is just so much going on that they live with heightened levels of stress that impacts all areas of their life. I now know that sometimes our 'unique wounding' when we're young holds clues about what we can do to make the world a better place. I found my clues while still an adolescent. My journey has been blessed since the day I almost left this world.

In my research I have come to understand why I struggled so much and why many of today's adolescents feel the same. I hope that I can give them hope that one day the fog does lift and they find they have value and are worthwhile. Simply reassuring them that everyone matters—those with big bums, noses, small boobs, and especially those with special needs—is a small thing, however it certainly impacts today's adolescents. Today's adolescents need more genuine kindness, compassion, connectedness and concern from significant adults in their families or communities.

My intention with this book is to help parents and teachers better understand what is going on in the minds, bodies, hearts and souls of adolescents so we will be better able to guide and support them so their journey into adulthood will be smoother.

Maggie

Chapter 1

What *is a* 'lighthouse'
and why do adolescents
need them?

Millions [of children] are growing up under conditions that do not meet their enduring needs for optimal development. They are not receiving the careful, nurturing guidance they need—and say they want—from parents and other adults.

The Carnegie Report, 1995.

In traditional kinship communities the responsibility of adults to prepare adolescents for adulthood is taken very seriously. Boys are mentored or guided by men, and girls are prepared by women. The tasks and life skills that young people need in order to be capable adults are taught until an adolescent has mastered the required skill and maturity level required by the tribe. Without these skills they're not initiated into adulthood. Initiations often take place through ceremony, after which adolescents are formally recognised as adults. This rite of passage sometimes requires physical challenge and pain, ensuring this step is not taken lightly.

In our modern world we have no formal rite of passage to acknowledge that an adolescent is now an adult, and many of our young people have been abandoned from the guidance required to grow into responsible adults. The development of the modern world has dissolved many traditional family and community structures that provided teaching and guidance for adolescents on their bumpy road to adulthood. This weakening of social capital has come at a high price with increasing numbers of depressed, unemployed and homeless adolescents, and a higher death rate from suicide and accidents. Adolescents need adults to help them build their resilience and competence at a time when they're pulling away from their primary guiding source: their parents.

A major contributor to the worsening mental health of Zeds (Generation Zed encompasses young people aged 17 and under) is less support from families, with fewer functioning adults around and a lessened sense of community.

Professor Ian Hickie, Executive Director, Brain and Mind Institute, University of Sydney.

This is not just within communities, it is also within families and schools—the two other main support structures for adolescents. Today's world functions at an unhealthy speed using technology that reduces human interaction. The vital window of adolescence is where the evolving child adapts to become more mature and adult-like. But, it seems the adult world has stepped back and left our adolescents without the guidance and support they need to grow into healthy citizens. You cannot learn about managing human relationships or develop life skills by watching *Home and Away*—or using Google™ to search for answers!

Never have so many people lived so far from extended family, or outside traditional communities where adults served as collective parents for all a neighbourhood's young people. These developments have reduced our social capital; the relationships that bind people together and create a sense of community. We must find ways to deal with our profound loss of social connectedness.

Father Chris Riley, Youth off the Streets.

Father Chris Riley works daily with adolescents and young adults who are lost. They are not bad, damaged or useless—they are lost. Their bumpy ride to adulthood was a journey without enough loving support and they have been scarred by their choices. Father Riley was asked, 'How can you help these no-hopers?' He replied, 'It's quite easy to help these young people. They all improve with compassion, kindness, food and a safe place to live.'

This is exactly what kinship communities offered when adolescents stepped away from their parents in their effort to claim independence and autonomy. There were other adults to keep an eye out, guide and support them. These other supports can be extended family, it can also be people who care enough to be there. I call them 'lighthouses'.

A lighthouse represents something that is strong, reliable and immovable, and shines a light showing safe passage. It does not tell you to do something, it simply shows you a safer way to go. A lighthouse says, if you want to do something really risky and smash on the rocks below where I stand, then be my guest, but

I won't rescue you. I will keep the light shining so that next time you remember how painful your last choice was and you might choose to follow the safer way where my light shines.

Key attributes of a lighthouse

- Solid and reliable.
- Offers protection.
- Well informed about adolescent development.
- Friendly.
- Shines a light in the darkness.
- Models healthy adulthood.
- Offers silent guidance.
- Gives hope.
- Committed to the greater good of all, not just the pursuit of self.

Lighthouses have to be able to develop a relationship that allows them to sow seeds of potential and shines a light on the invisible sign that hangs around every adolescents' neck:

Many adolescents feel invisible, unheard or that they just don't matter. It took me a while to realise this when I was teaching. It started to dawn on me when I noticed that some mornings as I headed from the staff car park to the English office, a student or two would be leaning on the brick wall that was on my route. These were students I had approached separately the previous day at lunch. They were not in any of my classes, but I had noticed how lonely they looked eating lunch by themselves. Recognising this reaction, I searched for the students who sat alone, had obvious physical challenges or appeared to be avoiding their mainstream peer groups. I learned their names and made sure I smiled when I saw them, and I even acknowledged them in the street. It didn't take long before the row of students who greeted me every morning grew to more than a dozen—some days up to 20. The simple act of being noticed made these students feel better. It may not have seemed like a big thing in the scheme of the curriculum, but it was huge for the students. This is an example of how we can all pause a little in our busy lives and shine that light.

Every adolescent needs a lighthouse to help them navigate the uncertain waters of adolescence.

Lighting the flame of potential, while being realistic about adolescent development, is extremely important. Young people are hard on themselves and adept at self-criticism and self-sabotage, and often get stuck in patterns of limitation. Lighthouses can help them see beyond these limitations. Lighthouses do not rescue, advise or make judgements on an adolescent's behaviour, instead they act as a mirror so the young person can see the world from a different perspective.

The benefits of a lighthouse

Many adolescents learn how to be trustworthy from the lighthouses in their life. These adults are helpful in the role they play by using good communication, helping to build life skills and having the courage to connect deeply. Lighthouses shed light on the pathway to adulthood and beyond. They are respectful, reliable, responsive and reciprocal. They provide an open door and retreat, no matter when, what or why.

During times of conflict lighthouses shine a light of reason, encouragement and acceptance. Adolescents often have poor skills around life management, planning for the future and coping with their chaotic emotional worlds. Lighthouses are like a personal life coach.

In my staff seminar I challenge teaching staff to take on a special 'project' every year. I encourage them to aim to connect with and shine a light on a student who has a bad reputation, or is obviously struggling on the bumpy road to adulthood. Immediately I see the looks on their faces as they recall a student whom they have helped in the past—and they know how good that connection made them feel. In the parent seminar I challenge parents to do the same for a niece or a nephew, a neighbour or any adolescent with whom they connect. Step forward and shine that light. You will be staggered by the potential it can activate in an adolescent who thinks no one cares.

> *People who have had a strong connection with a strong positive role model during adolescence are much more resilient throughout their life.*
>
> Bahr, N. and Pendergast, D., *The Millennial Adolescent*, (2007).

Lighthouses can be people who play a large role in an adolescent's life like a coach, teacher, aunty or family friend. Sometimes they appear only for a short time, but in that time manage to sows seeds of potential, give ideas or show through their actions and words something new and helpful.

A farmer approached me after a seminar one night and thanked me for helping him realise something important. He told me that many years ago a neighbouring father died suddenly, leaving behind a wife and three children—two girls and a 10-year-old boy. At times he would take the boy on long truck trips to Perth where they listened to whatever sport was happening—cricket or football. They would eat junk food and chocolate, drink soft drink, and fart and burp like young boys. The farmer would also take him to local sporting events, and sometimes just take him for a ride on the quad bikes. He never mentioned the boy's Dad or asked how he was coping, and for years had felt he had not done enough. When the boy left the farm and went to university he would still call occasionally and visit. He would throw a swag on the floor, stay a few days and ride the quad bikes or drive the trucks. Then he would leave again. The farmer finally realised he had been a lighthouse in this boy's life, and the fact the young man came 'home' occasionally just to spend time with someone who had cared meant the world to him. How important was that relationship in that boy's life? I'd say life saving! It's often not the big stuff, but the small stuff that can make a difference.

Human connectedness is a profound influence in all our lives and it's even more important during the years of adolescent change. Our individualistic material world has made it very difficult for adolescents to find their true selves because they have so many distractions overloading their mind. Having stable, charismatic adult mentors can make the difference between thriving and flourishing, or struggling and failing.

The influence of a potential role model is increased when, in the eyes of the young person, they fulfil the following criteria:

- Attractiveness—physical and emotional.
- Social power—reward and punishment.
- Status—perceived importance of the role model.
- Competence—specifically in the areas of shared interest.
- Nurturance—perceived concern for the observer.
- Interaction level—degree of contact.
- Similarity—characteristics in common or expected due to similar life experiences or genetic heritage.

Bahr, N et al. *The Millennial Adolescent* (2007)

The Lighthouse Model

Invisible sign: "Make me feel I matter..."

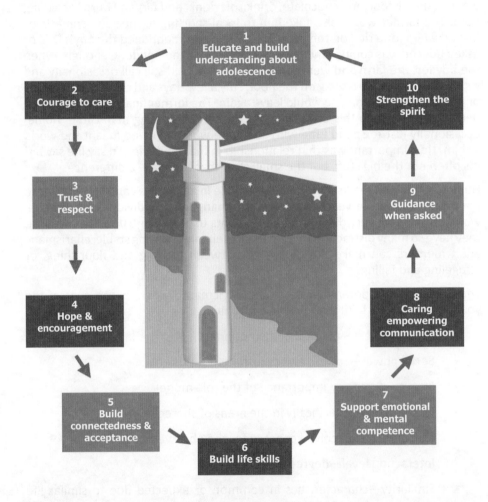

Our highest endeavour must be to develop individuals who are able out of their own initiative to impart purpose and direction to their lives.

Rudolph Steiner

10 supports lighthouses need to be able to offer adolescents

1. HAVE KNOWLEDGE AND UNDERSTANDING OF ADOLESCENCE

It is important to be able to share with adolescents some of the possible reasons for their moments of angst, confusion and emotional turmoil. Reassuring them that their brain is 'under construction' is important information. It is important to tell them that their past is just a story and it doesn't have to be the story for the rest of their life. Be careful not to stay too attached to sharing your story, because, that too, is over.

2. HAVE THE COURAGE TO CARE

Sometimes standing beside a troubled adolescent can be hard work—it may test you, and what you believe. Being able to care when they are walking on the dark side of life is challenging, and yet often the only reason they find their way back into the light.

3. BE TRUSTWORTHY AND RESPECTFUL

We must never lie, deceive or pretend to adolescents. It can be a tough call for any adult! Adolescents will break trust—sometimes more than once—and until they understand the value of it, they will seek to find it and know deep inside themselves that it's worth having.

A 13-year-old boy was transferred into my class once because his relationship with his teacher had become destructive. I was warned about how terrible he was. On his second day in my class I asked him to take a plastic bag of excursion money to the front office. He looked at me a bit strange as he left the room. When the bell went for recess, he stayed behind and shuffled to my desk and asked, 'Hey Miss, how come you asked me to take that money to the office?' I replied that I thought he had the face of a person whom I could trust. He mused for a moment and murmured, 'Trust. Is that what trust means? Hey, it feels good doesn't it?' And with that he left the room. I never had any problems with that student and he began looking for other ways to be valued and trusted. This is an example of realising that until we can embody values and virtues, we really are just talking words.

4. GIVE HOPE AND ENCOURAGEMENT

These are much more powerful tools than giving endless praise. It is very helpful if lighthouses and parents help adolescents imagine a preferred way of being or doing, because they often get stuck in negative patterns of self-fulfilling prophecies. If we keep telling ourselves that we are dumb and useless, or ugly and no one likes us, we are certainly creating a reality that supports that.

Directing adolescents, both consciously and unconsciously, towards a more positive solution-focused way of seeing themselves can have a dramatic impact on them. The simple act of telling them that in their 20s their brain will function so much better and the fogginess will lift, gives them hope by knowing the path ahead will be easier. Also, educating them that failure and setbacks are a normal part of life and that once something is learned from the experience we can move on.

5. BUILD CONNECTEDNESS THROUGH GENUINE ACCEPTANCE

This requirement is essential in being a lighthouse. It is especially important when we are working with adolescents from other cultures, those with special needs, those who have committed a crime, the homeless or those who are experiencing problems with addictive patterns of behaviour. Being non-judgemental and accepting helps adolescents feel safe. When we withhold love and affection because they are not meeting our expectations of how we think they should be, we invalidate them on a deep level. When we can accept them in their darkness they often feel safer because they may be hating themselves. If we still like them at their worst, then they often start liking themselves and the pattern of negative thought can be broken.

6. ENCOURAGE MASTERY AND TEACH LIFE SKILLS

Every adult on our planet should, in some way, mentor or guide adolescents to develop life skills and competencies that teach them to manage independently. The list of recommended life skills I believe adolescents need before they leave home is included in the chapter for parents.

7. HELP ADOLESCENTS MANAGE BIG, UGLY EMOTIONAL STATES

Suicide becomes the number one killer of under 35s

Dr John Irvine, 3 November 2009 (ABC blog)

There will be times when lighthouses have to help soothe and calm down angry, frightened adolescents because they cannot do it themselves. If we help them understand where some of their emotional intensity is coming from, it can help them develop emotional maturity and life-long coping skills. Most of all they need human connectedness and to know that people care. Dr John Irvine wrote in an article in 2009, that there were clear risk factors that were involved in youth suicide. These factors included:

- a loss of religion in family life
- divorce
- lack of family or community ties
- poor work or health prospects.

The Salvos Youth line found something similar, reporting that the kids just felt lonely, loveless and lost.

Having more support, especially lighthouses, could easily help more adolescents finish their bumpy ride to adulthood. Helping an adolescent overcome feeling 'lonely, loveless and lost' must be our number one priority at all levels in our modern world.

Supporting adolescents through their emotional upheavals can prevent further adversity. Being an emotional coach is part of a lighthouse's invisible role and can help a young person navigate the myriad of emotional challenges they face. Loving, caring relationships have a huge impact on the emotional stability of adolescents at home, school, sport and social activities. A sense of belonging feeds positive brain chemicals that help keep adolescents feeling optimistic and emotionally stable. Activities within the home or school that build inclusivity will support calmer, more compassionate and happier environments for young people. This is why connectedness is a vital protective factor in resilience regardless of a person's age.

When connectedness is combined with genuine compassion, concern, kindness, acceptance and understanding there is a much higher possibility of an individual healing from adolescent patterns of aggressive or angry behaviour. Lighthouses help this healing process for young people.

The adolescent journey is a passage from childhood to adulthood which every individual travels. The emotional unpredictability and uncertainty that happens due to brain immaturity is a normal part of the journey. Anything that can help adolescents diffuse or reduce their big, ugly emotional states will help prevent them getting into serious problems—such as alcohol or drug abuse, aggressive behaviour, self-harm and patterns of self-destructive choices. The pre-frontal lobe supporting this emotional maturity does not develop until over 20 years of age in the majority of adolescents. Keep this in mind and act accordingly.

8. PRACTICE CARING, EMPOWERING COMMUNICATION

Being able to communicate in a caring way that builds their sense of personal empowerment is a key aspect of lighthouses. *Never shame, blame, criticise, belittle or crush adolescents.* Lighthouses have a gift of communicating that builds connectedness and trust. There is more information on how to communicate in this way in the chapter for parents.

9. GIVE GUIDANCE WHEN ASKED

Lighthouses may want to give advice or tell adolescents what they should be doing, but they don't. They reassure, give seeds of potential solutions through telling stories and ask great questions that make an adolescent think. Always ask, 'Are you open to having me give you some feedback?' If they say no, respect that and shut up. These techniques will be covered in the chapter for parents.

10. STRENGTHEN THE SPIRIT—INCLUDING LAUGHTER AND LIGHTNESS

We can build an adolescent's connection to their inner world and their inner compass, as well as a deep connectedness beyond their physical self, by strengthening the spirit.

> *Each of us has a wise part within, an intuitive part that knows what is best for us. Contacting, listening to, and trusting that inner authority are important skills. They are invaluable when life presents us with problems whose answers are not found in the back of the book.*
>
> The Parent Talk System, Chick Moorman, (2003).

A 15-year-old once shared a story about an intriguing sense of 'knowing', in one of my classes. While she was at home in her room her father was working on his tractor down in the paddock. She became aware of feeling uncomfortable and uneasy. When she went out into the garden her unease became stronger. She clearly remembers the message, 'Something's happened to Dad', and headed off down the paddock as quickly as she could. She soon discovered that her Dad was injured and ran back home to arrange help. She returned to her Dad's side and waited until help arrived. Uncanny, yet true. From that point on in her life she believed that she had a guardian who kept watch over her (*Nurturing Kids' Hearts and Souls*, Maggie Dent).

In *The Soul of Education: Helping Students Find Connection, Compassion, and Character at School (2000)*, Rachael Kessler wrote:

> *When schools systematically exclude heart and soul, students in growing numbers become depressed, attempt suicide, or succumb to eating disorders and substance abuse.*

In his book, *Care of the Soul: A Guide for Cultivating Depth and Sacredness in Everyday Life (1992)*, Thomas Moore describes the symptoms of loss of soul as:

- emptiness
- meaninglessness
- vague depression
- disillusionment about marriage, family and relationship and life in general
- a loss of values
- yearning for personal fulfillment
- a hunger for spirituality.

This sounds very familiar to those who work with adolescents. The millennial adolescent struggles with a disconnection from this indefinable source of sustenance. Consumer pressures, messages that promote image over character and the general velocity of life cause many adolescents to become disillusioned and lost. The human spirit gets crushed from such a chaotic and troubled individualistic world.

There are seven gateways that allow young people to emerge into adulthood whole and healthy. Consider which of these gateways the adult world is offering today's adolescents.

Seven gateways to the soul of education

1. The yearning for deep connection.

2. The longing for silence and solitude.

3. The search for meaning and purpose.

4. The hunger for joy and delight.

5. The creative drive.

6. The urge for transcendence.

7. The need for initiation.

Kessler, R., *The Soul of Education: Helping Students Find Connection, Compassion, and Character at School, (2000).*

My concern is that many adolescents are feeling profoundly lost as these gateways vanish from our world. There is a serious hunger for the substance of each gateway, but without the adult world providing these opportunities with consistency, adolescents are seeking it for themselves. Many seek ritual or rites of passage, and when that is unavailable will take to body piercings, tattoos and other forms of markings. The profound sense of disconnection that these adolescents feel drives many of their poor choices. Our modern young people are eager to stop the numbness, confusion and loneliness.

Understanding deep connection

According to co-founder of the Rite Journey, Andrew Lines, a study[1] of 12,000 adolescents from 80 high schools across the United States found that 'young people who have a feeling of connectedness with parents, family and school have lower levels of smoking, drinking, other drug use, suicidal thinking, risky sexual behaviour and exposure to violence' (www.theritejourney.com.au).

---

1   *Study conducted by Doctor Michael Resnick from the Adolescent Health Program at the University of Minnesota.

Rachel Kessler validates the role of family, friends, lighthouses and community connections. She highlights the value of connectedness to the natural world and beyond by identifying the following types of deep connection people can have.

- Deep connection to self—nourishment of the human soul occurs when we really know ourselves, express our true self, and feel connected to the essence of who we are.

- Deep connection to another—authentic intimacy is a deeply caring, mutually respectful relationship with one other person. It can be a deep connection for anyone.

- Deep connection to community—a teenager's need to belong is seen by some as a form of spiritual hunger. For others, it is seen as a key to building authentic resilience. Close ongoing meaningful groups are important for developing deep connections to others.

- Deep connection to lineage—discovering a strong sense of family history can build a connectedness and a sense of belonging.

- Deep connection to nature—for some, the beauty and majesty of nature brings awe and wonder that satisfies and feeds the spirit.

- Deep connection to a power greater than themselves—this can be religion, other sources of spiritual sustenance and an awareness of the mysteries of life that simply cannot be explained.

Kessler, R., *The Soul of Education: Helping Students Find Connection*, (2000).

Spiritual intelligence

Life's true heroes. They carry a supportive and positive attitude that endures, especially in times of crisis. They do not drop away when the going gets tough or when there is a period of failure and struggle. They remain constant, seeing the best, supporting and accepting even when things are at their worst. They are good leaders, companions and friends.

Bloom, W., The Endorphin Effect, (2001).

Strengthening the spirit is an important role of lighthouses. Adolescents who have strong spirits have a protective mechanism that is difficult to measure, yet very clear when absent. Spiritual intelligence that parents and lighthouses can develop with children and adolescents includes:

- wonder
- respect and reverence

- awe
- relational spirituality
- lightness and laughter
- contemplation
- calmness, stillness and quiet
- tenderness and gratitude
- simplicity
- listening with the heart.

> *This is the first generation brought up on conspicuous consumerism. And they have no perceived guide to help them manage the new freedoms, cultural changes and technologies that have led to incredible individualism.*
>
> Professor S. Silburn, The West Australian, p. 8, 25 May 2005.

Building trust and being trustworthy

The role trust plays in an adolescent's development is enormous. When their trust is broken and they feel betrayed by the few people they have chosen to be trustworthy, adolescents are deeply wounded. Lighthouses must be completely trustworthy. The only time adults can break this confidence is when the adolescent expresses suicidal ideation, at which point duty of care must override confidentiality and a professional must be informed immediately.

> *Trust is a function of two things: character and competence. Character includes your integrity, your motive, your intent with people. Competence includes your capabilities, your skills, your results, your track record. And both are vital.*
>
> Covey, S. R., with Merrill R. R., The Speed of Trust, (2006).

If children have displayed a degree of trustworthiness while young, then a good starting point is to assume that, as adolescents, they can be trusted. Adolescents should be allowed to gradually assume responsibilities, both at school and home. Choose relatively safe things at first.

Adolescents cannot demonstrate responsibility if they are not given the opportunities to do so.

Be prepared for adolescents to make mistakes, bear the consequences, and trust them to learn as they go along.

Trust is important in adolescent-adult relationships because a high level of trust tends to bring out the best in adolescents. When they feel they have the trust of significant adults like parents and their lighthouses, adolescents are more likely to communicate openly and honestly, as well as to stick to rules and parental expectations. Research has shown that teenagers who feel they are trusted are less likely to engage in high-risk or delinquent behaviours.

As children grow up, it's natural that they gradually expect more freedom and independence. Adolescents, in particular, yearn for and require greater parental trust in their ability to make their own decisions. This is how they grow in autonomy. Fortunately, most parents adjust their parenting to accommodate their child's growing independence, quite often without even noticing.

Giving adolescents more freedom and loosening the reins is not easy for parents. The issue must be faced and a 'head-in-the-sand' approach is not the answer. Research shows that teenagers who are not given the chance to make decisions for themselves are more likely to rebel.

Good decisions involve rationally assessing the risks, benefits and alternative actions that are relevant to the case. While adolescents are beginning to think more like adults than children, they often still need help from their parents to make decisions that have serious or long-term consequences. This is because adolescents are:

- likely to be more impulsive
- lacking rational thinking strategies
- looking for novelty experiences
- less concerned about risk
- not thinking about the future
- more susceptible to peer pressure
- more concerned about physical appearance.

Developing trust with adolescents

- Share—share personal events and interests.
- Be available to listen—keep in touch via SMS, email and phone.
- Vulnerability—acknowledge that to err is human.
- Loyalty—stay committed to goals and visions.
- Accepting others—accept the unique qualities and behaviours of others.
- Involving others—ask others for input or decision making.
- Valuing—be willing to exchange ideas and ideals with others.
- Awareness—be sensitive to the needs of others.
- Communicating—give clear communications, both oral and written.
- Openness—be willing to explore new experiences.
- Honesty—be willing to share the truth.
- Shared positive vision—be willing to dream.
- Being accepting and non-judgemental—be aware that adolescents can be sensitive to criticism.
- Only give advice when asked—show respect for the young person's ability to make good decisions.

> *Trust is one of the most powerful forms of motivation and inspiration. People want to be trusted. They respond to trust. They thrive on trust. Whatever our situation, we need to get good at establishing, extending, and restoring trust – not as a manipulative technique, but as the most effective way of relating to and working with others, and the most effective way of getting results.*
>
> Covey, S. R. et al.

How a lighthouse can help adolescents

- Encourage adolescents to develop an awareness of their own feelings.
- Enable and encourage adolescents to become reflective regarding their own behaviour and the consequences of that behaviour.
- Enable adolescents to label feelings and know when they may or may not affect both work and relationships.
- Support adolescents to further develop personal insight.
- Develop adolescent's self-esteem and self-confidence.
- Enable adolescents to accept and use constructive, structured criticism and feedback.
- Encourage adolescents to develop their own self-control and self-management strategies.
- Encourage adolescents to develop empathy and authenticity.
- Enable adolescents to develop flexibility in order to cope more effectively with change, and new systems and ways of doing things.
- Help adolescents develop internal locus of control, i.e. encourage them to have a sense of control over their own actions.
- Encourage adolescents to develop self-motivation, resilience and a positive attitude.
- Encourage students to learn and make use of alternatives to physical or verbal aggression, and to express their feelings and views in a more positive and assertive way.
- Encourage parents and school staff to adopt a consistent approach to developing adolescents' emotional literacy, social skills and self-esteem.
- Further enable and encourage school staff to review current policy and practice in terms of managing the emotional, social and behavioural needs of students in their care.

There is no question that adolescents who feel respected, supported, understood and who have a place where they are heard, manage emotions much better than those who are not.

All adolescents will benefit from having committed, capable and compassionate lighthouses or charismatic adults who support their growth and development. These lighthouses need to guide, support and provide a safe harbour for young people while they discover their unique strengths, weaknesses and place in the world.

> *We're all here for a reason. I believe a bit of that reason is to throw little torches out to lead people through the dark.*
>
> Whoopi Goldberg, USA.

Lighthouses make a big difference even when they are not nearby. Here is a poem written to a friend of mine who is a lighthouse for many young adolescents. His name is Neville Dwyer and he works with a great team in the community of Griffith giving artistic opportunities for the local adolescents.

'Hey Neville, Just had to let you know.

I have broken up with an amazing girl, and on Saturday I was broken and in pieces. However, it was today that I said, 'Its a new day.'
And I was on a swing set at the park near my house, and, I'm not sure why, but I thought of you.

Turning Point.

It's kinda unusual, but thinking of the support you give me, made me appreciate. Appreciate everything. Opportunities, talents, friends and family, health, fitness, and everything.

And there and then this spilled from my mouth…

"In a world with no standards,
How can you know what's right,
and what's wrong?

In a system designed for you to fail,
How are you supposed
to succeed?

In a world that implements 'The Norm',
Is there a chance
For individuality?

In a mindset of 'being realistic',
Can you even dare
to dream?

Believe. In yourself. In dreams.
Take a risk.
Feel the rush.
And never be afraid to fall.

Because in falling,
You may just fly."

So Neville, thankyou.
For being there for me.
And for caring.'

Anonymous

My challenge to you is to step forward and be there as a guiding force of light in the lives of today's adolescents. The value to our world will be enormous and the shift in the self-centred, competitive paradigm that drives our world where value is driven by external measures will be weakened. We will value the quality of a person because of their character and on the quality of the deeds they do that serve others and make our world a better place.

I was lost
You reached up to heaven
And took down a star for me
A tiny one so perhaps
The angels wouldn't mind
It was such a small
And simple thing to you
But it was
All the light I needed
To find
My way back home

Source Unknown

The happiest and most fulfilled people I have ever met are those who have discovered how to be themselves, as honestly and authentically as possible. They have found a serious sense of meaning and purpose in their lives. They have found their own unique essence, as well as their own gifts and talents, and they are actively sharing that with the world. Their intention is to create something of value and worth for the greater good of the world we live in. These people choose to make a positive difference—and they do.

During my years of teaching I realised there was more being learned in my classroom than the English lesson I was giving. I had decided early in my career to make it easy for those who struggled with school, especially those who came to class without their files, paper or pencil cases because their home lives were difficult. Instead of beginning the class with negativity and a punitive focus, I created spare files, paper and a huge pencil case full of pens and pencils that students could use if they came to class unprepared. They didn't need to ask to borrow them, however most did.

This was such a small thing and I didn't think much about it after I stopped teaching. Then, one day I was stopped in the street by a tough looking biker covered in tattoos, rings and chains. He had a thick grey beard and wore a black leather jacket. He asked if I remembered him and I replied that he must have grown much bigger and hairier than when I taught him at school! He gave me his name and I was able to instantly recall a small, quiet, unhappy looking boy from a year eight English class 20 years earlier.

He had stopped me to thank me for the spare paper and biros that I had provided all those years ago. He explained that he had often slept in a park because of the alcohol and family violence in his home. My classroom was the only one he could attend where he wasn't punished or made fun of because he did not have his files and pens. 'You welcomed me just like every other student and for a time I felt my life was bearable. I learned what kindness was from you.' He went on to tell me that even though he looked tough and mean he always tried to be thoughtful to others and wanted me to know that he learned this from me.

> *When someone shines a light on that invisible sign of 'make me feel I matter that hangs around every adolescent's neck', we recognise the hidden goodness hiding within us just waiting to be found and shared.*

A key attribute of lighthouses is their ability to be caring communicators; someone who can be trusted and is committed to empowering an adolescent's ability to understand themselves, others and the world in which they live. They help build autonomy, personal responsibility and vital life skills through the art of caring and empowering communication. This aids in the lighthouse's ability to encourage reflective, flexible thinking to guide an adolescent's choices. By doing this, the lighthouse plays a key role in supporting the identity formation of the adolescent's 'emerging adult' into one that acknowledges their strengths and challenges. In turn, the adolescent realises the possible pathways of how their unique potential can make the world a better place.

A lighthouse has much more potential to be a coach than a parent because the adolescent is not stepping back as they biologically do with their parents. (Later in the book I discuss parents becoming more like coaches and the value that can have). Here are some coaching tips for lighthouses. These are about the questions we ask rather than any answers we give because we need to empower adolescents to find their own answers.

Remember, coaching:

- is a process that enables people to come up with solutions that suit them personally
- encourages individuals to work out the steps that suit their own circumstances
- promotes independent thinking and encourages people to take responsibility for finding their own solutions
- creates the climate for individuals to examine their own strengths and to use them to achieve their own goals
- avoids the pitfalls of advice
- engenders choice.

10 principles of coaching

1. Be non-judgemental.
2. Be non-critical.
3. Believe that people have their own answers to their own problems within them.
4. Respect a person's confidentiality.
5. Be positive and believe that there are always solutions to issues.
6. Pay attention to recognising and pointing out strengths, and building and maintaining self-esteem.
7. Challenge individuals to move beyond their comfort zone.
8. Break down big goals into manageable steps.
9. Believe that self-knowledge improves performance.
10. Hold a genuine willingness to learn from the people you coach.

Remember, the focus is always on putting things right, not what went wrong!

The power of questions: Seven question types for coaches

1. Future placing questions

These help to get people in touch with what they want to achieve and to motivate them. Examples include:

- What are you seeing, hearing or feeling now you are doing this new role?
- What is it like to be 'X' who already has this?
- Put yourself six months ahead. What decisions did you make along the way that got you to there?

2. Truth probers and dumb questions – often really obvious questions

These help people make insightful leaps forward in understanding themselves.

Examples of truth questions to help:

- What do you *really* want?
- What's actually stopping you?
- What's the truth here?
- What else is there?
- How will you look back on this?
- What gives you most anxiety here?
- What difference does this really make to you?
- Where are we?
- What's next?
- What's needed?
- Where do you want to go from here?
- What did you learn?
- What do you think?

3. Reframing questions

These are questions that encourage a different viewpoint.

- How else could we see this?
- How would this look from where your Mum sits?

4. Incisive questions

These stimulate creative thinking. The first part of the question suspends the limitation, while the second part encourages the search for solutions.

- What would you do if it didn't matter what others thought?
- What if there was a time in the past when you overcame a similar problem?

5. Permission and precision questions

This line of questioning needs trust and is not something to jump straight into. Build up to this level of trust.

- How would you feel about exploring this a bit deeper?
- Can you let me know when you are ready to look at this in more detail?

6. Commitment questions

These questions allow an adolescent to consider the present and near future and the pathways they might take.

- When will you know you have been successful?
- When will this start?
- What could get in the way of you completing this?

7. Distal questions

These questions extend beyond the coaching session and into the future.

- Imagine you are 25 years old. How would you like your life to look?
- Imagine you are 30....?

Young people require adults who can help them to find their own way in life.

- Teens do not want or need adults who tell them exactly how, what, and where to do this, that, and the other thing.
- Teens who feel heard and respected can more readily access their own sense of self and create lives of joy and meaning.
- When teens feel understood they work harder, display more interest and curiosity, and are far more compassionate and easy to get along with.
- When teens feel that they are seen as responsible, they become more responsible.
- When teens feel appreciated, they are more willing to feel and show gratitude.
- When adults open the lines of communication through the parent as coach/lighthouse role, the result can be harmonious and loving relationships that both parents and teens can treasure.

Sterling, D., *Parent as Coach: Helping Your Teen Build a Life of Confidence, Courage and Compassion*, [online] http://www. parentascoach.com.

My work as a resilience and parenting specialist has helped me reach many others who share a similar passion of making a real difference in the lives of young people. We all hold that potential to help someone find that special and unique part of themselves they bring to the world. Anyone can do it. When we give the gift of hope to others, we also give ourselves the gift of hope that we are getting closer to being the best person we can be. To all our lighthouses, I thank you deeply.

To the lighthouses who supported my sons on their road to manhood, I am very grateful for the role you played. Thank you to the following teachers from Albany Senior High School in Western Australia for being lighthouses for each of the Dent lads on their bumpy ride through adolescence:

- Mr Gillies
- Mr James
- Mr Ritchie
- Mr Johnson
- Mr Lucas

And to the many others who have touched our lives—too many to name— thank you.

Key Points

- Adolescents need significant caring adults on their bumpy ride.

- Traditional communities prepare adolescents for adulthood over a number of years.

- Lighthouses need to be many things.

- Lighthouses have enormous potential to positively influence adolescents.

- Building trust is essential in adolescent-lighthouse relationships.

- Lighthouses can contribute to building emotional, social and spiritual competence.

- Lighthouses act as coaches and mentors on the bumpy ride.

- The more support adolescents get, the better.

Chapter 2

The
millennial
adolescent

Adolescence refers to the multifaceted set of maturational sequences and elements that impact on life for people moving from childhood to adulthood.

Bahr, N. et al.

Adolescence is the bridge between childhood and adulthood. It is a stage that can positively or negatively shape the rest of an individual's life. Unfortunately, there is no clear line that defines exactly when adolescence or the process of puberty starts. These days, it appears that bodies are developing earlier—especially for girls. However, this does not mean that the developmental changes of the brain start any earlier. Adolescence is a much better description of the process of maturation than puberty because the physical changes can be almost over by the late teens, yet the final stages of brain development are still incomplete. So I will use the term adolescents rather than teenagers because they are still on the bumpy ride well into their 20s. Each child seems to have their own blueprint of when they begin adolescence and when they complete it, as well as the unique challenges they will meet on their bumpy ride. Every child is different and the maturation rate of every adolescent is different. This means there are no clear markers or boundaries for qualitative dimensions. There are two main theoretical schools of thought around adolescence:

1. Those that examine biological parameters.
2. Those that consider socio-cultural parameters of maturation.

While this book will concentrate on the 12- to 25-year-old age range of adolescent development, there is still significant evidence that shows that adolescence can be considered as young as 10 years of age, and sometimes continues beyond 25, depending on the inhibitors that may have delayed healthy development.

> *The United Nations (2005b, p2) makes an important observation fundamental to the global decision making about young people. 'A simple but often ignored fact; young people today are different from any of the previous generations of youth. It is essential that youth interventions are relevant and valid for the current young generation in society and not mired in the realities of times past'.*
>
> Bahr, N. et al.

Adolescents are learning how to manage their rapidly changing minds, bodies and emotions while navigating their way through the most important years of their education. They are developing key skills that will enable them to manage life, and at the same time are exploring their identity and potential. The strong drive to become independent is matched in intensity by the drive to belong with their peers, as well as wanting to step back from parental influence. The world that surrounds them today offers so many more stressors and a lot less support than 20 years ago. However, the main drivers of adolescence are still the same as they always have been. There are six main drivers of adolescence.

Six main drivers of adolescence

1. Seeking autonomy and independence

From the time that the body starts changing physically, adolescents need to gain more choice to empower them to stand on their own feet. Autonomy needs to come gradually and we must be mindful that mistakes and poor choices are quite normal during adolescence. The big part of the learning with this driver is that every choice will have a consequence of some kind—sometimes positive and sometimes negative. The exploration of making choices with an understanding that decisions may have far wider consequences than may seem evident at the time is the role of good parenting. Few adolescents are capable of making enlightened decisions that can explore both choice *and* consequence. This is a pre-frontal lobe activity that is far from complete. They can even repeat the same really risky or dumb decision within the same week for the same reason!

I have worked with parents who have threatened to ground an adolescent for the rest of their life when they have broken a curfew or deliberately lied to them about where they have been. This may not be the best way to help the adolescent learn from the experience. They may just become angry and resentful, which tends to make them rebellious. Remember, every experience will have a learning opportunity, especially the failures, disasters and muck-ups. There are some helpful tips in this chapter on caring and empowering communication to help you if this happens. Mother Nature needs adolescents to step up and take more responsibility in order to create more adults to take care of the older people in society in the future.

> *Please be kind to your adolescent—they will choose your retirement home one day!*

2. Identity searching.

The search for identity and belonging and having a place in a consumer driven, high-tech, fast-paced world is difficult. The search for identity is one of the most important jobs that teenagers have and, in order to complete this search, they need to step back from their family—especially their parents.

According to Martin Seligman (1995), one of the reasons why young people are less resilient today than in earlier generations, is the change in parenting styles.

> *[Seligman] argues that parents have focused too much on trying to make their children happy. He believes that out of misguided love parents have given their children the message they should be happy, and that it is terrible and abnormal to feel unhappy even for a short time, and that something must be done to 'feel good' again.*
>
> McGrath, H. and Noble, T., *Bounce Back: Teachers Handbook*, (2000).

This touches on the overprotection of children so that they are given treats and quick fixes to make them feel better after being disappointed or hurt by normal life experiences. This behaviour does not help children or adolescents learn that they can overcome setbacks and failures themselves. Managing and learning from failure is a huge life skill, as is recovering from a painful experience. These patterns, whether healthy or unhealthy, will tend to stay with individuals for life if they are not given some support to change them during the vital teenage years. Autonomy can only occur when an individual has overcome challenge, or achieved a success because of their choices and behaviours independently of others—sometimes in spite of others!

The search for 'Who am I?' is a huge part of the bumpy ride to adulthood. Some adolescents want to follow the tribe at any cost, while others want to follow no one. Remember, the things they do with their hair, no matter how bad it looks, will grow out one day. Hold your tongue and breathe deeply when they do strange things—although, it is helpful to let them know that some forms of personal expression are more preferable than others. One mum told me that her daughter had her upper arm tattooed with 'I love Ross'. Unfortunately Ross dropped her three days later. It was a painful way to learn about how some choices can be more permanent than others.

> *Maggie's tip: The louder you complain about their hair, clothes or make-up, the longer it will stay. Don't you remember hating being told what to do as an adolescent?*

3. Needing to belong: The importance of peers and deepening friendships

This is a very important stage of adolescent development.

> *Just hangin' and talkin' is healthy teenage behaviour and actually has an important purpose in an adolescent's development.*
>
> Feinstein, S., *Parenting the Teenage Brain: Understanding a Work in Progress*, (2007).

Being connected to friends and peers has the added advantage that an adolescent will be in touch with the parents of those friends. These friendships help develop social skills, help modify the 'dark moods' of adolescence and usually enhance moral development. Through friendships, adolescents learn unspoken codes of conduct that they will take with them throughout life.

This does not mean that friendships are easy! Being sanctioned by peers is one of the fastest ways to create the catalyst for an adolescent to change an unhelpful behaviour or uncaring communication. Also, friendships can make or break an adolescent in many ways.

Positive friendships are a powerful protective factor that will help adolescents avoid unlawful, risky behaviour, especially those involving addictions. This time is a window of sensitivity. Never will addiction to alcohol, drugs or tobacco occur more quickly than during the teenage years. This is a double whammy, because they are also much more resistant to recovery (Feinstein, 2007).

Positive friendships help young people develop a sense of belonging. This builds their inner sense-of-acceptance, as well as their extrinsic sense of 'I am acceptable.' Lighthouses need to help adolescents form friendships with peers, this is vitally important for their social and emotional development on many levels.

> *A study of resilient and optimistic teenagers noted they belonged to a group of friends, particularly those in high school. More than 90% of the young people reported that being connected to peers was the second most important protective factor during crises and applied to most young people.*
>
> Worsley, L. *The Resilience Doughnut: The Secret of Strong Kids*, (2006).

As a child morphs into an adolescent on the way to becoming an adult, the biological drive to survive as a species begins to kick in. We need to have other people to maximise our chances of survival and so the need to have friends becomes stronger. Adolescents have a deep need to just 'hang out' together without necessarily having a sense of purpose. If you want to do family things like holidays away or visit old family haunts, consider allowing your adolescent to bring a friend. They simply need to be with other young people as you become more 'boring'.

Create a space like a garage or a den where your adolescent can have their friends over. They will hang out together, plus it is much safer keeping them around a home than it is to have them wandering the streets. It is a good idea to get to know your adolescent's friends' parents so that you can take turns at having 'overs' (that's a sleepover without much sleep!) Often an adolescent will listen to a friend's parent's advice more than their own parents'—even if they say the same thing!

> *Maggie's tip: Turn your garage into a safe gathering place for your adolescent. Make it comfortable with the basics to make toasties and cups of Milo. Have a TV to watch movies and mattresses to throw down for extra friends. If it's for boys, get a pool table, table tennis table, dartboard or a Wii. This helps them burn up their competitive urges with real people.*

4. Immature brain driving a mature-looking body

There is no doubt that puberty is happening earlier, especially with girls, and many adolescents look much older than their years but do not be fooled! The changes taking place in their brain have not moved at all. Many will be like an L-plater driving a Porsche which is why they need to have vigilant, loving care in the adolescent years.

5. Separation from parents

When an adolescent steps back it is a sign that the child–parent relationship is fading (as it should) and a new relationship with an adolescent is forming. It is healthy for them to question your values and beliefs because they are searching for their own way of interpreting the world. And, yes, they could

be a bit kinder sometimes in how they tell us that we don't know what we are talking about.

While stepping back from parents is healthy and normal, research shows that adolescents with positive parental involvement travel better on the bumpy ride. Parents living busy lives while raising a new generation of adolescents makes for interesting times!

> *Expecting the adolescent to forever remain a child sets you up for disappointment, disillusionment and hurt. Accepting the fact that the child–parent relationship is over and embracing the different but potentially wonderful one that lies ahead is a giant leap toward getting along with a teenager.*
>
> Feinstein, S.

There is a biological reason for this separation from parents that is very reassuring. When we lived in kinship tribal communities, the adolescent stepped away from his parents to find his own 'new' tribe so that he never mated with his parents. This helped keep the gene pools healthy and avoided in-breeding.

6. Forming deep relationships

Another part of the developing adolescent is the deepening of friendships after 16 years of age. This occurs when boys catch up with girls and stop being 'so immature.' Things change when they start to bond, even across genders, based on shared values and interests. It is helpful for boys to develop 'girl mates' that are not their girlfriends because they can help boys decode the 'girl world'. The reverse can happen as well, and these friendships are particularly beneficial in the transition years as an adolescent prepares to leave home and stand on their own feet.

Adolescents are not really supposed to share their first sexual encounters and or disasters with their parents. This can be much healthier with someone their own age whom they know and trust. This driver is one of the reasons why it is helpful to keep adolescents engaged at school for as long as possible, even if they are not performing well academically. Leaving school early can alienate an adolescent from their key friends and they can miss this deepening of the friendship process. Many boys have had this occur and I have worked with many who fell into depression during this vital window because they were feeling separated from peers by being in an adult work environment with no one their own age, and definitely not any friends.

In my work as a marriage celebrant I often see male 'bride mates' and female 'best bitches.' This shows a healthy honouring of the friendships that develop on the bumpy ride from home to the real world.

It is important to note that these drivers are biological and they occur for adolescents everywhere, even for those with special needs, and they occur according to each individual's unique inner programming. Adolescents do not ask for these changes to happen, however they need to happen to allow a child to begin the changes necessary to become an adult in the future. There has always been a generation gap between parents and adolescents; however, since the new millennium it has become more of a chasm. Today's and tomorrow's adolescents, sometimes called Gen Y, Digitals or Millennials, not only have to cope with their own rapid physical, mental, social and emotional changes, they are doing so at the same time as the world goes through massive transformation.

A new millennium

The year 2000 saw a new millennium begin. Even though every generation of parents may have found adolescents confusing and challenging, the current generation of young people who are now entering adulthood have created a unique set of concerns and challenges for parents and teachers. According to Peter Sheahan in his book, *Generation Y: Thriving and Surviving with Generation Y at Work*, (2006) there are nine character traits that define the Y Generation (those born between 1978 and 1994):

1. Street smart
2. Aware
3. Lifestyle centred
4. Independently dependent
5. Informal
6. Tech savvy
7. Stimulus junkies
8. Sceptical
9. Impatient

This means that the normal generation gap difficulties have become a chasm for many well-meaning parents of Generation Y, Generation Z (born from 1995 to 2009) and beyond. It is important not to categorise young people as all belonging to one homogenous group with these characteristics. Today's adolescents are going through their own life transition right in the midst of a time of unprecedented societal change. These two concurrent change processes have impacted deeply on young people. New media, information technologies and the Internet have changed the context of adolescents' lives and the nature of interpersonal relations.

> *Technosavvy, image driven, develop graphics skills before literacy skills, do not think in a linear fashion but rather think non-linear, loopy, in hyperlink hopscotch fashion. Time for them is measured in microseconds and survival of the fastest, not the fittest. They have a strong sense of immediacy, a desire for instant gratification, and a low boredom threshold. They learn by interaction and doing rather than sitting and listening and they prefer to experience and feel rather than think and analyse.*
>
> Donnison, S., *The Digital Generation, Technology, and Educational Change: An Uncommon Vision*, (2004), [Online] http://www98.griffith.edu.au/dspace/handle/10072/2085.

Both parents and teachers know about the unique characteristics of today's adolescents. Our classrooms are struggling to engage the modern adolescent because they are still using many methods that may have worked 20 years ago, but are no longer reaching across the chasm of change. Just managing the presence of mobile phones that can allow students to keep track of their emails and social networking during class is enough to challenge our most competent teachers. Also, we have students whose expertise with the Information Technology (IT) world far exceeds their teacher's by the time they are 14 years of age—they know how Internet security works and seldom pay for any program because they know how to download things illegally for free. Try questioning the legality or morality of such actions and you will quickly discover the chasm that exists between today's students and teachers.

In every era there are advantages and disadvantages to living during that period. In this modern age advantages include the ability to connect globally within seconds and the availability of massive information pathways no matter where you live—provided you can access the Internet. Disadvantages for today include the massive social change that is occurring, plus the increase of abuse of children and adolescents, and the increase in aggression and bullying using cyberspace and mobile phones.

The need to be 'technologically savvy' is another pressure today's adolescents have to deal with. The need to be connected via Facebook, YouTube and Twitter puts time-poor adolescents under a lot of pressure. For example, some adolescent's self-esteem is influenced by how many friends they have on Facebook on any given day! That is so sad.

The pressure for adolescents to be conditioned by the consumer driven 'must have' mentality has created many levels of social alienation. The price of affluence for some families has been the breakdown of healthy family relationships. The pursuit of financial prosperity has come at the high price of alienation from their Millennium Generation (MilGen) children. Those without the financial means to meet the demands of the massive consumption patterns often end up with 'plastic money' or credit card debt.

> *Young people addicted to technology are dialling up debts that will take a lifetime to overcome [...] peer pressure on young people to incur debts for goods and chattels in a 'must have now' society is driving the upswing in personal debt.*
>
> D. Passmore, Lifelong debt only a mouse click away, *The Sunday Mail*, (7 August 2005).

Lower social and emotional competencies have impacted on the Y Generation with an increase in illicit drug use, alcohol abuse, road rage, intentional delinquent behaviour (that is often repeated), mental illness, eating disorders, obesity, homelessness and premature deaths as a result of poor decision making. The breakdown of family and community has impacted enormously on the healthy raising of children. This, coupled with a massive expansion of the television and film industry, has meant that many children's values and beliefs are now more shaped by soap operas and fiction than by reality. Exposure to violence on television and in films definitely changes children's behaviour and their understanding of human relationships.

Why we are concerned about millennial adolescents

- Up to 300 per cent morbidity rate increase (400 per cent in rural areas).
- Mental illness has increased among this age group. In 2008, 26 per cent of people aged between 16 and 24 (about 650,000 people) suffered mental illness in Australia, and 14 per cent of Year 8s self-harmed.
- There has been a huge increase in binge drinking and drug taking at earlier ages.
- Twenty-six thousand people aged under 18 are homeless in Australia each night.
- Twenty-thousand adolescents aged between 12 and 18 are reported missing to police every year.
- More 30-year-olds are still at home than ever before.
- There has been a massive increase in violence among young people, especially among girls.
- Abortions have doubled in girls aged 14 and under in the last four years.

Many adolescents struggle with problems of enormous magnitude. Some of the things they are struggling with are quite invisible like:

- stress from being pressured by social networking sites
- over dependence and addiction to mobile phone communication
- too many things happening at once and very little down time.

Many adolescents struggle with hidden pressures of body image that are perpetuated by the endless magazines and websites—boys as well as girls. Relationships are often confusing and challenging for adolescents and they often struggle to manoeuvre themselves in the large communities like schools, colleges and universities. They have too many choices on what to do with their time and money before they are capable of good decision making.

Problems adolescents face in the new millennium

- Overall morbidity and mortality rates increase significantly between middle childhood and late adolescence/early adulthood.
- Onset of problems such as nicotine dependence, alcohol and drug use, poor health habits, and stress-related challenges often will show up as mortality in adulthood.
- Eighty per cent of teenagers are reported as engaging in one or more risky behaviours over a period of one month.

Feinstein, S

Mental illness

Many adult onset problems such as depression can be traced back to similar early episodes in adolescence. In all Australian states the mental health facilities for adolescents are struggling to cope. If mental illness episodes can be detected early and adolescents are given appropriate care, often it will not become a life-long illness. However, much mental illness goes undetected in adolescence and when it is finally diagnosed, it has often become a life-long concern.

A serious effort needs to be made around setting up adolescent wellness centres that offer medical support in an environment that is welcoming and supportive of young people. This will ensure their health concerns can be addressed as soon as possible. Mental health facilities must be set up so adolescents can receive the best care possible in environments that offer more than just a locked ward for those most at risk. In these centres there would be opportunities for the recovering adolescent to attend resilience and life skills programs with other young people.

I have had clients who have been admitted to mental health facilities when at risk of suicide, or after a suicide attempt and after a week or two on high medications, they are released back home with no follow-up support—often with no counselling because of high numbers of high-risk patients. Adolescent mental health centres would be able to better support those both at high and moderate risk by building positive connections with adult allies. Adults can also run programs to build their life-coping skills in a holistic way. One initiative that appears to be meeting the needs of young people is the federal government program, Headspace. There are now around 30 centres across Australia to offer support for adolescents who are experiencing problems. I do hope these centres will continue to be funded for the long term and not get cut off just when they have finally built relationships with young people. For more information about these centres go to www.headspace.org.au.

New research shows that the years of adolescence are most critical in the development of mental and emotional competence that impacts on resilience for the rest of a person's life. The unique changes in the brain impacts enormously on an adolescent's thinking, moods, behaviour and ability to communicate.

In promoting resilience in adolescence, adult carers, parents, teachers and others working with them must have a mature understanding of what is happening. With this knowledge they will be able to better support adolescents as they navigate this time of massive change.

Given the nature of the modern world, the MilGen adolescent needs more support than ever before. They need more than family and friends to guide them on their bumpy ride to adulthood. They also need lighthouses who can care for them while being a solid, reliable source of comfort when the ride gets rough. It is essential that we increase the social capital of our communities so we can practice more collective, positive parenting.

Never before in the history of Australia have young people been told so much, but never before have they known so little, they are drowning in an information explosion that is unique to our time, yet wisdom has never been so sparse a commodity. We seem to have created a generation of young people who's alleged street wisdom is nothing more than a flimsy covering, over an aching void of vulnerability. They are only 18% of the population, but 100% of the future - a future that is very much in the hands of the middle schooling movement. As Martin Luther King jr once said, '...we shall have to repent in this generation, not so much for the evil deeds of the wicked people, but for the appalling silence of the good people.'

Carr-Gregg, M., [online] http://www.michaelcarr-gregg.com.au.

Key Points

- Adolescence lasts much longer than the teenage years.

- The maturation rate of every adolescent is different.

- There are six drivers of adolescence that happens to all adolescents.

- Massive social and technological change can create unique challenges.

- Some MilGen adolescents have less social and emotional competence.

- The modern consumer-driven world creates unique challenges for children and adolescents.

- There are more invisible threats than ever before.

- We need to build social capital to better support today's adolescents.

Chapter 3

Resilience
and why it is
Important

The complexity of the types of development that help young people toward resilience indicate that any approach needs to be proactive, holistic and part of an on going ethos rather than a program for implementation.

Bahr, N. et al.

Resilience refers to the ability of a person to successfully manage their life, and to successfully adapt to change and stressful events in healthy and constructive ways. It is about survivability and 'bounce-back-ability' to life experiences—both the really advantageous ones and the really challenging, traumatic ones. Other definitions include:

A universal capacity which allows a person, group or community to prevent, minimize or overcome the damaging effects of adversity.

The International Resilience Project, (2005).

In humanistic psychology resilience refers to an individual's ability to thrive and fulfill potential despite or perhaps because of stressors or risk factors.

Neill, J. T., [online] http://wilderdom.com, (2006).

In traditional kinship communities adolescents were separated by gender so that girls could be trained to do what women needed to do and boys could be trained to do men's business. When they had mastered the competencies needed, they would undergo an initiation ceremony to signify to the rest of the community that they were ready to become an adult with adult responsibilities.

Boys were taken by the men to learn mens' business—and they had to learn fast or they could be killed by a mammoth or a sabretooth tiger on a hunting trip! This pathway for boys meant that risk-taking was a key element of the maturation process and we must not forget that some of these biological drivers of human survival are still playing out in the lives of today's adolescents. Unfortunately, boys have few valid pathways in which to follow these instincts other than doing dangerous things with their bodies with modern lethal weapons like cars, knives, guns and drugs.

These words came from Melanie Woss, a Perth girl who struggled with depression before finally taking her own life when it got too hard:

> *Why not be proactive instead of being reactive? Why not implement a program where school aged kids learn skills to help them cope with stress? Decision-making skills. Problem solving strategies. Relaxation activities. Communication skills. Why not address the issues that kids talk about today? Sex; drugs; politics both within the community and the school, family life, racism etc etc etc. Why not give kids the skills that generate confidence, the ability to speak articulately, how to present oneself for different occasions, how not to put your foot in your mouth. Kids need to be taught that stress exists and it is very real, and most importantly, that they can cope with it.*
>
> Giles, F., [ed], Melanie, (1992).

We almost expect adolescents to work out what they need to learn by accident rather than by a conscious education about life and the required skills they need to master to be considered an adult. Schools have placed such a huge emphasis on learning that can be measured and assessed, and many people think this is where adolescents will magically learn everything they need to become a worthwhile member of society. This is a serious flaw in our modern world. Life skills that will impact on the type of competencies an adolescent should learn and master must be given a much higher priority. Many get to adulthood with few skills, especially social and emotional skills, and they struggle with relationships, managing money and coping positively with positions that require responsible choices and consideration for others. They may have all the modern gadgets that they believe show they are part of the adult world, but they may lack the mature mind and ability to make sound decisions because they were not given these skills by significant adults.

> *Thirty years of research tells us that resilient people are happier, live longer and are more successful in school and jobs, are happier in relationships and are less likely to suffer depression.*
>
> Werner, E. and Smith, R., *Journeys from Childhood to Midlife: Risk, Resilience, and Recovery*, (2002).

Resilience refers to a person's capacity to manage life and to overcome adversity or challenge. This is something that many of today's older adolescents lack. They are not totally responsible for this lack of skills and abilities because the adult world has stepped back from the place it used to have in providing the environment and experiences that build mature individuals.

> *Living in a secular, disconnected society, the global economic downturn, terrorism, record levels of bullying and cyber harassment, family breakdown, peer pressure to dress provocatively, perform academically and become sexually active along exposure to a veritable smorgasbord of alcoholic and narcotic seductions, mean that there will be many voices in the ears of our children and it is our job to ensure ours is the loudest.*
>
> Carr-Gregg, M., *When to Really Worry: Mental health problems in teenagers and what to do about them, (2010).*

Father Chris Riley who works with a project called Youth Off The Streets in Sydney wrote the following in his document Towards a National Strategy for Young Australians Nov 2009 (online: http://www.youthofthestreets.com.au/downloads/2009_november_national_strategy.pdf).

> *'When we see troubled kids we begin the journey to understand the quality of their early relationships, the psychological condition of their inner life and the development of their spirit. At the heart of the matter is whether the child is connected rather than abandoned, accepted rather than rejected, and nurtured rather than neglected and abused.*

Virtual world versus real world

Today many young people have a social and moral code that has been downloaded from the virtual world full of poor-quality television, films and DVDs of a violent and mind-numbing nature. Then there are the new entertainments that engage delicately developing minds in games and online activities that are often competitive and require a victor at the cost of all other players. The time wasted on these forms of entertainment is never recaptured because the maturing adolescent and their capacity to develop the social and emotional skills of a fully mature adult are delayed, if not missed completely.

This has helped to create a fascination of 'celebrity status' where adolescents are often infatuated with actors and sporting heroes with very questionable morals. Online activity, especially social networking sites, also distracts adolescents from their school and further education studies, as well as time spent learning artistic or sporting prowess. The adolescent brain is very easy to be distracted because it is still developing the emotional competences of delayed gratification, impulse control, self-motivation and self-regulation of desires. It's a little like putting children in a lolly shop that has one small basket of fruit and saying, 'Go for it!' Their choices are often driven by a child's sense of uncontrolled desire and instant gratification. The adolescent is still being driven by similar urges.

To support adolescents on their bumpy ride from childhood to adulthood, they need to be guided and taught how to manage themselves, interact with others positively and accept responsibility for their place in the world. This has always been seen as the responsibility of parents, extended family, schools and other significant members of the community in which the adolescent lives.

In many ways the modern world has devalued the role of significant adults in young people's lives because the information-rich environment appears easier to use than the time honoured way of teaching and mentoring. It is easier to simply Google™ information than seek information from parents and other adults. The qualities that a person needs to become competent, confident and resilient requires human interaction because they are social and emotional skills and no computer, iPhone or mp3 player is capable of these skills, no matter how many applications you download.

Characteristics of a resilient person

- The ability to bounce back and recover from almost anything.
- Optimistic and flexible thinking skills.
- Have a, 'Where there's a will, there's a way!' attitude.
- Tend to see problems as opportunities to learn and grow.
- The ability to hang in there, persevere and persist.
- Have a healthy, authentic self-esteem.
- Capable of setting clear, realistic and attainable goals.
- Have a healthy social support network.
- Practice assertiveness rather than aggression or passivity.
- Seldom dwell on the past or the future.
- Have well-developed emotional and spiritual competence.
- Learn from previous challenges and mistakes.
- Have a capacity for detachment.
- Have a well-developed sense of humour.
- Have meaningful involvement with others or their community.
- Treat themselves and others with respect.
- Have problem solving and conflict resolution skills.

Characteristics that break down resilience in adolescents

- Destructive relationships: As experienced by the rejected or unclaimed child, hungry for love but unable to trust, expecting to be hurt again.
- Climates of futility: As encountered by the insecure youngster, crippled by feelings of inadequacy and a fear of failure.
- Learned irresponsibility: As seen in the youth whose sense of powerlessness may be masked by indifference or defiant, rebellious behaviour.
- Loss of purpose: As portrayed by a generation of self-centred youth, desperately searching for meaning in a world of confusing values.

Brendtro, L., Brokenleg, M. and Van Bockern S., *Reclaiming Youth at Risk: Our Hope for the Future*, (2001).

British psychiatrist Michael Rutter identified the following risk variables in children who developed psychiatric disorders and delinquency in adulthood:

- Marital discord.
- Low socio-economic discord.
- Large family size.
- Paternal criminality.
- Maternal psychiatric disorder.
- Removal from home by local authorities.
- Major loss experience not resolved (death, moving home, major illness).
- Being male.
- Repeated bullying or harassment.
- Low literacy skills.
- Negative school experiences.
- Low social competence.
- Lack of significant caring adult relationship.
- Contrasting and conflicting experiences between home and school.
- Highly spirited/energetic children.
- Ethnic/cultural differences.
- Disabilities of any kind.
- Uncertain/different sexual preferences.

In *Parenting the Teenage Brain: Understanding a Work in Progress* (2007), Sheryl Feinstein identifies the following danger signs of teens at risk:

- Isolation from family and friends.
- Sudden changes in schoolwork, job performance or athletic activities.
- Drastic mood swings.
- Lack of interest in outside school activities.
- Family conflict.
- Living in a community with high crime and easy availability of alcohol and drugs.
- Delinquent friends.

- Academic failure.
- Change in eating and sleeping habits.
- Cutting or hurting themselves.

The essentials for troubled adolescents and ones who seem to be travelling well are exactly the same. They need charismatic, caring adults or a lighthouse who can act as an anchor; much like young babies and toddlers who need a secure base. Without these adult influences we leave adolescents to flounder in a confusing world full of change.

In today's modern world we are seeing more adolescents who are living in regular families struggling where they should be thriving. With a better understanding of what is really happening for the MilGen adolescent we can step forward to support them so they may reach their potential.

Social capital means positive social interaction at many levels in a community, from the family through to school and out into the wider community. This needs to be a conscious action of placing the needs, firstly of children, then young people as a priority like it used to be in traditional communities. By doing this, no adolescent should fall through the cracks of apathy and dislocation. There is an enormous potential to throw lifelines to adolescents that may help them find a more positive life direction. In adulthood the potential for change diminishes greatly.

The world experienced by today's adolescent is very different to the one in which many of their parents were raised. The rapidly changing world has created a dilemma for those who are responsible for raising children and, even more importantly, adolescents. The generation gap is now a chasm that makes it harder to communicate due to the modern context that our young people live in. This is why it is so important to lift the awareness in communities and homes on how resilience is built or promoted in today's children and teenagers.

Matthew's story

In my first year of teaching as a high school English teacher I met a wise teacher in one of my classes. His name was Matthew. He was thirteen and he was illiterate. I can still remember clearly his cheeky smiling face and the most beautiful brown eyes peering out from under his long fringe. Matthew was always restless and found it hard to concentrate.

One afternoon after helping him with some work I offered to drop him home as it was really hot. When I arrived at his home he asked if I would like a cup of tea. His manners and his courtesy took me by surprise. Once inside he turned the kettle on and excused himself for a few minutes and soon returned with the washing off the line—neatly folded. Anyone who has sons will know this is pretty unusual. Washing brought off the line usually still has the pegs attached— if they voluntarily do it at all!

Then Matthew said, 'I am home first, so I help Mum get things done as this is her late day and Paul, my brother, has basketball training. I just have to put a chicken in the oven and then I will make your tea. Is that alright with you?'

I watched as this capable young man took a chicken out of the fridge and put it into the oven for his sole-parent mum and, obviously much loved, brother. Then we had a cup of tea made with a teapot and a strainer. We chatted about many things from friends to pets and to his favourite foods. It was a very comfortable experience and I felt I was in the company of someone much older not the restless lad who was in my class who often grunted, 'Yep', 'Nup' and 'Whatever Miss.'

The following week I showed the class a video that was an introduction to a topic on tolerance. It was a symbolic presentation that simply showed different coloured dots that moved around with background music. When it had finished I asked the class what the video was about. There were many confused faces in the room and my 'A Level' students had no idea what the video was about.

Matthew put up his hand and said, 'Miss, it's easy. The video is about colour prejudice and shows how some people think they are better than other people because of the colour of their skins—and that's not true. We are all the same really.'

The class was stunned and so was I. Here was the boy who couldn't read and could only write a few words showing us that true wisdom cannot be measured by grades or assessment. Matthew showed me that day something that all teachers need to know: Students cannot be judged by their academic performance, dress, hair or the way they behave. What is important is that we believe in the inherent goodness and wisdom that lies within, maybe dormant, but still present nevertheless.

From that day on Matthew was respected in our class and that meant the world to him. He felt he belonged and that people cared. His behaviour was never a problem and the other students helped him with his literacy and always turned to him to listen to how he viewed the world.

Unfortunately, having poor literacy skills meant that life outside of school was much tougher. Without a supportive network that cared about him Matthew struggled in life and numbed his pain of believing he was dumb and useless with drugs and alcohol. This journey took him into mental illness and deep depression and Matthew took his own life when he was just 23 years of age.

I hold Matthew as one of the wisest teachers I ever met and I feel I failed him in some way by not building his resilience while he was with me for that year of his life.

From birth, we are building personal resilience through the acquisition of various life skills. The better the quality of parental care that children are exposed to, the stronger their resilience—provided the care has allowed for children to have opportunities to explore the world, make mistakes and learn how to overcome adversity.

I have created a model of 10 essential building blocks from birth to 12 years of age that explore how the small things in childhood can become big things later in life. For more information refer to *Real Kids in an Unreal World: Building Resilience and Self-esteem in Today's Children*. These essential building blocks in childhood will build the capacity for children to better manage adolescence and adult life.

Adversity is not all bad. Many of the most successful, competent and influential people in the world are that way *because* of adversity in childhood. This is where we can develop a social conscience and understanding of the need for change to existing cultural attitudes.

The ability to overcome setbacks, disappointments or failure can be determined by minimising risk, building protective factors and/or patterns of behaviour acquired by a person. Any adolescent can suffer from depression, even high achievers. Any adolescent can make a spur of the moment decision that can be fatal regardless of school grades or prior patterns of behaviour. We must not assume that any adolescent is reliably and consistently resilient and able to make decisions that guarantee their safety. Neither vulnerability nor resilience are fixed constructs. We are all at risk of life and my unplanned suicide attempt is an excellent example of that.

Resilience should be understood as a vital ingredient in the process of parenting all children. It is a process that directs our interactions as we strengthen our children's ability to meet life's challenges and pressures with confidence and perseverance. The most potentially dangerous time in an adolescent's life is between 14 and 16 years of age due to the biological changes happening in the teenage brain. However, I would argue that 18 to 25 years of age is equally as dangerous because many adolescents have left the safety net of school, are legally driving, drinking alcohol and have stepped back from parental influence. This window is one where many parents think they can breathe a sigh of relief. But sometimes they breathe that sigh too early.

The lighthouse model clearly focuses on how to support our young people by building strengths and competencies rather than focusing on the flaws and problems that may be present. Every adult can benefit from having positive, supportive people in their life no matter what. Until that adolescent brain finishes its final stages of maturation into an adult brain, young people are still at risk of making irresponsible decisions that can hurt or kill themselves or others.

Review of resilience research

Bonnie Benard, considered by many as the mother of the concept of resilience, has worked for many years with children considered to be at risk. Rather than focusing on what was wrong in these children's lives, she explored what was working, and what was helping them to cope with their very dysfunctional lives. This study led to her developing a list of protective factors that were needed in all communities to promote resilience.

Protective factors that enrich resilience in 12-year-olds and above:

- Increasing bondedness.
- Learning life skills.
- Establishing and maintaining clear boundaries.
- Providing care and support.
- Communicating high and positive expectations.
- Creating opportunities for participation and involvement.

Michael Rutter, an English expert, identified the following protective factors for young people:

- Stresses fewer in number and shorter in duration.
- No genetic disposition.
- Easy temperament.
- Being female.
- Positive school climate.
- Successful mastery and self-efficacy.
- Warm, close relationship with an adult.
- Planning/goal setting as a coping skill.

Norman Gazey's research found the following protective functions as being valuable in developing resilience:

- Effectiveness in work, play and love.
- Healthy expectancies and a positive outlook.
- Self-esteem and internal locus of control.
- Self-discipline.
- Problem solving/critical thinking skills.
- Humour.

Steven and Sybil Wolin described the following goals of resiliency:

- Master painful memories rather than the victim trap of rehashing the past.
- Accept that the family left its mark.
- Get revenge by living well and not squandering energy blaming and finding fault.
- Break the cycle of family trouble and put the past in its place.

Factors identified by MindMatters, an Australian national initiative to build resilience in schools, are:

- Connectedness.
- A relationship with caring adult.
- Support, belonging and role models.
- A good self-esteem.
- A belief in one's own ability to cope.
- Handling the demands of school.
- Having a sense of control.

Robert Brooks PhD and Sam Goldstein PhD, identified the following 10 ways to help build a resilient mindset in children:

1. Be empathetic.
2. Communicate with respect.
3. Be flexible.
4. Give your undivided attention.
5. Accept your kids for who they are.
6. Give kids a chance to contribute.
7. Treat mistakes as learning opportunities.
8. Stress your children's strengths.
9. Let your kids solve problems and make decisions.
10. Discipline to teach.

Nan Bahr and Donna Pendergast in their book, *The Millennial Adolescent,* believe that identifying resilience for adolescents as a competence is useful because it's something that can be actively developed, taught, practised, demonstrated and deployed. This means we can impact young people's lives by providing the right configuration of experiences and learning events. If we don't provide these experiences then we are dooming people to suffer the nastiest consequences of adversity. It seems a callous approach to refuse to actively attempt to develop resilience attributes because it is assumed to be an immutable trait.

The more positive resilient protective factors or patterns of behaviour you have, then the better your chance of overcoming setback, disappointment or failure of any kind. The choice to fight everyone who may represent the perceived cause of your life challenge, like authority figures, is simply that: a choice. The choice to make a positive difference by accepting your share of the responsibility (if there is any, because young children are innocent), and then finding ways to prevent that happening to another, is a sign of high resilience with good character.

> *It is therefore safest to assume that all young people, regardless of whether they seem vulnerable or not, could benefit from a focused attempt to develop resilient attributes.*
>
> Bahr, N. et al.

An interesting irony in life is that when adolescents can learn rapidly from adults they develop scepticism towards them. With troubled adolescents, they often resist help that is offered and this is why many get lost. This is one reason why having significant meaningfully involved adults as a part of their lives before they stumble into the hormonal vortex of puberty is so important. When they crash their dad's car he will be the last person they will want to call. However, they may call an uncle, a sports coach or the father of a mate. This connection of having people who know you and care for you, no matter what, is a key aspect of resilience. Adolescents who have no such people are at most risk in our modern world.

Ideally, adolescents need to leave school with as many of the following as possible:

- An optimism about finding a place in our world.
- A hope that they have something positive to offer humanity, no matter how small, so they know they have value.
- A positive regard and appreciation of themselves.
- A healthy sense of humour.
- A significant adult who loves and cares for them.
- At least three real friends.
- Survival skills like self-care, decision-making abilities, money management.
- Mastery in a learned skill or other activity.
- Self-respect.
- An ability to manage their emotional world.
- A sense of security in the future.

I would like to mention the excellent work of Lyn Worsley and her Resilience Doughnut model of exploring resilience in young people. Lyn shares my perspective that 'if something is working, do more of it' and also to allow an adolescent to give feedback on how they see their world, rather than assume what's happening. So often well-meaning counsellors and teachers make decisions about what's best for an adolescent without really understanding how the adolescent is seeing the world. An adolescent may be using a map of the world that might need adjusting, but it is their unique view of the world. Lyn has created an online game for young people to play that helps them explore their own resilience. For more about Lyn's work, the book, resources and seminars go to www.theresiliencedoughnut.com.au.

We must collectively focus on building resilience in children and adolescents so they can better manage living in this chaotic changing world.

> *People who have had a strong connection with a strong positive role model during adolescence are much more resilient throughout their life.*
>
> Bahr, N. et al.

Consider the following 16 fundamental facts about adolescence:

1. A mother's education is the greatest indicator of a teenager's future success.
2. Teenagers function mainly via the amygdala—the emotional centre of the brain.
3. During the teenage years there is a huge window of opportunity to learn key life skills like impulse control, developing relationships and communication skills.
4. Massive pruning of the brain occurs during adolescence.
5. Short-term memory increases 30 per cent during adolescence (after the initial pruning).
6. The closer a girl is emotionally to her father, the later she enters puberty.
7. The teen brain craves novelty.
8. Teens need more sleep than pre-teens or adults.
9. 70 per cent of teens have difficulty waking up in the morning.
10. Students with close bonds to their parents are less likely to drop out of school.
11. Only five hours of playing violent computer games will show brain activity with aggressive thoughts.
12. 40 per cent of adolescent deaths are caused by vehicle accidents.
13. 50 per cent of teens have tried drinking by 14 years of age.
14. Adolescents often misinterpret body language and the spoken word.
15. Computer games emphasize rapid responses in the teen's brain instead of encouraging thoughtful decisions.
16. Children who are born prematurely are at high risk for dropping out of school as teenagers.

Feinstein, S. *Parenting the Teenage Brain* (2007)

'When you are really angry or unhappy with your teenager close your eyes, take three deep breathes and imagine how you would feel if suddenly you had been told that they had died in an accident - then bring your awareness back into the present moment, now, how do you feel? How serious was the issue really? What would you now like to do about resolving it? At the end of the day what really matters?'

Key Points

- Resilience can be built in childhood and adolescence.

- Adolescents need positive adult involvement to develop life skills and social and emotional competencies.

- Adolescents at risk can come from regular homes as well as dysfunctional homes.

- Helping adolescents build life skills builds resilience.

- Academic ability is not a guarantee of resilience

- We must not assume that any adolescent is reliably and consistently resilient and able to make decisions that guarantee their safety.

- Caring adults in a child's life from the early years are powerful protective factors in adolescence.

Chapter 4

The adolescent brain: What is going on up there?

The new knowledge about the teen brain shows us that adolescence offers perhaps a second chance—or at least an additional one—to unleash the enormous potential and possibilities that lie within a person's brain and to shape positively that person's social, emotional and intellectual development. It means that what happens during their adolescent years is very important and can have a considerable and long-lasting impact on their lives.

Corbin, B., Unleashing the Potential of the Teenage Brain: 10 Powerful Ideas, (2008).

I have worked with adolescents for 30 years and taught them for 17 years, yet the information quoted above was certainly news to me. In my classes, I only occasionally saw behaviour that remotely looked anything like 'unleashing enormous potential and possibilities'—other than the unleashing of inappropriate words and gestures! However, the longer I taught the better I found these possibilities because I invested heavily in improving my capability as a teacher. I am still waiting for a student to find me and tell me that I changed their life by how I taught them to write essays. I spent hours researching experts and finding techniques that made learning interesting. I used the hamburger metaphor when teaching how to write essays and I have had students tell me that even at University, there were times they reflected on that metaphor to find they had a topless essay without the hamburger bun at the top!

The importance of communication

Learning how to effectively communicate, encourage, connect and understand different learning styles all helped—things I didn't learn at university. Then I discovered Edward de Bono, a physician who taught students how to think and develop techniques that gave them a chance to improve their academic performance. Then, accelerated learning techniques came under my radar and they made the classroom more interesting. Also, Jack Canfield's work on building self-esteem in the classroom allowed me to build self-belief and acceptance both within and between students. I recommend visiting Jack's website to view the class resources, or attending Jack's intensive training seminar. I completed this training in 1998 and learned more than 245 techniques to use when teaching or facilitating. Afterwards, my students' performance accelerated, as did their personal and interpersonal growth. They came to a better understanding on how to learn best, think and be mindful. More importantly, they understood how they were all a valued part of a 'classroom family'.

But, I wish I'd known what was really happening within the brains of my students so I could have helped them better understand why they sometimes drowned in self-doubt, felt vulnerable and had melt-downs in front of their peers. The information I am sharing will answer so many 'Why?' questions for both parents and teachers.

Keep in mind the difference between boys and girls during puberty. There is a 'boy delay' in terms of brain maturation, as well as a definite difference between how a boy's and a girl's brain functions. However, brain changes happen in both sexes, although it usually starts earlier in girls.

Towards the end of primary school when our children are around 11 to 12 years of age they can be quite agreeable people. They can be pleasant, polite and predictable and many parents are lulled into a false sense of security that they have this parenting business figured out. By this age some children may have noticed body changes, and some girls will already be menstruating. It's important to note that puberty now starts earlier than in previous decades, yet the brain still doesn't begin its biological changes any earlier. Don't be fooled by what the body is doing. It's the brain that's to blame for so much of the random and sudden adolescent angst.

Let's pretend that we could draw the pre-adolescent brain, keeping in mind that there are trillions of neurons and brain cells, not just the few I have pictured below. The adolescent brain is essentially a large brain that is poorly organised and it is in need of some serious tidying up in order to be more efficient.

This unwieldy mass of writhing chaotic cortex must be trimmed and pruned and streamlined until it has the potential to think like Newton, a Picasso or a Presley.

Bainbridge, D.

Adolescent
Brain Development

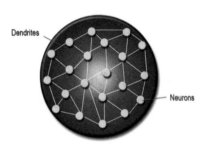

Four factors of brain development

1. Pruning—use it, or lose it.

There is a massive pruning that occurs in the brain during the early teenage years, anywhere up to 15 to 20 per cent. Information that is used often is deemed important and becomes stronger and is easier to remember. Information that is not used often is deemed unimportant and is forgotten. This can happen without warning and it impacts in many areas of an adolescent's life. These are unexpected changes that the adolescent did not ask to have happen. Mother Nature is preparing the child-evolving brain to become smarter, faster and to function with more maturity. In order to do that, it must prune those things that it decides a young person may not be using enough. Some pruning activity impacts across other competencies in an adolescent's life that can be unhelpful.

> *Every area of the teenage brain is pruned [...] this may sound like troubling news but in actual fact it's just the opposite—the brain becomes more efficient discarding some of its inconsequential information.*
>
> Feinstein, S.

Parents and teachers know this pruning has occurred when monosyllabic grunts replace articulation in communication with many adolescents, especially boys. I have worked with boys who were absolutely confused when instead of full sentences coming out of their mouth, an abbreviated 'lump' of sounds come out. Some boys have shared with me that the full sentence was inside their head, and yet what they heard was nothing like what they intended. How confusing and potentially embarrassing would that be for anyone? To cope, many boys stop trying to respond and put the metaphorical paper bag over their head and avoid talking as much as possible. This makes many boys feel dumb and stupid. Being wired to be warriors rather than wimps, they often cover this vulnerability with aggression, physical power threats or by hiding under their caps, fringes and behind the wall of their mp3 players. Then there are the deepening of boys' voices which does not happen in an instant. There are times that a boy's voice will almost come out like a squeaky mouse and three words later it will sound like a growling bear. No wonder some boys disappear behind a mask of indifference and apathy.

Adolescent
Brain Development

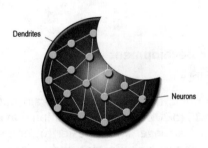

20% pruning of neurons-
pruning what is not being used- use it or lose it!

Another common unhelpful change that occurs at this pruning time is the drop in short-term memory—they become more forgetful. Even organised students can forget to hand in assignments or do homework when they were quite capable before the melt-down. Both girls and boys lose clothes, shoes, mobile phones and school bags during this time. (As an almost menopausal woman with similar problems with forgetfulness, I really can understand how these young people feel).

I have known of adolescents who will get off a bus and leave their school bag behind, or leave a lunch table with their mobile in clear view, or forget to meet parents or friends at clearly defined locations. We must reassure them this is normal, albeit frustrating!

An adolescent's skills in general can go awry, and messy bedrooms are often a product of this. They simply find managing their world harder and more challenging, and will often seem to forget simple things around the house, especially when it's their turn to do the dishes. This is when parents can ask the question, 'What were you thinking?' The answer for many is: They were not thinking!

Note that there are more stressors in today's world that add to an adolescent's sense of feeling pressured, stressed and overwhelmed. Many adolescents tell me that anti-depressants help them manage their stress as it 'sorta numbs things.' I am concerned that some adolescents may believe they are clinically depressed when they are simply overwhelmed by life. This also means they may be delaying the learning that is required: 'How do I cope with stress and change – without chemical support?'

2. Emotional overwhelm—strong stressors

This occurs when we feel overloaded by life. The more things that occur simultaneously, the more overwhelmed an adolescent can feel. There are things they cannot resolve by themselves and this lack of resolution causes further stress on their confused, vulnerable psyche. The younger adolescent is closer to the brain pruning process and can feel even more overwhelmed than adolescents aged 17 to 18 years. Some things that can overwhelm adolescents include:

- Car accidents.
- Bullying and harassment.
- Nasty, malicious gossip.
- Failing at school.
- Depression and other mental illness.
- Death of a loved one.
- Loss of a job.
- Abuse of any kind.
- Teenage pregnancy.
- Betrayal.
- Criminal activity.
- Alcohol or drug abuse.
- Gender confusion.
- Concerns about sexual orientation.
- Discrimination.
- Serious illness.
- Personal injury.
- Family disharmony.
- Sudden unexpected life change.
- Unresolved conflict.
- Pressure of expectations.
- Perceived failure.
- Continual forgetfulness
- Getting lost

- Being late.
- Living outside your honour code.

Constantly feeling out of control or disempowered makes many adolescents believe they are in some way at fault. An emotional melt-down that occurs quite unplanned at home or at school can impact on their confidence in all areas, including school, sporting, work or artistic pursuits. An adolescent will be wary of taking risks in case they look stupid again and it can change the way they behave in class.

An adolescent who is struggling will be reluctant to get help, which makes it challenging for those who care for them. They often search the Internet for answers and self-diagnose what's happening to them. Remember, an adolescent's capacity to think things through with maturity and objectivity is limited, and when this coincides with huge shifts in their emotional intensity, then feeling a small moment of vulnerability can become a huge emotional challenge. This is why many molehills become mountains (and many small zits look as big as Mt Vesuvius). If parents' expectations are inflexible at this time, they can feel even more threatened and challenged. (This was the time when I believed my bum was well out of proportion—but it was my reality).

This is a time when many adolescents are making decisions about managing money because many are buying mobile phones and other electronic equipment. As they lack the mature brain to think things through wisely, and they are driven by the strong herd mentality of 'must look cool' they are having big problems with debt. Some late payments for mobiles can damage their credit ratings for up to 10 years. This may not seem important to a 15-year-old, but when they are unable to take out a loan to buy a car when they are 24, it will be a problem.

Recent studies have found that as children reach puberty their ability to interpret and understand social situations and emotions in others can drop by up to 20 per cent. In one study, adolescents at 12, 14 and 18 years of age were shown photographs of facial expressions. At 12 the adolescents were accurate about 86 per cent of the time. This dropped to around 60 per cent at 14 and didn't ever return to the previous level of accuracy until 18. What does this mean? This means that in the window of 12 to 15 years of age when the brain does its automatic pruning, young adolescents often misread facial expressions and misinterpret body language that they could read much more competently before. They badly misread people and other adolescents. I have had adolescents say that someone 'looked at me like I was a dickhead', or 'like I was a fat ugly slut'.

Adolescents often misread parents and teachers. Some have admitted that when a teacher has growled at a class for poor effort, they are sure the teacher meant just them. Adolescents have told me that they're sure their mum hates them, when she may simply be premenstrual and maybe a little grumpy. This sensitivity when combined with a few other changes makes our confused adolescents very susceptible to self-criticism and self-judgement.

In 2008, SBS Television's *Insight* program ran a story about eating disorders. A couple of the sufferers recalled how someone making a comment about the way they looked is what helped tip them over into anorexia. Many overly personalise comments and especially criticism. This change causes many adolescents to feel ugly, stupid, useless and incompetent.

This can be a very frustrating time for parents and adolescents, but it is simply a biological process, not an intentional choice by adolescents.

Many adolescents struggle to get schoolwork done, be motivated and stay focused on their purpose. Remember, this coincides with a drop in short-term memory of up to 15 to 20 per cent around the same time, so losing and forgetting things is very common—and very frustrating!

It is important to again emphasise that these changes are not something adolescents asked to happen and they are often equally as confused as the parents. When I explain this stage of adolescent brain development to students there is a noticeable sense of relief on their faces. Many parents think their adolescents are being difficult just to annoy them, however confusion and frustration with things they have no control over is a perfectly normal response. There is very little intentionality in the adolescent world. They do not get out of bed in the morning deliberately planning to 'piss off' their parents—it just happens. The good news is that this mental and emotional processing gradually returns to the level of a 12-year-old by 18 years of age and full functioning is possible from around 22 for girls and much later for boys.

There are more factors to throw into the recipe of adolescent development that explains the chaos they perceive. The next brain change is a 'good news/bad news' scenario. The pruning of the 'grey matter' is occurring in order to smarten up the adolescent brain and make it work more efficiently. Unfortunately, it tends to make things worse before it gets better. Then the brain decides to amp up the 'white matter' in the brain, otherwise known as the overproduction of dendrites and synaptic connections.

3. Overproduction of dendrites and synaptic connections.

There will be billions of synaptic connections in an adolescent's brain by the end of adolescence. Synaptic connections are created and learning occurs when neurons communicate with each other. The more you engage in an activity, the more dendrites grow and the stronger the synaptic connections become.

Adolescents can acquire learning, knowledge and skills at an unprecedented rate. This window of opportunity is a vitally important window in the journey of human development. Learning, especially that which is based on real experiences, will happen faster than at any other stage in life (other than the first four years of life). The massive increase in dendrites will allow an adolescent to master new skills like playing a guitar, taking up sport, learning a new language, doing a triple flip on a skateboard or even learning to cook faster. However, if they are not engaged in their education or in positive pursuits like music, reading, sport, creative arts or practical skill development, they may be learning things that can impede their development for the rest of their life. This is why the role of caring adults is vital in helping adolescents to develop social and emotional skills, as well as thinking skills which enhance their capacity to predict, plan or make measured choices.

Adolescents need help managing their emotional world and the effects of surging hormones to help them build social and emotional competences. This, in turn, will help them build positive connectedness with others on their journey towards adulthood.

Adolescent
Brain Development

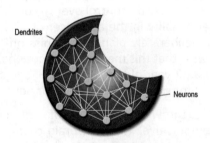

Massive overproduction of dendrites-
"enormous window of potential."

During this period adolescents can learn something quickly and with more ease than any other time in life, especially practical things like how to fix a car, surf, develop deeper relationships and expand communication skills. Never will it be easier for them to learn these skills and never are they more motivated to do so (Feinstein, 2007). This means that we need to ensure that adults are available to share this vital stage of their growth so adolescents can learn something they are interested in. Parents can use this window of fast learning by teaching them many practical life skills they will need when they leave home.

Regrettably in many secondary classrooms today adolescent students are still doing things and learning in ways that have characterized classrooms for decades and that unfortunately, have long been shown to be ineffective

Corbin, B., *Unleashing The Potential of the Teenage Brain: 10 Powerful Ideas*, (2008).

The adolescent brain is highly malleable with a high degree of plasticity. This means that it can change more easily than an adult brain. This is happening at the same time they have all the other crazy influences like hormones, the pruning process and the maturation of the emotional centres of the brain—the amygdala. For the adolescent boy who had to become a competent hunter back in the days of the mammoth, this overproduction of dendrites meant he could quickly learn how to be a competent hunter, or he would die.

> *Trying to warn adolescents off rash and suicidal behaviour doesn't work. Adolescence has always been a time of risk taking and more traditional societies were wiser than ours in that they created fitting tests and challenges for teenagers to face, and turned these into rites of passage.*
>
> Oldfield, David.

Fast forward to today and the same potential to learn quickly is still unfolding, but there are no mammoths to hunt and few ways to become the warrior that a young man is still hardwired to be. Instead, he can become addicted to other activities that he pursues during this window. This can mean criminal activities, sport, driving fast, doing risky behaviours and becoming hooked to online computer games. (More about that in the chapter about Secret Boys Business).

All adolescents can become addicted during this window faster than at any other time in their life. This is one of the main reasons why all adults need to work hard together to prevent exposure to smoking, drinking and other drugs. New evidence suggests that the later adolescents get a taste for alcohol the better they manage alcohol consumption as an adult. Addictions developed in young adolescence can become life-long addictions more easily than those addictions that occur after 16 to 17 years of age. Adolescent experimentation is one thing; however, buying alcohol for your adolescents during this time could be the catalyst that builds their addiction for life. I don't know any parent who would want to do that.

> *A mother called me one day and said she was really worried about her two teenage sons aged 13 and 15. She said they were tying pillows to themselves and throwing themselves out of trees. I was a little mystified for a moment as to why she was worried? 'And you are worried because...? Mine used to do that without the pillows.'*
>
> Maggie Dent

This opportunity to learn fast is one of the reasons why Indigenous football programs have the degree of success that they do. At a time that is full of risk and potential danger, young men are given a tight structure in which they can play lots of football, be supervised by significant role models and still get to play rough and tumble in a socially acceptable way. Their rapidly improving ability builds their sense of being capable and competent, which also weakens the pattern of early adolescent self-doubt and self-criticism that many numb with alcohol and drugs. They also have a boundary they learn to respect—no school, no play!

Of particular concern is that while this window is open, today's adolescents are rapidly consumed by SMS and chat room communication. There have been many who have shared with me how consumed they become because of their need to stay connected in case they miss something. This sense of immediacy develops stronger during this window of rapid growth and can become a major stressor for life. Try taking a mobile off an adolescent for 24 hours and watch how uncomfortable they feel. The need to be plugged in either via mobile, the Internet or to an mp3 is concerning because it's a way of inhibiting human connectedness. I know adolescents argue that they feel more connected, but it is not genuine human conversation and it's shallow and rapid.

When we chat online, everyone weighs less because we have a tendency to embellish ourselves. This sensitivity to chat rooms has lead to many girls being groomed by paedophiles, and due to their gullibility and connection to this artificial way of communicating, they are at so much more risk. I recently worked with a 14-year-old girl from a Christian family who was not only groomed, she met this person, and even though he was obviously much older than the 14 years he said he was, he convinced her he really loved her. The end result was that she lost her virginity, and if it wasn't for a text message that went the wrong way, she may still be meeting him secretly. Young adolescent girls have a very immature brain that can be easily manipulated, yet they believe they have it all worked out.

The inability to objectively see the situation especially when she was faced with a 30-year-old not a 14-year-old is a sign of how vulnerable today's adolescents are when they add these new forms of communication into the mix. She genuinely found it hard to see that the man had done anything wrong.

> *Concerns range over the abandonment of grammar through SMS shortcutting, to the risks of child exploitation, and perversion through Internet chat sites, from the loss of childhood to the explosion of knowledge widely available on the net, to work intensification and the expectation that people are available instantly, either by phone, fax or email. All these changes impact on what it means to be a member of the Y Generation as a millennial adolescent.*
>
> Bahr, N. et al.

I am so glad I am not teaching English anymore. It was hard enough 10 years ago to get adolescents seeking university admittance to be able to write in a mature fashion with full words, and now I know from my teacher friends it is even more challenging. Even with my own sons I sometimes have to SMS or email asking for more vowels!

Parents need to use this window as positively as possible by offering opportunities for participation in clubs, sport, art and dance classes and by encouraging adolescents to take a wide range of options in high school. It is yet another irony of adolescence that right when they could take best advantage of their potential, many are feeling dumb and terrified of looking stupid in public. I know many a frustrated parent who has done everything they could to get a reclusive adolescent out of their bedroom without success. This is where the role of friends and family can help.

I live by the adage that within every child ever born are unique gifts and talents that are meant to be shared with the world to make it a better place. Many adults can look back to their adolescent years and nod in wonder at what made them pick up a guitar, fall in love with long-distance running, take up dancing or become passionate about the environment. For me it was basketball and writing. If my body would still allow it, I would still play basketball today such is my love of the game. Obviously, I am still writing!

On my bumpy ride through adolescence I struggled and felt like the world was against me many times. I wished my ride had been smoother and that I had made fewer mistakes. Only as an adult did I realise it was *because* of my bumpy ride that I am who I am today. I will always stay committed to being a person who will support adolescents to better understand their search for themselves, and that having bad things happen when you are a child or an adolescent is just part of a unique journey that shapes you—it's not good or bad, it just 'is'. Helping young people find their own call to greatness, despite what hand they're dealt, is what life is all about.

> *Life will throw you a curved ball from time to time. It's what you do with it that makes all the difference.*
>
> Maggie Dent

The window when adolescents can have a lust for risking, playing, experimenting and exploring who they are is one that doesn't last forever. *Much more* at risk are the adolescents who are lost in virtual worlds in their bedrooms being numbed and distracted by the screen world. We need to keep an eye on our pre-teens to see where their interests lie and notice any experience that they seem very excited about, because it may be a clue to what they may like to pursue when the massive overproduction of synaptic connections occurs.

We can over-worry and keep our adolescents too safe and over-protected, and on their bumpy ride to adulthood they may simply get lost on a road they were never meant to travel. They have *an amazing capability to learn and cope.*

In previous eras many adolescents had left school at 14 years of age and worked very hard. They developed a tolerance, wisdom and resilience about life by experiencing it, which is much different to being shown or told how life can be. I know of 14-year-olds who care for invalid parents or look after younger siblings, and they do this quite competently.

When adolescents know what biological changes are happening in their brain and why, they can better understand some of the confusion they feel. It can empower them to know they are not alone and that Mother Nature is preparing them to become wise adults. The ride has been bumpy for everyone—especially their parents!

Dear Mrs D

I'm sorry if I spell a bit rong but I have improved so much because of you. I have lurnt more off you than I have off anyone else in my holl life. Mum was so proud of my report. Do you rember when I first cam to you I had no friends, I hated myself and I didn't want to live? I lied to myself and everyone all time, now I hardly ever lie at all. I have so menny friends its hard to keep up with them all. Befor I met you I had tried to kill myself so many times. Now I never even think it.

Thank you for not doing what evry other teacher did to me – give up on me.

Thank you so much for believing in me.

4. Myelination—insulating the neurons and synaptic connections.

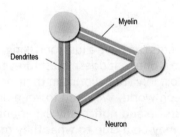

Myelination
Finished prefrontal lobe- adult reasoning brain

This is the final stage of brain development and involves the thickening of the white matter, or myelin, on the axons. This is the process of insulating the neurons and synaptic connections, which allows more connections and more efficient usage. This means the quality of thinking improves, and from 22 to 28 years of age the pre-frontal lobe (the executive function of the brain) will be mature enough to ensure that improved decision making can take place. This generally indicates less emotional unpredictability, more impulse control and better organisational skills.

> *The frontal lobes are the section of the brain responsible for abstract thinking, good decision making, analysing and problem solving are among the last parts to receive myelination. As the frontal lobes mature during adolescence the quality of thinking increases.*
>
> Corbin, B.

The myelination process is negatively affected by alcohol and drug abuse. Marijuana is essentially a fat loving substance and in the rapidly developing brain it can eat up the myelin and thus slows down the thinking, and weaken motivation. Binge drinking can strip new learning from the brain—what a waste that would be in the final years of school!From 22 to 24 years of age for girls, and 26 to 28 for boys (allowing for boy delay, although some may argue it takes much longer for boys!) is when parents can start to breathe a sigh of relief. At this time there will be less emotional unpredictability, more impulse control and better organisational skills. This can only happen if the developing brain in that critical window of pruning and overproduction of dendrites has not been damaged by accidents, addictions or lack of positive experiences to grow positively.

> *The immediate social environment of any learning setting reflects values, beliefs, habits, ways of being and discourses of contributing culture.*
>
> Nuthall, G., *Commentary of learning, and language and understanding the complexity of the classroom*, (1996)

This is why so many youth programs that create opportunities for adolescents can turn their lives around. The time of this significant adolescent brain development means that adults—especially parents, teachers, youth workers, counsellors and coaches—hold the key to an adolescent's future life success on all levels. Even for those who have had challenging childhoods with abuse and deprivation, this time presents an opportunity to reshape themselves if they're given optimal opportunities by adults who are prepared to act as lighthouses. They need to offer not only safe places to live and basic care, they also need to offer positive experiences that can reshape the adolescent brain.

Many adults wrongfully step back out of their adolescent's lives thinking they need to develop autonomy, or maybe they find they are just too hard to manage. But, we now know that adolescents need support and guidance, not control, well into their 20s. The perception that they will be fine after 18 years of age is a fallacy. You will know when the pre-frontal lobe has finally grown because they will not only thank you for a delicious meal they will *offer* and *do* the cleaning up with a smile on their face.

Some of the things that support adolescent social and emotional as well as cognitive learning for the MilGen are:

- the WIIFM factor (What's In It For Me?)
- genuine compassion
- authenticity.

The MilGen adolescent wants to know 'What's in it for me?' and that means that there has to be a high degree of relevance for anything they do, whether it's at home, school or work. They value genuine compassion that is non-judgemental and accepting of where they are at, not just where they could be. Finally, today's young people hate inauthenticity, even though they find it hard to define, and if they're aged under 17 they will find it hard to notice. Being accepted as they are at any point in time helps them feel safe, which means being less stressed.

The inner critic in adolescents is working overtime, especially since the growth of the emotional domains in the brain. They are beating themselves up most of the time. Having significant adults who can validate their emotional state without judgement, and accept they need to find their own solutions or pathway in order to grow is vitally important to all adolescents—even those who look like they are doing OK. Remember I had all the external signs of a capable successful adolescent and I almost killed myself over a failed essay!

On Listening

When I ask you to listen to me
and you give me advice,
you have not heard what I asked of you.

When I ask you to listen
and you tell me why I shouldn't feel as I do,
you are trampling on my feelings.

When I ask you to listen
and you feel you have to find solutions to my problems
I feel let down, strange as it may seem.

Please listen. All I ask is that you listen—not talk or do or advise: Just LISTEN.

Advice is cheap. I can get that anywhere.
I can do for myself. I'm not helpless;
maybe discouraged and faltering, but not helpless.

When you do something for me
that I can and need to do for myself,
you contribute to my fear and reinforce my weaknesses.

When you accept as a simple fact,
that I feel what I feel,
however irrational it may sound to you,
then I can quit trying to convince you and I can then explore this irrational feeling.

When that's clear, the answers are obvious
and I don't need advice.
My irrational fears make sense when I can discover what's behind them.
If you listen and understand I can work things out for myself.

So I ask again. Just listen and hear me,
and if you too have something to say
be patient, then I'll listen to you.

Dr Ralph Roughton (Adapted)

Key Points

- The adolescent brain is large and poorly organised.

- Pruning aims to improve the functioning of the brain by decreasing grey matter and increasing white matter.

- Pruning can make adolescents forgetful, disorganised, emotionally unpredictable and more likely to misread facial expressions.

- Pruning can make adolescents feel vulnerable, incapable and less confident.

- At the same time as pruning occurs, the brain also over-produces synaptic connections and dendrites.

- Adolescents can learn faster during this window of opportunity, as well as become addicted faster and develop unhealthy thinking patterns.

- Many adolescents flourish despite all the changes that are happening to them.

- The brain does not finish its myelination process until the 20s, at which stage an adolescent develops better reasoning, problem solving, impulse control and the ability to reflect.

- The final stages of the brain's development can be hindered by alcohol and drug abuse.

- Most adolescents have no idea what's happening in their brain and it can help if they know 'what's going on up there'.

Chapter 5

Why the emotional chaos and confusion?

I see them staring, laughing, pointing, looking at me. It happens every day, not just once every so often but every single day. Now when I wake up in the morning I look in the mirror and I see a person I hate.

Covich, S. (ed), *A Circle in a Room Full of Squares*, (2002).

Adolescents can struggle enormously with their emotional world. During my time in classrooms over the years I sometimes wondered why a boy would suddenly punch a wall over something quite minor. I discovered in my counselling that adolescents could be drowning in the emotional sea of something that happened months ago, but had already been considered to be resolved. I also found that when I read a story from *Chicken Soup for the Soul* to a class of supposed tough students, they all had tears in their eyes and were moved by a collective emotion.

Emotion is a term that describes certain feelings and bodily changes that occur when the brain is aroused. Emotions are often aroused from an unconscious level of the brain. Biological changes during adolescence show a growth of the amygdala, which is considered to be the emotional epicentre or gatekeeper, especially around fear and anger. Adolescents rely more on the emotional part of their brain.

Emotional illiteracy

Gayle Greogry PhD identified the following key elements in violent male adolescents who conducted mass murders in US school:

- Kids were ignored as children.
- Very little play activity as a child.
- Average age 13–14 years.
- Typically very bright.
- Usually overweight or underweight.
- Absent dad or poor relationship with dad.
- Don't know how to lose.
- Have few emotional breaks.
- Members of groups with like interests, for example, gangs.
- Have no fear.
- Desire to use power with violence.
- Often TV, video or computer over-users, especially with a violent preference.

We must accept responsibility as adults who care for children, and aim to build the emotional intelligence of our children so they do not have to become violent, anti-social cripples capable of hurting others. Emotional competence includes many areas and doesn't just appear in a box on the 16th birthday. This is why the value we place on the first five years of a child's life reflects the value we hold as a society about life in general.

Qualities of emotional intelligence

In Daniel Goleman's *Emotional Intelligence,* the following qualities of emotional intelligence (EQ) were identified:

- Awareness of feeling states.
- Being able to motivate oneself.
- Persistence in the face of frustration.
- Impulse control.
- Delayed gratification.
- Regulation of one's moods.
- Keeping distress from swamping one's ability to think.
- Ability to accurately empathize.
- Hopefulness.

Adolescents can be very short of some of these characteristics and yet some people have them in abundance. An adolescent can appear to lose the EQ that had prior to adolescence and we need to know, this is part of the bumpy ride! The fully developed brain certainly helps when wanting to be emotionally literate. For more information on how to build emotional, social and spiritual competence in children and adolescents check out *Nurturing Kids Hearts and Souls* by Maggie Dent.

The adolescent response to threat

Adolescents use the amygdala to interpret the same information that an adult would interpret using the pre-frontal lobe. This is why they have such difficulty with misreading social situations, communicating with others, emotional vulnerability and impulse control. It also influences such aspects as hunger, thirst, sleep, sexual response and hormone production. The limbic system is particularly affected by the great surge of sex hormones.

This is also partly why so many adolescents can be obsessive about clothes, music, personal image, peer pressure and infatuations with others. This heightened sensitivity can appear quite irrational at times to adults because we have a pre-frontal lobe that allows for reasoned thinking. They also experience big highs and lows that occur rapidly. This can be very confusing and confronting for adolescents.

Here's a classic example of how an adolescent brain functions without a reasoning pre-frontal lobe:

There was a 15-year-old boy who had ADHD. He decided to graffiti the principal's car after the principal had words with him about his behaviour. Unfortunately, the lad's graffiti included his name so he was easy to identify!

> *When we feel unsafe, physically or psychologically, impulses from the reptilian and mammalian parts of our brain override our higher functions, and we can behave like a threatened animal.*
>
> Sunderland, M., *The Science of Parenting: How today's brain research can help you raise happy, emotionally balanced children*, (2006).

So many of an adolescent's responses to their world are coming from the least developed part of the brain. The amygdala is supposed to have the capacity to size up situations and take control of them instantly so that it will work faster than the slower thinking parts of the brain. For example it will quickly initiate pulling hand away from a hot stove without needing to think about it. John Joseph in his book, *Learning in the Emotional Rooms: How to create classrooms that are uplifting for the spirit,* sums it up as:

> *This is good for survival because while the thinking parts of the brain are still trying to size up the situation and come to a decision about what to do, the amygdala has already coordinated an instant bodily response about what to do, the amygdala has already coordinated an instant bodily response that will keep it safe.*

When confronted by a threatening situation, the primitive brain tends to respond automatically in one of three ways:

1. Flight.
2. Freeze.
3. Fight.

During my seminars I ask students and adults to imagine that they have been asked to go to a work place to collect something at night. They have to enter a code into the alarm system within 30 seconds of opening the door. I then suddenly and very loudly make an alarm noise designed to scare them. I then ask, 'What is your first reaction?' We will always tend to do one of the above responses.

If you are a 'flight' person (whom I call a 'runner') you'll be home on your lounge within two minutes. Runners will also tend to lie about being there at all out of fear of being disclosed. If you are a 'freezer' you can stay stuck for quite some time immobile and unable to think. If you are a 'fighter' you're likely to keep on punching in numbers on the alarm pad, albeit quite irrationally.

With adults who have pre-frontal lobes, after a period of shock the brain will kick in with some strategies like, 'Take a breath and think!' or 'Maybe there's a number to call for the alarm security people,' or 'Who would know the number?'

Adolescents do not have this capacity to reason and do not have it until their 20s at the earliest.

Adolescents struggle with situations of perceived threat. Remember, they can perceive threat where it may not exist because of the pruning[2*] process that has occurred in their brain which means they can misread things.

David's story

I remember a 14-year-old boy called 'David' who had experienced a very tough childhood. He was a fighter and was always ready to fight over everything he was asked to do, even with teachers who treated him well. His brain had a habitual response to figures of authority because he had been subjected to many experiences that were painful. It takes time to change the core concepts or thinking patterns and this is one of the reasons why adolescent behaviour can be so challenging.

David did make some changes in my class because he finally realised he was safe. A sense of safety can allow the brain to come off guard and be less likely to react from an irrational place of threat. Unfortunately, he did not have the same good fortune in his physical education class.

The tough male teacher tried to make David be more cooperative by shaming, yelling and using threats. He also would hit David with cricket bats as though it was a joke. One day David snapped and punched the teacher to the ground. He came and saw me just after the incident and said he thought it was best if he left town because he couldn't take any more.

---

2   * NB: Pruning seems to curb ADHD symptoms and Tourette's Syndrome. Disorders such as schizophrenia and OCD get worse with pruning.

How many students have been pushed to breaking point by teachers who do not understand how the brain works during adolescence?

The emotional barometer

Emotions can continue to exist within our nervous system long after an event that has triggered them. Anyone who has lost a loved one will know that grief and sadness, and sometimes anger, can last a very long time.

To show how adolescents struggle emotionally draw a diagram of a barometer. Pretend that it belongs to either a boy or girl. Imagine that at the bottom of the barometer bulb that there are some emotions that are still in a girl's nervous system from early childhood.

Let's pretend that at one time she was the baby of the family and loved being seen as special. Then along comes a sweet little sister who not only takes her place, she also appears to have become Dad's little princess. Colour in the bottom layer of the barometer.

Then, just before her second birthday, another older sister decides to cut off all her lovely golden curls while she was playing hairdresser. Now she looks like a boy in all the photos taken at her second birthday party. She's not happy about that!

Then, when she was four her older brother stole her Barbie doll, cut off its head and buried it in the back yard—and Dad never growled at him. She's very unhappy about that. It's time to colour in more of the barometer.

Now she is 14-years-old and has found it really hard to wake up on this day. After three attempts her mum has yelled at her to get up, which is not a good way to start the day. When she gets down to the kitchen to have breakfast she has found that Daddy's Princess has just eaten the last of her favourite cereal. Then when she gets to the bathroom, as she is the last person in the house, there is no hot water left. By this stage she's very unhappy. Colour in more of the barometer.

By now, the young adolescent girl has had to put on her dirty gym gear that she flicked under her bed last week because it's gym day. Then she's had to run for the bus, but realises that she has left her completed maths assignment on her desk and forgotten her lunch.

Normally her friends keep her a seat at the back of the bus, but today they didn't. The only seat available is next to the ugliest boy on the entire planet. Not only does he have braces, he has food hanging out of them. He also has such greasy hair that the grease is dripping on his shoulders and his BO is so bad that she has to hold her nose. Her day is unfolding in the worst possible way. Time to colour in more of the barometer.

At school she gets into trouble for leaving her maths assignment at home, and worse still, the teacher thought she was just making an excuse and didn't believe her. More things happen during the school day that make her feel worse—plus she's very hungry. She can't find her friends at lunchtime and the negative self-talk in her head really amps up—'Maybe they don't like me? Maybe they think I am fat, ugly and stupid? I have no friends, no one who cares'. Then she sees someone who looks at her like 'You are a fat slut' (remember, adolescents misread facial expressions badly).

The downward cycle rapidly gets worse with an intensity that few adults can understand. So, when she accidentally bumps a small Year 8 girl outside the library and her books fall everywhere she explodes. She calls the small girl all sorts of names and makes a total scene. This is the boiling point of her barometer and the incident with the Year 8 girl is the final straw. The final straw that overloads the nervous system, can be quite small.

This metaphor shows how we all can become emotionally overloaded and the tipping point can trigger a huge response that is way bigger than what the stimuli warrants.

Adolescents have difficulty managing their emotional world and need to know that they can do things to help diffuse their emotional barometer. The tipping point was when David assaulted the teacher; however, it can be quite small like with the imaginary girl above.

We have real concerns for adolescents because mental illness appears for the first time for many people during this vulnerable window. I remember speaking to a mother of a 16-year-old son at a suicide prevention conference. She said her son had walked in after school and eaten two biscuits out of biscuit barrel. When he went to get the third she asked him to put it back because dinner wasn't far away. Without her noticing, her son walked down the back yard and hung himself from a tree. He had reached his tipping point and couldn't take anymore. His mother said if she had known he could have eaten the whole barrel.

We must be very aware of an adolescent's enormous emotional vulnerability and ensure we don't make assumptions about understanding what is happening inside their confused minds.

When you add other stressors like rejection, failure or lack of sleep an adolescent can reach their tipping point quite quickly or unexpectedly.

I can't remember what my first word was, but I am pretty sure it was probably 'dunno'. When I got home from school with my parents fresh off the phone from an angry teacher, I'd just shrug my shoulders and say, 'dunno' to Dad when he asked why I'd been naughty this time.

I suppose it was easier to formulate words as to how I felt. Even then, I don't expect I could have mustered anything more enlightening than the 'd' word. Truth is, I was as much a mystery to myself as I was to everyone else.

Creed, L., A *puppy called aero: How a Labrador saved a boy with ADHD*, (2009).

These insightful words come from a boy who not only had adolescent turmoil going on, he also had ADHD. His story of how he was helped by taking part in an out of school program with dogs is full of amazing experiences seen through the eyes of the boy. His descriptions of his emotional melt-downs are so realistic that it is like being in the mind of an adolescent boy. This is an excellent book to read for adolescents as well as adults.

Anger and frustration

There is no question that adolescents who feel supported, understood and have a place where they are heard, can manage emotions much better than those who are not. Emotions need to be diffused from the body or they will remain in the nervous system. Vigorous physical activity is the preferred mode for diffusing the big emotions such as anger and frustration, however, there are other ways to do this.

Anger is an emotion that involves two notions. First, a perception of some wrong, or problem in the world, committed by someone else, and second, a sense of the unfairness or the injustice of this wrong.

Currie, M., *Doing Anger Differently: Helping Adolescent Boys*, (2008).

As people develop emotional maturity, they are often better able to use their 'executive function' (the frontal lobes) to interpret potentially unfair experiences. However, for the adolescent brain it is clear: it's about them, it's wrong, it's unfair. This leads to them getting very angry very quickly.

Understand that anger is a symptom, not the problem.

Many parents want their adolescent to stop being angry because they see the anger as the problem. The parent does not understand that anger is a response, and is often a reaction to feeling disconnected, useless, powerless or out of control. Once again, lighthouses in an adolescent's life can help them explore the deeper issues that drive their big feelings. Often, anger, which is accepted more easily among peers, is a cover up for sadness or depression, characteristics which can be perceived as weaknesses.

Another key area to understanding anger is conflict about the adolescent's own sense of identity. Repeated acts of aggression, especially with a key figure of authority where an adolescent is made to feel bad or hopeless, can be a way of him defending or attacking his wholeness, or how he sees himself. He must attack so that he does not succumb to 'disintegration' (Currie, 2008).

> *Anger is an emotion that emerges when the stability of one's self image is threatened from without. Aggression, the act of physically damaging or destroying something or someone in the world, emerges when this threat becomes unbearable.*
>
> Currie, M.

This is a vitally important understanding for lighthouses as they can be that one person who can help an angry adolescent find reassurance that their core identity still has a potential for goodness, or there are parts that hold positive value. This is why a relationship built on trust and acceptance can be such an important buffer against the confusion of an adolescent's world.

Michael Currie believes that helping aggressive adolescent boys with a 'cycle of identity' will help them grow emotionally and enable them to better manage their apparently irrational aggression. The cycle of identity contains three steps that build an adolescent's capacity to find meaning in their world:

1. Perception of the event: By describing the actions that took place from their place of reality.
2. Meaning-making: From description to constructing meaning. Be an emotions coach and help them identify the positive and negative consequences of his actions.
3. Performing meaning: From constructing 'meaning' to 'action'. Help them identify any attempts to change their previous choices. This can help them understand ethical behaviour, accepting responsibility, and learning about the value of growing awareness of how social interaction occurs.

This approach is similar to Ian Grant's 'CPR' approach with boys:

C — Consequence: A penalty that will teach.

P — Plan: How to put it right.

R — Reconciliation: Relationship restored.

Too often adolescents, especially boys, are shamed, lectured and punished without being allowed to explore what was wrong and how to fix it. This feeds their low sense of self and their inner anger at themselves. This increases the pressure in their emotional barometer thus increasing the chance of a major melt-down, and so the cycle continues. Instead of shaming and judging, work with an adolescent so they can see how they can make better decisions next time. They have such an intense self-critical voice playing in their head all the time, so why make it worse?

When an adolescent is angry, upset or feeling threatened their brain is being swamped by stress hormones such as cortisol, which is produced by the hippocampus. Cortisol is a slow acting chemical that can stay in the brain at high levels for hours, and in clinically depressedpeople for days or weeks (Sunderland, 2006).

> *There is a mass of scientific research showing that quality of life is dramatically affected by whether or not good stress-regulating systems are established in the brain in childhood. Research also shows that it is very hard to reverse an over-active stress response system.*
>
> Sunderland, M., *The Science of Parenting: How Today's Brain Research Can Help You Raise Happy, Emotionally Balanced Children*, (2006).

This flooding of cortisol makes people feel anxious and stressed. To avoid such emotional pain individuals can act impulsively and rashly. Just as for children, the stress hormones in the adolescent brain need some help to change so as to stimulate opioids, dopamine, norepinephrine and serotonin—the calming brain chemicals.

Serotonin is responsible for improving mood, emotional stability and sleep quality. This again reaffirms the vital role of lighthouses in adolescents' lives. The lighthouse offers safety, trust, unconditional acceptance, and gestures of reassurance and kindness that can help the adolescent alter the chemical reactions in their brain. Unfortunately, most troubled and distressed teenagers are met with quite the opposite, which further adds to their inability to manage their big feelings without causing more problems.

Mental illness and emotional response

> *Various neurotransmitters (brain chemicals) that control and regulate such things as moods, impulse, motivation and emotional excitability are greatly influenced by sex hormones produced during this emotionally explosive time in an individual's life. Because of this teenagers often experience emotional highs and lows more quickly and at the same time have less control over these emotions.*
>
> Corbin, B.

Parents need to be vigilant for any signs of mental illness. Nothing is as frightening for a parent than to know that their child may take their life, despite the love they give their child. Sadly, a parent's love is sometimes simply not enough. Adolescent depression is a huge contributing factor in suicide. Lower levels of serotonin during adolescence can contribute to depression, especially for those with negative thinking loops. This further feeds the low serotonin levels and makes adolescents feel worse.

You are the **neurotransmitter source** in the home and classroom

Positive	Negative
• Serotonin	• Cortisol
• Dopamine	• Adrenaline
• Endorphins	• Noradrenaline

Neurotransmitters influence both explicit and implicit memory

Adults need to be aware that they can profoundly influence the emotional state of adolescents both positively and negatively. This is why schools need to rethink their raison d'être. If schools aimed to create inclusive caring cultures ahead of academic grades, then they would improve their academic grades while keeping more adolescents engaged at school. When students feel safe, valued and worthy of being part of a school community—even when they make mistakes, have low literacy or have special needs—they would be able to learn better with more positive neurotransmitters, and have less emotional overwhelm, irrational behaviour and mental illness.

Micahel Carr-Gregg in his book *When to Worry* explores adolescent mental illness so that parents can better understand what it can look like! Some adolescents disguise depression with lethal consequences. There are times that can definitely be more dangerous than just normal adolescent 'bumpiness'. So be particularly mindful around the following challenges during adolescence;

- Serious problems at school or a cluster of problems
- New incidents of bullying

- Unresolved grief over death of parent, sibling, friend or relationship ending.
- Ongoing violence or conflict at home
- Family break-up
- Drug and alcohol use and abuse
- Suffering long term illness or injury

Healthy activation of positive brain chemicals can help in the prevention of depression as can healthy nutrition, plenty of exercise, loving relationships, meaningful involvement and a strong spirit. Parents and lighthouses can help adolescents keep healthy in mind, body and spirit. Adolescents are often their own worst enemy and vigilance is essential in keeping an eye on their well-being.

It takes the development of the pre-frontal lobes of the brain for an individual to have the capacity to make a different choice, although the automatic response will most likely always be the first choice anyway. Think about how often adolescents get into fights, whether verbally or physically, and how many run away and disappear. Adults who act as lighthouses need to be aware of this behaviour in young people and know how to support both them and their families to negotiate these detours and bumps in the road.

Now just a little more about the primitive responses that govern much of adolescent behavior:

Flight

For the adolescents most likely to go into flight response when threatened, also known as the 'runners', we need to ensure they have somewhere to run. This may help explain why over 26,000 adolescents aged between 12 and 25 are homeless in Australia on any given night. This also explains why so many are reported missing to police. The most common reason families and friends believe adolescents go missing (at the time of going missing), and the most common explanation given afterwards, is conflict about authority, rules or independent behaviour. When an adolescent is threatened and they've reached their tipping point they will run away from the threat.

When there is a serious conflict or fight that sees an adolescent leaving the family home we all must work hard to help reunite that family.

Adolescents are often much more at risk in the outside world. Sadly, some are safer.

In the many reconciliations I have supported I have noticed that it really helps if an adolescent knows that if ever a tough moment happens and they need 'time out' from home for a while, it helps if they know where to run.

A group of parents, or a family, need to have an understanding that an adolescent needs to know where they are welcome if they decide to run. The other home will—without judgement—let the parents know their child is safe and then try the magic three-day window.

If you have had some very hurtful things shouted at you in the heat of the moment you can forget that you love your adolescent. The same goes for your emotionally challenged adolescent. Leave everything for three days because it takes about that long for both sides to calm down. Also it takes around three days for an adolescent to miss their bed, their bedroom, their stuff, the dog, Mum's cooking and maybe their freedom. They will eventually miss home.

For the parents it may take every minute of the three days to remember how much they love their adolescent and then acknowledge that they have the pre-frontal lobe and their adolescent doesn't. A parent needs to act like an adult and call their child and accept ALL the blame for the conflict. This is much more successful than telling them to apologise for things they said and rehashing the awful things said.

This may sound like giving in, but surprisingly, if a parent accepts all responsibility, an adolescent will often disagree and see that their parent is doing the essential bridge building that they themselves are not capable of doing.

Freeze

The 'freezers' who bury their emotions and disappear sometimes can become potentially more at risk later. Adolescents who freeze emotionally can risk an even bigger melt-down than those who run or fight because they hold enormous emotional distress under a calm or dreamy exterior.

I have worked with many 'freezers' who end up very sick physically, or when they snap they can kill because their emotional intensity is so much higher. These adolescents are often introverted, keep to themselves or hide in their bedroom away from the stressors of the world. They survive by escaping in their dream world, TV world or computer game world.

I have found that a very high percentage of cutters or self-harmers are 'freezers' who feel so numb to pain that it's only when they cut themselves they feel better. In my work I have found that a high percentage of self-harmers have been victims of abuse, particularly sexual, that has created deep shame. This shame can sit quite dormant until the amygdala develops and then things get much tougher.

Male shame from childhood can turn into deep despair and self-hatred and can result in suicide attempts. This pattern often happens to gentle sensitive boys who were shamed for not being tough by a significant male figure early in childhood. I worked with one 19-year-old who had made several attempts at suicide. He remembered his dad not only teasing him when he cried, he also took his comfort blanket and teddy bear off him well before he went to school to toughen him up. This lad was able to overcome his deep patterns of shame and inadequacy, and has grown up to be a very loving, committed father to his own children.

Fight

The final group are the fighters and that's exactly what they do—fight! They will fight verbally, physically, psychologically or emotionally, and there is a distinct difference between girls and boys.

Boys will tend to quite suddenly resort to aggression or violence when they reach their tipping point. Some are triggered by frustration or confusion rather than anger per se. Boys are more likely to use anger and aggression to cover feeling dumb, useless or vulnerable. However, it is often interpreted as normal male aggressiveness.

Girls who are fighters will fight by arguing, being incredibly bitchy and nasty, and by practising female tactics of freezing out or ignoring others. When girls fight physically there is often a high level of planning and intentionality about it. This is not the same as boys who tend to just explode and fight.

Adolescents who have lost a loved one when they were children can often struggle with deep sadness and grief when their amygdala grows, even though they seemed to have coped with the loss as a child. The grief can surface as deep irrational anger. Many adolescent boys or young men will become aggressive and get into fights very easily to cover up their sense of feeling so weak and vulnerable. They can also use binge drinking or other drug use to cover up the grief and they create more risk for themselves but they are simply struggling with deep emotional states that frighten them. Unresolved grief can easily turn into depression during adolescence.

Things to help protect and nurture adolescents

In the *Kit Bag*, the product I have created for adolescents, there is a list of things that young people can do to help move their emotions safely.

There are positive ways and life-negating ways of overcoming the effects of major stress and emotional overwhelm. Encourage adolescents to try the positive ones often so they can avoid getting used to the quick fixes like pills, binge drinking or lots of chocolate.

Safe stress-busters:

- Get active—especially outside—doing something you enjoy like walking, riding, yoga or Tai Chi.
- Call a friend—especially one you can trust.
- Do a guided relaxation like *Relax and Escape*, or *Dare to Dream*.
- Play uplifting music that you enjoy.

- Play calming music that you enjoy.
- Read a book that is pure escapism from life.
- Drink four glasses of water.
- Make a juice with fresh fruit.
- Do something creative—paint, draw, play music, take photos.
- Get out family albums with your baby photos.
- Watch a positive film like *Lion King*, *Shrek* or *Forrest Gump*.
- Share your emotional state with a family member who loves you.
- Cook something for the family like cookies or melting moments.
- Go to the park or beach.
- Go to your special place in nature.
- Read a great kids' picture book or cartoon book.
- Read a joke book.
- Write in a journal.
- Do something for someone who needs help.
- Arrange to speak with a school chaplain or counsellor.
- Have a long bath or shower and wash everything really clean.
- Try some energy releasing techniques.
- Get as many hugs as you can.
- Write a letter to someone special.
- Watch ants.
- Find a butterfly.
- Look at the stars and count them all.
- Pretend you have just fallen in love with your fantasy.
- Wash your sheets and clean the windows in your room.
- Light a candle and pray for help.
- When all else fails, walk at least three kilometres to buy a small bar of chocolate that has fruit and nuts in it—this is really a health food! Eat this very slowly and then walk home.

Even with this information we know the ability to take action is difficult because it takes a mature adult brain with reasoning powers. This is one of the reasons why adolescents choose ways to numb deep emotional pain by using alcohol, drugs or by doing risky things. They are seeking ways to change their emotional states. They are seeking transcendence, an expanded state that makes them feel 'more' or 'better' than what they felt before. Even adults do this.

Emotional Freedom Therapy

Emotional Acupressure
Release Points

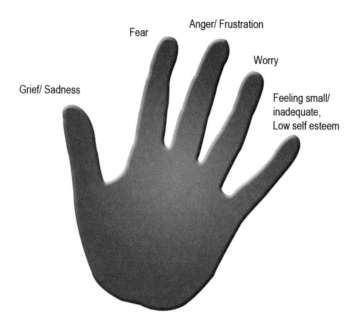

I am an advocate of Emotional Freedom Therapy (EFT) as a means of removing emotions from our nervous system. It is the quickest way to improve how a person feels emotionally, plus they can do it for themselves.

In EFT there are tapping points on the face that release emotion, they are the end points of the energy meridians within the body. There are also points on the fingers just next to the nail, but not the fatty bit, on the side closest to the thumb. Adolescents find it quite amusing to find that the middle finger is the 'anger finger'! I have suggested that if they see their parents busily tapping their middle finger, it's probably not the best time to ask for anything.

Patricia Mathes Cane PhD works with traumatised children after disasters like civil wars, earthquakes and tsunamis. She uses the same EFT techniques because they can work with a large group of children at a time. There are huge benefits that young people can gain by deep quietness and stillness. With the modern world moving so fast and filled with so many distractions, many adolescents never stop. There is enormous pressure to stay connected to friends via technology and because of their brain immaturity they have trouble maintaining boundaries. This means that they have very little time 'off the grid' where they can rest, go slow or take some time out from their busy day.

This is one of the reasons why I use calming CDs with adolescents. When used often the unconscious mind creates a pathway to relaxation that soothes a busy psyche. The brain will produce serotonin and other dopamines that soothe the body. Much of the time when adolescents are experiencing stress they are creating hormones and chemicals that make them stay alert to threat. The cortisol that's produced can be a threat to well-being if it is never switched off.

With the simple functioning of an adolescent brain going though its biological changes and having a newly developed amygdala coupled with a body doing strange things, it is easy to see why adolescents can be so unpredictable. When they discharge their excess emotional angst from their nervous system, it's often Mum on the receiving end. Maybe mums should see this as a sign of how much their child really loves them by simply trying to empty their emotional barometer. I believe there is very little intentionality to these outbursts, they just happen.

Daniel Goleman writes about 'emotional contagion'. This is the concept that strong emotions can influence others. This is why some enthusiastic and optimistic teachers can totally change a student's perception of not only their subject, but also of themself. It's quite a good thing when the emotional contagion is an uplifting one, however it can be very dangerous when it is negative. This is one of the reasons why deep grief can be so debilitating for adolescents- it also can effect friends of the same age.

An adolescent brain mainly processes through the amygdala rather than the frontal lobes, but it is still not mature and an adolescent is more susceptible to being influenced. This may be one reason why they can follow peer behaviour that is driven by strong emotions; for example, like those experienced in gangs. It may also explain why clusters of suicides can happen after a single suicide. Adolescents like to connect with others who feel the same, and with websites that encourage anorexia and self-harm, we have more reasons to be worried about our young people.

There is much happening in the emotional world of adolescents that is quite irrational and unpredictable. This spills over into the virtual world where adolescents can get lost to point where they can have the same responses to something that happens on TV as they do in the real world. I can remember days when it was difficult to engage students in class because a major character had died on *Home and Away*. Adolescents can be deeply affected by what happens in the world of TV and we must accept that is a sign of the immaturity of their brain. When we say how silly they are, or that it's just TV, we can contribute to overloading their nervous system. It may also add to an adolescent's view of the world where they believe that no one understands them. This sense of feeling alienated and disconnected drives a lot of adolescent negative thinking. This can lead to irrational thinking loops that can lead to mental illness—'No one cares' and 'I don't matter.'

Many times an adolescent who has attempted suicide mentions to me that they never told their parents because, 'I would just be another disappointment to them,' or 'They would be better off if I wasn't there as I don't matter.'

Everyone in an adolescent's life matters. Even if they think they matter to a teacher, their nana, or the friendly man in the newsagent who chats to them whenever they go into the shop. I know how this feels. I had a boyfriend, lots of friends and was part of a basketball team and club. But, there was no one I had let get close enough to allow genuine affection to occur because I really believed no one could like, let alone love, someone as damaged and ugly as me.

When an adolescent has done something inappropriate or stupid like punch someone, jump off a double story balcony or fart loudly in class, it can take their inner world on quite a ride. Often they just did these things without thinking and had no thought to the possible dangers, or whether others may be unhappy. When they have been made aware of the true nature of their misdemeanour they can often have a huge rush of feeling stupid. For boys this is often followed by anger at themselves for being so stupid, and it's usually when they get a well-meaning lecture about their inappropriate actions. This often takes their emotional barometer into overdrive, and if it's poorly handled then a melt-down can occur. Their inner thoughts can make them feel worse than they need to and they may simply react with the automatic flight, freeze or fight.

> *It is important when handling adolescent indiscretions that we don't blow them up from molehills into mountains. I once worked with a homeless girl who left home because an argument went badly about who left a wet towel in the bathroom! She had simply run and kept on running. In her reality her parents hated her and were just too hard to live with. She had struggled with living in squats around drug addicts and drunks. She had been beaten up, raped and used by many unsavoury adults. But her pride and her inability to manage her emotional world meant she preferred to stay there than go home. Fortunately, she had found a lighthouse in a youth refuge and was getting back on a safer track.*

Other than EFT and the finger tapping, I show young people other simple ways to move big emotional states. These include:

- Laughter and lightness.
- Athletic success.
- Artistic and creative expression.
- Deep relaxation and stillness.
- Safe, honest human connection.

- Significant immersion in nature.
- Acts of service.
- Discovering new purpose and meaning.
- Ritual and ceremony.
- Celebration activities.
- Gratitude.
- Kindness.

Understandably, emotional illiteracy is common in all young people, especially troubled adolescents, and an important role for parents, teachers and lighthouses is to help build these competencies. Many adolescents take things very personally. Many struggle with strong, irrational, ugly emotional states and need safe adults to help them move through these without triggering the primitive brain responses of flight, freeze and fight.

Techniques to Manage/ Transform Emotional States and to support adolescent emotional and social growth......

- Colour/ breath clearing.
- Staying in the moment – is it really happening?
- Magic Eye Scramble.
- Taming the negative critic voice with circuit breakers
- Becoming grounded.
- Deep breathing
- Creative visualization.
- Safely expend excess energy.
- Caring, empowering communication.
- Allow nature to nurture you.
- Calming CD's especially creative visualisations
- Energy therapy techniques incl finger tapping
- Emotional freedom technique.
- Being really heard and understood.
- Avoid sleep deprivation.
- Neuro Linguistic Programming (NLP) techniques to reframe or hide the painful experience.
- Ask 'what would love do right now?'
- Be mindful of 'awfulizing'.
- Artistic effort – dance, paint, draw, sing.
- Make another choice.
- Find resolution through some action (eg. truth letter, see appendix).
- Practise honesty.
- Safe, reassuring touch.
- Ensure healthy nutrition.
- Reduce other stressors in an individual's life.
- Build sense of humour and learn to laugh

With multiple stressors like relationship problems, identity confusion, school challenges, bullying, image issues and illness, many adolescents struggle with emotional overwhelm. They can become very vulnerable and distressed, and parents need to be as supportive as possible. This is another place where lighthouses can be life-saving.

Hope is recognised as a serious emotional state-changer in an adolescent's life. Amidst the chaos of an immature mind, hope can transform doom and gloom into light. We all need to believe that adversities or challenges can be diminished. This optimistic thinking pattern is characteristic of resilient people. Lighthouses need to harbour hope, especially when the adolescent appears to have given up. They also need to sow possibilities of hope into the psyche of adolescents. Germination of this hope may not be readily seen, however, there is a strong possibility that in the future the young person may look back and remember quite clearly a time in their life when a positive influence helped them through a difficult time.

The power of hope

- Hope can be defined as: Believing you have both the will and the way to accomplish your goals, whatever they may be.
- Hope makes all the difference. Given roughly the same range of intellectual abilities, emotional aptitudes can make the critical difference.
- Modern researchers are finding that hope does more than offer a bit of solace amid affliction—it plays a surprisingly potent role in life.
- Students with a high level of hope recover quicker from poor school grades.

People with high levels of hope share the following traits:

- Are able to motivate themselves.
- Feel resourceful enough to find different ways to accomplish their objectives.
- Reassure themselves when in a tight spot that things will get better.
- Are flexible enough to find different ways to get to their goals, or switch goals if one becomes impossible.
- Have the sense to break down a formidable task into smaller, manageable pieces.

Goleman, D. *Emotional Intelligence* (1999)

Hope is a powerful motivating force

Having hope helps people from overwhelming anxiety, a defeatist attitude or depression. Optimism works like hope—it can lift performance in life. Hope and optimism can be learned just like helplessness and despair.

Peterson, C., Maier, S. F., and Seligman M. E. P., *Learned Helplessness: A Theory for the Age of Personal Control*, (1995).

Our daily and hourly life experiences, thoughts, emotions, and behaviours can modulate both gene expression and neurogenesis in ways that change the physical structure of the brain.

Factors such as stress, nutrition, exercise, social issues, trauma and extended emotional states can influence gene expression. The environment affects our cells. Is it any wonder that adolescents from violent homes bring violence into schools and future relationships?

The science of hope suggests that hope, affirmations, prayer, celebration and expressions of gratitude may do more than make you feel good—they may be changing your brain (Jensen, 2006). Lighthouses need to be people who are optimistic and aware of the infectious nature of hope.

> *Emotions are contagious. Most emotional contagion is subtle. People who are able to help others soothe their feelings have an especially valued social commodity; they are the souls we turn to when in greatest emotional need.*
>
> Jensen, E., *Enriching the Brain: How to Maximize Every Learner's Potential*, (2006).

The essential supports for adolescents are exactly the same for those who are troubled and those who seem to be travelling well. They all need charismatic, caring adults who can act as an anchor, a safe base—much like young babies and toddlers who need a secure base. Lighthouses are even more critical for adolescents, because their adult-like, highly aroused bodies are akin to very fast cars being driven by inexperienced and unlicensed drivers. In addition to adults they need skills and strategies that really work.

My heart goes out to any parent who has lost a child to suicide; this is every parent's worst nightmare. In various ways the modern world has diminished the value of human life. Rampant consumerism and the massive advances in technology need to be seen for what they are: ways for others to benefit financially, socially or from an inappropriate place of notoriety or power. Instead, let's acknowledge the true value of human life and the value of human connectedness that happens between people who are present, not virtual worlds.

It is not just nostalgia that drives my message to focus more on building meaningful relationships in our homes, schools and communities. I almost took my own life at 17 years of age because of a sense of profound disconnectedness where my tipping point was simply failing an essay. I was also a successful student, school leader and capable sports person who had experienced life success. This was all well before the Internet and mobile phones.

Please tell people you care. Yes, you may hear your adolescents cringing and rolling their eyes, but I know that deep affection and love can bring people back from near disaster. The human spirit can be activated in moments of crisis by the power of love, as discovered by:

- Jamie Neale, the English bushwalker who was missing for 11 days in the freezing Blue Mountains.
- Stuart Diver, the lone survivor of the Thredbo disaster.
- Todd Russell and Brant Webb, survivors of the fatal Beaconsfield gold mine collapse in Tasmania.
- Lincoln Hall, the mountaineer who was left for dead on Mt Everest.

A mum who attended my Adolescence Unplugged seminar took my advice of standing in front of your adolescent, hands on their shoulders, looking deep into their eyes and telling them how much you love them. She said her son rolled his eyes and looked quite uncomfortable and then went to bed. Next morning as he was leaving for school, he came over and put his arm around her shoulders, made eye contact and said, 'See you Mum.' She said he had not touched her for years. It made such a difference to both of them.

If you have adolescents in your home, share a story you hear in the media about adolescent suicide and then tell your children how devastated you would be if anything like that happened to them. Tell them how much you love them and value them and that if you could, you would lay down your own life to save them. Adolescents often feel that because you keep telling them to clean their room, stop hitting their sister, wash their hair, always asking if they've done their homework and so on, that somehow you don't love them and they don't matter. Their adolescent brains are undergoing major reconstruction and they are simply misreading your intentions.

Maybe write them a letter to tell them how much you value them. Then they will be able to read it again later. See appendix for draft letters.

So much of the pain of the bumpy ride comes from mis-communication from both sides and from both parents and adolescents reacting when they are tired, stressed and ungrounded. There are many tips and suggestions that follow in this book that can help – however managing our busy stressful world needs to be the first base for parents!

Key Points

- All adolescents struggle with their emotional world.

- Adolescents use the amygdala to interpret the same information that an adult interprets using the pre-frontal lobe.

- When we feel threatened we automatically switch to our reptilian brain and react in a primal way in order to survive.

- Adolescents can struggle with melt-downs when their nervous system gets overloaded.

- The emotional barometer can be used to help an adolescent understand how their emotional world can impact on their behaviour.

- It's often only a small event that's the final tipping point that triggers a serious primitive response like fighting, running away, self-harm or suicide.

- Added stressors like rejection, failure or lack of sleep can cause an adolescent to reach their tipping point quite quickly or unexpectedly.

- Healthy activation of positive brain chemicals, good nutrition, plenty of exercise, loving relationships, meaningful involvement and a strong spirit can all help in the prevention of depression in adolescents.

- There are huge benefits that young people can gain by deep quietness and stillness.

- The techniques to help adolescents diffuse emotional energy from their nervous system are very simple—try using them.

- Adolescents can have difficulty separating the real world from the virtual world.

- Parents need to beware of the enormous damage cyber-bullying can do.

- Take the time to tell your adolescent that you love and value them no matter what.

Chapter 6

Other
interesting
things about
adolescence

Teenagers have difficulty comprehending that bad things can happen to them; in their minds, they are sheltered from harm's way. Neuroscientists believe that this is due to the many changes experienced in the teenage brain. The oblivious mind-set explains the risky behaviour they actively pursue, such as unprotected sex (I won't get an STD) driving recklessly (I won't be injured or killed) and smoking (I won't get lung cancer).

Feinstein, S., Teaching the At-Risk Teenage Brain, (2007).

Adolescents and their search for identity

Discovering their own identity is an essential part of the journey for an adolescents, and to do it well means stepping back from family, especially parents. But, for parents, this is easier said than done. For them, this step involves the art of letting go and allowing the adolescent to become more responsible for their own life choices, including managing mistakes and failures.

During an adolescent's search for identity it may mean ignoring the rat's tail, the tongue ring, the endless assortment of black clothes or the interesting hair colour. These are normal expressions of their search. Sometimes an adolescent learns helpful things about boundaries when they get detention for wearing inappropriate clothing or jewellery—and that's OK. Every child has joined the planet to be themselves, not a clone of a family member.

Be yourself, everybody else is taken.

One of the frustrating things parents struggle with during this search is an adolescent's poor attention to body hygiene. It can make them quite disagreeable to others, yet they think they have dressed to be cool. Body odour, greasy hair or too much perfume or makeup can cause others to make unfair judgements about them. The same goes for their passion for wearing favourite clothes for weeks even when they smell and are covered in dirty marks.

I find it humorous that two of my sons who wore long ponytails in early adolescence have commented to me as adults, 'What was I thinking not to tell them how bad they looked? Why didn't I tell them?'

Maggie's tip: The more noise you make about something like greasy hair, dirty clothes or black nail polish, the longer it will stay there. If you use parent power around the non life-threatening things, the more they will fight for autonomy and independence. Save your parent power for the big things like boundaries around drugs, drinking and driving.

Adolescents do a lot of work around trying on identities, especially in classrooms. When they are feeling confused, dumb and vulnerable, they try on masks to cover their vulnerability. For example, my protection was to assume the academically superior 'bitch' mask. It meant I was always trying to make my grades give me a sense of worth and value because I didn't have any. I diminished and belittled people with my comments on others' achievements or failures on tests and assignments. I did the 'eye rolling' thing if I heard someone received a low mark, purely to make them feel dumb so I could feel better. It was bullying and I excelled at it (I sincerely apologise to anyone I may have scarred during my own bumpy ride to adulthood). Other masks that adolescents may try are:

1. The computer geek who seldom communicates with anyone other than those similarly masked.
2. The invisible mouse. The student who doesn't want anyone to notice him or her and seldom speaks in class.
3. Princess Bitchface. She wears makeup, jewellery and files her nails in class and thinks she is best looking girl on the planet.
4. The jock. This is the sports freak who just loves wearing tracksuits and playing sport—can be male or female.
5. The smart Alec. They usually try to disarm teachers and big note themselves to be seen.
6. The drama queen. Oh my God! *Everything* is *always* a negative drama or a potential moment to perform so *everyone* notices ME!

7. The clown. Always trying to make people laugh, although usually at someone's expense—slightly less painful than the smart Alec.
8. The bully. Deliberately shoves their power around either physically, verbally or psychologically.
9. The gigglers. Always girls who avoid being taken seriously and just giggle instead of being involved in real interaction.
10. The affluent spoilt I-Have-Everything brat. Always bragging about latest iPhone, computer, mp3 player or gaming console they have, as well as other stuff money buys.
11. The know-it-all. The one who always knows something about everything, and then makes up what they don't know.
12. The confronter. Argues about everything, disagrees with everything and always challenging the teacher's authority.
13. The people pleaser. Always sucking up to adults to make people like them.
14. The victim. Everyone else is to blame and they have a 'poor me' mask.

These were just some of the masks that I found in my classrooms, and adolescents tell me I am pretty accurate even today. When I was teaching, once a cooperative, caring classroom environment had been fully developed I always noticed that students would come without their masks. They might behave like their mask, but they stopped believing they *were* the mask they projected. This was the result of building trust and respect.

Sometimes an adolescent may want to drop their mask, but others find it difficult to accept the change. For example, a student may want stop being a bully but their reputation makes it hard for others to trust them. I have worked with adolescent boys who wanted to stop fighting and bullying younger students and it is hard work for them to drop their mask. Their peers often find it hard to accept they have changed and, unfortunately, so too do the teachers. This is partly because we form concepts and beliefs that influence the way we think and behave. These concepts become unconscious and it takes time or a powerful new experience to change them. Sometimes, it's easier to just keep playing the game if an identity appears fixed.

Sometimes an adolescent saves their worst behaviour for home because they have been the 'perfect student' at school. This happens when they swallow their frustrations and angst at things that happen at school under a mask of 'I am fine'. However, when they get home that emotional barometer needs some discharging and it's often their siblings or Mum who are on the receiving end. I have found that these 'perfect student' adolescents run a cycle of: perfect student → unrealistic expectations → frustrated → discharge at family → feel guilty → need to be perfect student to feel better → unrealistic expectations → frustrated → discharge at family... We must remember they are managing the best they know how. We must teach adolescents effective ways to discharge their emotional garbage otherwise they will struggle.

With the pressures of our modern world—especially from consumerism and body image—today's adolescents have enormous challenges to either follow the 'perfect body' path or the 'absolute grunge' road to rebellion. It is concerning to see adolescents undergo breast augmentation, massive orthodontic work to achieve that perfect American smile, or spend lots of money on makeup and clothes believing they will be happy and feel better, or be more accepted.

Authentic self-esteem is about self-efficacy and self-respect and acceptance. It is about becoming capable of taking care of yourself and developing life skills that ensure healthy independence and the growth of authentic self-awareness and appreciation for who you really are. It honours the *journey* to that place of finding worth and value, not just the destination. Some really rocky moments in adolescence can shape who we become and determine the way we make choices.

The modern world and its pursuit of perfection are flawed. We need to honour each child's unique gifts, talents and flaws, and the interplay of these unique abilities on their journey. Some gifts are hard to find, especially in adolescence, which is why it is important to have adults who can help adolescents find their spark or potential call to greatness. We need to embrace the whole diversity of difference that exists during adolescence especially for those adolescents with special needs. They still experience so much of the bumpy road just with more obstacles.

Peter's story

Peter was a very quiet student in my Year 8 class who was illiterate and academically challenged. He would sit quietly and smile at me when I looked his way, but he didn't learn much due to the huge delay in his learning. I wondered how he was going to create a worthwhile life when he left school with so few skills.

Years later I came across Peter again. He was working at a service station—it was still the good ol' days when you were personally served. He came out so enthusiastically when he saw me and filled my car while we chatted away. He washed my windscreen, my side mirrors and even my back window. If he had more time I think he would have washed my whole car while it refuelled. As I drove off I thought he had treated me special because I was his old English teacher.

The next week I went back and to my surprise, discovered that I hadn't been given any preferential treatment. Peter treated everyone with the same enthusiasm and genuine human concern. When people drove away from him they felt the world was a better place.

One day I noticed cars lining up on Peter's side of the service station just so they could be served by him. People preferred to wait so they could experience this man doing what I then saw as unbelievably valuable work.

Later, I almost cried tears of joy when I pulled in to get fuel. There was an elderly person's home just up the street from the service station and I could see three elderly people with their walkers coming through the station. Out Peter rushed with a cloth and he wiped over their walkers and chatted to them and patted them on the back. Their faces shone with delight as they toddled off. I then saw that Peter was doing sacred work. Daily, he was making a positive difference in the lives of so many people by being kind and caring.

Peter may not have been given a big intellect, but somehow on his journey, he had found his gifts and was sharing them with our world. How perfect.

Everyone Matters

no matter what

The search for identity and autonomy in a consumer-driven, high-tech, fast-paced world is so confusing for today's adolescents. There is a glut of movies, documentaries and television programs that show so many permutations of how adolescents could be—including wizards and werewolves. But, true autonomy and growth of identity can only occur when an individual has overcome challenge, or achieved a success, because of *their* choices and behaviours. It's important that this is done independently of others, and sometimes in spite of others.

The modern world's 'parenting competition' is putting incredible pressure on adolescents to achieve high grades. I have worked with many final year students who burn out or succumb to serious illness like chronic fatigue syndrome, glandular fever or depression. They tell me that from as early as they can remember they have shouldered their parents' expectations for high grades. They have been deeply hurt at the look in their parents' eyes when their grades were less than they had hoped. That deep sense of letting down parents can become very terrifying for adolescents. For some, they strive so hard that they lose friends and stop doing healthy things like playing sport or music.

> *The pressure to achieve high marks has the corresponding expectation that if you get good grades, you will somehow have a better life because of your better education. This is not always true.*

Being well educated cognitively will not necessarily prepare an adolescent to manage living independently in today's chaotic world. Their capacity for resilience has nothing to do with grades or intellect. How they manage being sacked, losing a loved one to death, or moving to a new job in a new location without support is determined by their resilience. I have worked with so many adolescents with depression that was partially triggered by their profound sense of being 'ripped off' when their university degree did not deliver the good life that was promised by their parents.

I remember a young man who worked really hard in his final year of school. He had planned to become a maths teacher, however, when he received his results they were much higher than he had expected. His parents felt that he should do an engineering degree rather than a maths degree because his marks were so good. So he transferred to engineering. It took about six weeks before he realised he hated engineering. In a way he felt trapped and troubled, and he became deeply depressed and suicidal. Finally, he came home and admitted to his parents he hated engineering and he wasn't going back. His deep depression took almost a year to become manageable before he could go back to university to study what he had originally wanted.

Adolescents can be very accurate and they can be totally off the mark about their parents' expectations of them. It is their reality – and not yours that matters while they are navigating adolescence. There is a fine line between healthy, positive expectations and unhealthy expectations. If parents want their children to grow up happy and healthy, and become who they really are then they must allow flexibility. This will help adolescents better manage the transition from school to work/career.

Having goals and high, positive expectations for yourself can be healthy or unhealthy. I once taught a dynamic, bright girl who was determined to become a doctor. To support her dream, she moved to the city to ensure she would get the best education. Unfortunately, she missed the cut off for entry into medicine by .05 of a mark! She crashed and became bitterly disappointed. With her dream now pushed to one side, she went to university and studied law instead, but like the boy who started the engineering degree, soon realised it was not for her. She ended up struggling emotionally and psychologically, but she didn't give up. She worked in a café for a couple of years before applying to another university. Her courage to try again paid off and she is now almost a fully trained doctor.

She was one of the most confident and competent adolescents I have taught. To see the bumpy ride she endured when her planned goals were not met was a valuable insight for me, even though it was a painful experience for her.

We must be careful of linking an adolescent's search for identity too tightly to their school results. Whether they are getting excellent or poor grades is not a reliable indicator of who they are or who they can become. In my presentation to adolescents I show them a list of famous people, then I share some of their flaws as students—especially those of Kerry Packer, Richard Branson and Kerry Stokes who all struggled with dyslexia. Despite their learning difficulties these people have become extremely successful.

If we link the identity search with academic results we negate those who struggle academically and make them feel 'less than'. A student who came runner-up in two subjects in his final year of school said to me the final graduation evening made him feel a bit of a loser because he didn't receive an award or any recognition. He wondered how those who had done a lot worse than him felt.

This is an example of the effects of our society kneeling at the altar of external signs of success. It shows how our current mindset can potentially have a negative effect on most adolescents who 'fail' to make the benchmark. Adolescents have an incomplete reasoning brain and many struggle with the perception that they are 'not enough'. We need to help them understand that they have other abilities that will never make it onto their report card. Only 30 per cent of students ever make it to university. What do the other 70 per cent perceive of themselves when they leave school? Remember, they have an unfinished brain that's still incapable of mature thinking.

An example of how mastery on any level builds self-esteem

Thirteen-year-old Zarah came to see me because she was unhappy and very homesick after moving from her farm to our local hostel. Her mum asked me to help her build her self-esteem and bounce back from this big change in her life. Her mum said Zarah had not had an easy life. She had been born premature and was very sick early in life. She found it challenging when she started school because she was short-sighted and wore thick glasses. She also had problems with concentration and coordination. On top of this, Zarah had a nasty motorbike accident and lost all the fingers on her right hand—her dominant hand.

When I first met Zarah she was timid, shy and very self-conscious of her disfigured hand. She always had her hand hidden in pocket and spoke in a tiny voice that was difficult to hear. However, in a short time she became confident, cheerful and so comfortable with her injured hand that it was hard to notice she had ever felt self-conscious.

She happily told me one afternoon she had asked to lend a teacher a hand and said, 'I only have one hand so that's all I can offer!'. Her wonderful sense of humour had been set free and she used it to great effect. She became a goal setter and an avid reader of books about health and happiness. With some memory training she increased her ability to concentrate and improved her grades in some subject areas. Soon Zarah was modelling and dancing thanks to her newfound confidence. She became a champion for the underdogs at school, and won three citizenship awards for her commitment to supporting charities and good causes.

Zarah graduated high school filled with guts and determination, and a citizenship award. She has since gone on to get her driver's licence and tackle life with a fierce determination seldom seen in one so young. Once she discovered the qualities and abilities that made her special and unique, she transformed her life—despite her physical challenges. Today, she continues to live with enthusiasm and positivity. She certainly taught me and many others, a lot about courage, faith and hope.

The importance of peers and deepening friendships

The social dynamics of the adolescent world is fraught with challenge and delight. We know that stable, reliable friendships will support an adolescent during their ride to adulthood. It is a major protective factor in terms of resilience. Friendships help develop social skills, modify the dark moods of adolescence and enhance moral development.

Through friendships, adolescents learn unspoken codes of conduct that they will take with them throughout life. This does not mean all friendships are plain sailing. Being sanctioned by your peers is one of the fastest ways to create the catalyst for an adolescent to change an unhelpful behaviour or uncaring communication. Friendships can make or break an adolescent in many ways.

Positive friendships are a powerful protective factor that can help adolescents avoid unlawful or risky behaviour. It can be hurtful when your adolescent no longer wants to go on family outings because he or she would prefer to hang out with friends. However, it is a sign of healthy adolescent development as they unknowingly prepare their own future tribes.

> *Maggie's tip: When adolescents stop wanting to spend time at Grandma's or go on family holidays because they prefer to be with their friends, relax, this is healthy. Instead of saying 'No', ask them to bring a friend on holiday. The double bonus is they often behave better when they have a friend around!*

There can be enormous volatility in friendship links between 12 and 15 years of age. Many parents have stories about the cruelty of certain friends and the devastating impact they had on their growing adolescent. Adolescents are particularly sensitive to the barbs and wounds of friendship conflict—girls can be particularly brutal. When friends spread malicious lies that destroy reputations the damage can be fatal, demonstrated by the suicides of those who have been cyber-bullied.

We learn the value of friendship many times in our journey through life. True friendship is knowing you are never alone, and that right beside you is someone you can lean on, talk to and cry with. It's also about knowing that there is someone to share the joy, laughter and achievements with.

Friendship means everything to an adolescent. To be socially and personally acceptable they need to be seen to have friends. The biological urge to belong is so strong that adolescents will do anything to be part of the crowd. They can easily take up with a group engaging in risky or criminal behaviour, and many have come 'off the rails' in such circumstances. Poet John Dunne's famous words, 'No man is an island entire of itself' certainly apply to teenagers. Nothing is as threatening in the social network of adolescents as 'the loner'. Being a loner occasionally is not unusual, but it is developmentally unhealthy to be alone all the time.

For adolescents, having fun is almost unheard of in a singular sense. Parties, sleepovers and get-togethers are their ways of celebrating and finding enjoyment. This is why it's important for communities to offer safe, appropriate places where they can get together and be noisy.

Within the school environment, friendship groupings—especially for girls—can change quite fast, and for the most amazing reasons. Often adolescents can be very judgemental and a friend can be ostracised from a friendship group on the basis of a fabrication. In other words, someone can create an untruth about another in the group and the tribal mentality will decide to dump that person. If we feel trial by media is something abhorrent, trial by friendship group can be much more damaging. Usually the supposedly 'offending' person is given no chance to defend themselves, and the resulting damage to self-esteem and social standing is considerable.

Teenagers can also use colourful language and be amazingly cruel when they have group support, adding to the damage that the exiled adolescent experiences. Caring parents and teachers often are the ones to pick up the pieces and help the shattered adolescent on the road to recovery. As this involves a loss experience, many adolescents experience a grief response, which often affects school-work and behaviour at home.

Somewhere along the way adolescents need to be made aware of how it feels to be hurt, rejected or wrongfully accused. Role play, story telling and circle work in the classroom are great ways of exploring this as a group. It is essential to encourage adolescents to learn that honesty with compassion is a tremendous personal quality. Help them understand that any personal gain made at the expense of another is absolutely false. Remind them that they will get back everything they put out at least 10 times over. Imagining how it is to walk around in someone else's shoes, and being non-judgemental are also key qualities of a true friend.

> Breathless
> I am unable to fit in
> Like a picture frame
> Without a picture
>
> Trying to fit in
> When no-one talks to you
> Is like trying to breathe with no air
> The kids are staring
> The teachers aren't caring
>
> I am alone
> Like the fame
> Without a picture

Louise Miniken
Covich, S. (ed), *A Circle in a Room Full of Squares*, (2003).

Learning to trust is an important part of friendship. Some adolescents carry deep scars from having their trust betrayed in childhood, particularly those who were abused. As adolescents they need to learn how to begin to trust again. If their trust is shattered again, they will struggle in their adult years to overcome the powerful belief that no one can be trusted. It is very difficult to form a deep, long-term, intimate relationship without being able to trust. Parents and educators have a responsibility to let our youth know that betrayal of trust can cause deeper damage than they realise.

Encouraging our adolescents to become good listeners is another facet to consider around issues of friendship. We have been born with two ears and one mouth, and should use them in that order. Having a safe place to dump emotional pain and feelings of insecurity is one of the most important reasons for having friends. Many adults are poor listeners and adolescents often give up trying to be heard. This can create a sense of powerlessness, which gives rise to anger and resentment. Lighthouses must be good listeners and hear when nothing is being heard elsewhere.

The inability to see social threats objectively can lead to poor decision making during friendship squabbles. To be ostracised is a serious threat to an adolescent's survival and they will fight to prevent that happening. The effects of social rejection can last for life. Bullying and physical violence has increased in our schools and communities partly because of the decreased emotional literacy, the increased stress levels, less resilience and desensitisation to violence from the screen obsession of many adolescents .

The following email is from a student I taught over 26 years ago. This is exactly the type of wounding and damage that adolescents can experience at school and the result it can have on their life after school.

> Hiya
>
> You might not remember me, but I certainly remember you. I was a student of yours at Mirrabooka High in 1979.
>
> I have for many years, wanted to thank you for making my final few months of high school bearable. I don't know what would have become of me if you hadn't stuck up for me one day in class. I was the one who used to have a chorus of barking dogs whenever I entered the room, was constantly teased, and basically, had my self esteem crushed at quite an early age.
>
> I endured years of bullying from those in my school, and in my class especially. I still remember their names, all of them, and to this day am still haunted by the years of humiliation.
>
> As a result, I have not managed to develop many friendships, been quite a shy person, dislike social activity, and have ended up pretty much a prisoner to my own fears of being embarrassed and humiliated.

I was diagnosed as social phobic at 19 after spending three months in prison for bouncing cheques (my own) and well, now 40 has arrived, and it finds me still unmarried, still a social cripple, and living a life which is far from exciting.

Seems you have been very successful in your career, and I wanted to let you know how much I appreciated what you did for me all those years ago. It was probably something quite insignificant to you in the scheme of things, but to me, it was like a life raft.

I think I probably would have taken my life at the tender age of 15 if it hadn't been for you Maggie.

I've wanted to thank you for many, many years, and now I have.

Thankyou!!

Robyn, 27 November 2005
Dent, M., *Nurturing Kids' Hearts and Souls*, (2006).

Parents can unwittingly strengthen a negative relationship by telling an adolescent they don't like a certain friend. It's a bit like the rat's tail: quietly tolerate it until they realise that person is not a good friend. It may take time but it's essential social development that needs to happen. Remember, the more adults criticise or resist something, the longer it stays.

Positive friendships that are formed during primary school need to be preserved if possible. The impact of moving an adolescent from a long-term location needs to be considered very carefully because such an experience of social dislocation can be like death to them. When they arrive in a new community it's hard to break into existing friendship groups. Unless the adolescent has some obvious attraction, like being competent at sport, music or academically, this can be a difficult transition. If you have adolescents aged between 12 and 17, then please consider very carefully before relocating your family. At this age adolescents *are most at risk of suffering from losing the protective net of established friends.* The grief they feel can easily turn into deep resentment and anger towards their parents for 'ruining their life'.

We opened our home to one of our son's mates when his parents moved to another town because he asked if he could stay and finish his last year at high school with his friends. We were a bit worried because he was not doing the tertiary bound course that my son was doing and wondered if he would be a distraction. We gave him clear directions that if he mucked up or distracted our son he would go back to his parents. He didn't put a foot wrong and was an absolute delight. I still love him as one of my boys and it is a year I remember fondly.

Being connected to friends and peers means an adolescent will be in touch with the parents of those friends. Encourage the role of shared parenting among the circle of your adolescent's friends if you feel the parents are good role models. This gives parents a chance to have the odd weekend off, also your own adolescent behaves much better when there is a visitor in the house. Shared parenting helps with activities such as trips to sport, beaches and camps, and collecting adolescents from parties. This is healthy on many levels for parents, adolescents and their friends.

Positive friendships help young people develop a sense of belonging which builds their inner sense of acceptance, as well as their extrinsic sense of: 'I am acceptable'. Lighthouses need to support adolescents as they form friendships with peers. This is vital for their social and emotional development. The lonely adolescent is at risk for many years, not just during adolescence.

All adolescents are consciously or unconsciously shaping their evolving identities around the significant adults who are present in their lives.

Friendship is one of the most wonderful rewards in this journey of life, and the experiences our young adults in transition have can set them down the road to the beautiful sunrise or down the road to the long dark night. Loving and supporting each other will give them the strength and courage to deal with each and every challenge that life has to offer, positively.

Side by side

Don't walk in front of me
I may not follow;
Don't walk behind me
I may not lead;
Walk beside me
And just be my friend.

Author unknown.

Window of Sensitivity

There is a unique window of sensitivity during the adolescent years of brain pruning and massive over-production of the dendrites. There are rapid changes noted in the levels of neurotransmitter chemicals such as serotonin and dopamine, which control and regulate the pleasure response in the brain. Alcohol, nicotine and many other drugs appear to trigger the same responses in the brain as serotonin and dopamine.

Our young people can learn much quicker during this window and never will addiction to alcohol, drugs or smoking occur more quickly than during adolescence. This is a double whammy because they are also much more resistant to recovery. Research suggests that adolescent addictions are more likely to last for life and are very difficult to cure. This is why we must fight as hard as possible to maintain tight boundaries to prevent adolescents having easy access to alcohol, cigarettes, and prescription and illegal drugs because their brain is hard wired to learn fast to be dependent.

Avoid giving adolescents the 'taste' for alcohol during this window of sensitivity and collectively encourage the same vigilance among their friendship group. The marketing of sweet alcoholic drinks towards adolescents, particularly girls, is blatantly aimed at encouraging teenagers to drink at a younger age by offering a sweet introduction to the taste.

Adolescents will still want to experiment; however, when parents start purchasing alcohol for their adolescents they are opening the door to alcohol addiction. The binge culture has serious long-term effects on the developing brain and it impairs learning at a vital time of accelerated learning potential.

> *We know the teenage brain is different, and one way that it's different is that it seems to be more sensitive to alcohol. New studies show that alcohol and nicotine cause permanent damage to the adolescent brain.*
>
> Strauch, B., *The Primal Teen: What New Discoveries About The Teenage Brain Tell Us About Our Kids*, (2003).

The same extreme caution applies to marijuana. A dependency on this drug can delay key brain development and the growth of the pre-frontal lobe. It is particularly toxic to young adults because it can de-motivate. Marijuana combined with the lack of motivation already present in many adolescents puts a huge obstacle in the middle of their bumpy road to adulthood. There are enough potential blockages without adding any more.

Marijuana is a fat-loving substance that is very damaging to the developing brain. It strips away the myelin that the brain is trying to cover the axons with in order to prepare it to be more mature. There is more about how to help adolescents understand the dangers of drugs in the chapter on Sex, Drugs, Rock and Roll, and Cyber Space.

Most psychiatric and mental disorders first appear during adolescence, especially depression, bipolar disorder and schizophrenia.

> *26 per cent of people aged between 16 and 24—about 650,000 people suffered mental illness last year. 14 per cent of Year 8s in Aust self-harmed in 2008.*

These figures only represent those who were diagnosed—adolescents with mental health issues often find it hard to seek professional help and this is another reason why lighthouses can be such a vital help in supporting a struggling adolescent. It is excellent to see Professor Patrick McGorry be acknowledged for his brilliant work at addressing the mental un-wellness of young Australians by being honoured as Australian of the Year. He helped to create the program called HeadSpace and coordinates the Orygen Youth Health Institute that helps in the prevention as well as the diagnosis of mental illness among adolescents. He is committed to the early intervention of mental illness in adolescents. Schools and communities need to step forward and help us all take better care of our young, and to be proactive if we find a young person who is struggling.

Positive psychology, optimistic and enthusiastic thinking patterns, and deep human connectedness can also help adolescents avoid or minimise mental illness. Positive psychology is a field of study that investigates how individuals can overcome life's challenges and increase their mental health by using their strengths to perceive life as meaningful. Researchers at Monash University in Melbourne are currently working on a study on adolescent well-being. The purpose of the study is to identify the factors that contribute to flourishing, or high functioning in young people, and to see how the characteristics of adolescents with high well-being might be taught to other adolescents so as to improve their well-being and mental health.

Schools can contribute to this development of more resilient factors by building a more inclusive, caring culture. I have noticed that high schools with the most effective student services team often have above-average school results. When adolescents feel cared for and supported, they will feel safer. This reduces stress and the brain learns better in less stressed and less fearful environments.

We need to set up 'adolescent only' wellness centres where they can visit and get help and support from people trained to connect with youth. Such a centre could offer medical, financial, social and emotional support. They could run programs and have information available to address most adolescent challenges.

Adolescents have a strong resistance to getting professional help, especially within the school system. Comments from students reflect this:

- 'I would solve my problem myself.'
- 'I think I should work out my own problems.'
- 'I'd be too embarrassed to talk to a counsellor.'
- 'Adults can't understand adolescent problems.'
- 'Even if I wanted to, I wouldn't have time to see a counsellor.'
- 'A counsellor might make me do what I don't want to.'
- 'I wouldn't want my family to know I was seeking a counsellor.'
- 'I couldn't afford counselling.'
- 'Nothing will change the problems I have.'
- 'If I go to counselling, I might find out I'm crazy.'
- 'If I went for help, the counsellor would not keep my secret.'

Wilson, C.J., Rickwood, D., Ciarrochi, J. & Deane, F.P. (2002). *Adolescent barriers to seeking professional psychological help for personal-emotional and suicidal problems.* Conference Proceedings of the 9th Annual Conference for Suicide Prevention Australia, June 2002, Sydney.

In their examination of barriers to medical service use, the Australian Access to Service and Evaluation Research Unit (SERU, 1999) found that young people identified cost, communication, compassion, confidentiality and convenience as the major barriers to seeking help from general practitioners. With regard to mental health services, Sawyer et al. (2000) found that parents cited practical barriers such as:

- the cost of attending services
- not knowing where to get help
- long waiting lists.

Donald et al. (2000) found that young people reported that the most common barrier to formal service utilisation was concern about confidentiality, followed by cost barriers and fear about what the service would do. In a study of Australian high school students' barriers to help-seeking, Wilson and Deane (2000) found that students emphasised the importance of fear, anxiety, shame and adolescent autonomy. Students also revealed that three important barriers to formal help-seeking related to: beliefs that prior professional help had been of little use; limited knowledge about the help that professionals provide; and concerns about not having a relationship with available professional help-providers. Additional barriers included concerns about trust and confidentiality.

If an adolescent's first attempt at getting help is unsatisfactory, they may never reach out again. Their fear of betrayal of trust and negative consequences of public knowledge of their vulnerability is paramount. When they have found a place that really offers support in an adolescent-friendly way, they will refer other adolescents and they *will* turn up. It is incredibly important to ensure that issues that arise during this window of sensitivity get the attention and support needed before they become permanent—especially issues around mental and physical health.

My vision is for centres where adolescent-friendly GPs, alcohol and drug counsellors, family planning, career and social workers, and mental health professionals are all available free of charge with after-hours crisis support.

Friends will call for help when they know people care about them. I was able to intervene in a number of suicide attempts and potential runaways because their friends asked for help. We must develop relationships before we can support them, and we need places outside of schools or other learning institutions that look user friendly and welcoming to young people. The Headspace initiative of Professor McGorry is aimed at addressing this but so far has only 30 centres established for the whole of Australia. For excellent facts sheets about mental illness and adolescents please go to the Orygen web page http://tc.oyh.org.au/ InformationResources/factsheets.

This window of sensitivity has another new phenomenon to cope with: the addiction to online computer games. Boys are our primary concern because the window of sensitivity is when they are fine tuning their competitive edge. The desire to compete is not unusual because the need to prove oneself was always a part of the traditional community's rite of passage or initiation; biologically it is to ensure they can attract a mate. However, highly addictive computer games have been created where lone competitors play with or against unseen others around the world. This has led to the identification of a new form of mental illness that can occur.

Boys can become so addicted that if they play often enough for long periods of time their brain, being highly plastic at this age, can permanently change. Instead of just being aggressive for a short time after playing the game, their personality can be changed long after they have stopped playing the game. They become the character they have been playing. There have been accounts of academically capable, well-liked boys who have changed so much they never return to school. They lose their friends and require medication to manage living. In some ways it is like your son having an accident and getting a brain acquired injury. He may look the same but part of his brain has been damaged and he is no longer the boy he was.

Please tell at least five people of this dangerous damage that can occur during the window of sensitivity in adolescence. It is a tragedy to lose our boys during the time in their life when they have the greatest potential to learn.

Adolescents are experiencing massive change on all levels physically, hormonally, mentally, socially and emotionally, and they need proper nutrition and rest. The better quality food they eat, the better all these changes can occur, and some things are very important for the optimal brain development. Having breakfast, especially with some protein helps adolescents concentrate better and maintain moods while at school. A balanced diet with as little sugar, saturated fats, over-processed ingredients, preservatives and colourings is best. Also, a diet that includes plenty of fresh fruit, vegetable, and essential amino fatty acids like Omega 3 and 6 will help with brain integration.

Boys who undergo very fast growth spurts can consume enormous amounts of food because the growth exhausts their supplies of energy. However, eating massive quantities of poor-quality food like pies, chips and burgers will often simply make them fat no matter how fast they are growing.

I feel for anyone with three or more adolescent boys in their house because the fridge is empty within hours of being filled. We would often have to cook a kilogram of pasta or rice for each meal just to try to slow down the fridge snacking, and often it made no difference at all—whole loaves of bread simply disappeared.

Not only does food give the body the energy to sustain the changes that are occurring, it has a huge influence on mood and emotions. Sugar is particularly bad for massive shifts in mood and is to be avoided as much as possible, especially if it's from soft drink or sweet drinks like chocolate milk or high energy sports drinks. They will be OK if they drink it before a marathon or high energy sporting event, but to consume these products and then just sit on the couch is asking for trouble—physically and emotionally.

The final piece of information is about 'hot cognition'—thinking under conditions of high arousal and emotion. This can be very risky for adolescents. Computer simulation performances of risky driving scenarios, such as running orange lights, were compared between adults and adolescents. Both parties were similar when tested alone. However, when tested in the company of friends adults showed no change, but adolescents showed clearly increased risk of accidents. When adolescents have friends in the car their ability to make good driving decisions drops by up to 40 per cent. The same applies to being distracted by mobile phones—especially if texting while driving.

On an ABC television program about adolescence called, *Whatever: The Science of Teens* they compared an adolescent and an adult male doing a driving test. They had to drive around a course without hitting any traffic cones. The results of their first attempt was quite similar. The second time they did the test, there were three very beautiful adolescent girls watching. The adolescent boy went faster but collected a couple of traffic cones, while the adult performed very similar to the first attempt. The boy said he felt pressured to perform better and show off with the girls there.

This is a key aspect of the capacity of the adolescent brain and it relates to most risk-taking behaviour of adolescent boys, whether it's driving, taking drugs or jumping off tall buildings. Remember, it is partly linked to the biological drive to get a mate where the best performance will guarantee a partner. But, the primitive biological drive to reproduce and survive has a higher price in our modern world because of the man-made riskier activities that tempt and lure adolescents, especially boys.

Key Points

- Adolescents are biologically wired to search for identity.

- Social cohesion is important for adolescent survival.

- Friendships can be a protective or destructive factor in an adolescent's life.

- The more adults criticise and complain about something, the longer it will stay.

- Adolescents try on 'masks' and often think they are their mask.

- Every adolescent has strengths and flaws.

- We must help adolescents recognise their innate strengths.

- Excelling at school only works for some, not everyone.

- Over-emphasis on achieving grades can cause adolescents to create a skewed sense of self.

- Everyone matters no matter what.

- The window of sensitivity in early adolescence is a time of great threat to adolescent health and well-being.

- Adolescents can become addicted faster than at any other time in their life.

- Adolescents are at a greater risk when driving cars with company.

- Healthy food and nutrition maximises adolescent potential on all levels.

- Addictions to violent games can cause personality change.

- There are differences with hot cognition between adults and adolescents.

Chapter 7

The nightmare *of* adolescent sleeplessness

One clear casualty of sleep deprivation is learning. That's a tragedy—a recent tragedy.

Professor William Dement, Stanford University, (considered to be the father of sleep research.)

I recommend that every high school should run an awareness program about the importance of sleep, especially during adolescence. Why? Because poor sleep impacts on every level of an adolescent's health and well-being.

Consider how you felt the last time you were seriously sleep deprived. Have you ever experienced jet lag, where your sleep clock is set to a different time zone to the one you have just arrived in and you are wide awake until 2am because it's really 11pm in your normal time zone? You will remember being grumpy, frustrated and irritable. The up side is that you have a pre-frontal lobe to manage these emotional states.

Adolescents need more sleep than pre-pubescents or adults. This is a biological need due to the massive changes happening physically and within the brain. With sudden growth spurts, particularly in boys, adolescents experience huge waves of intense lethargy. Hormonal changes create more melatonin, which means, chemically, the body is demanding more sleep. The next big shift is with the adolescent circadian rhythm. Suddenly, they are more alert in the afternoon and evening, and need more sleep in the morning. For approximately 75 per cent of adolescents, their sleep clock moves up to 1.5 hours later, which means they are not ready for sleep until much later.

To beat the frustration of sleeplessness, adolescents will often go online to entertain themselves or play games. This re-stimulates them and when their body is finally ready for sleep, it will be even later than the 1.5 hour difference. This is why adolescents can be so difficult to wake up in the morning. I have had adolescents sleep through incredibly loud car-horn alarm clocks because they are so deeply asleep at 7am.

Most adolescents run on a 'sleep deficit'. This has significant negative affects on their well-being on many levels. An article in *The Weekend Australian Magazine* (24 November, 2007) highlighted research that showed when more is learned during the day, then more sleep is required at night. This is so the brain can process and consolidate the memories. Vital gene activities need to occur during Rapid Eye Movement (REM) sleep to ensure synaptic plasticity, or the strengthening of neural connections. Without deep sleep these activities do not occur. The storing and processing of the day's learning is a vital component of REM sleep. If an adolescent is not getting sound REM sleep then this information is not stored effectively and the brain will not be able to create the new brain cells required for the next day.

New spaces for learning grow every night after the existing spaces for learning have been filled. Without REM sleep, there are no new cells, and adolescents arrive at school tired and with a brain that is like a motel with a NO VACANCIES sign up. Without the right sleep there is nowhere for the new learning to go, and unless the adolescent reviews the learning on another day after a good night's sleep, then that learning has not been retained. This information is critical for adolescents to know because they often think they are dumb when they don't retain information, or fail tests when they have simply not given their brain a fair go.

Many adolescents sleep with an active mobile phone, are easily distracted by their friends on social networking sites on the Internet, or play games that engage them far too much for them to want to sleep. When I share this information with students, they often tell their friends that their mobile will be on silent for school nights. We must remember that time management is not a strength that has developed with adolescents and they can genuinely waste hours in the middle of the night without realising it.

The easy-to-distract and poor impulse control tendencies of adolescents, when wired with a need to be entertained, explains a lot about why their sleep patterns can be disrupted. The consequences of insufficient sleep in adolescents can be frightening; they include:

- Missed school and less attendance
- Sleepiness—including micro-sleeps
- Negative synergy with alcohol
- Decreased creativity
- Tiredness (decreased motivation)

- Lower school grades
- Irritability and low-frustration tolerance
- Higher risk of car accidents
- Increased anxiety and stress symptoms
- Over-eating, and yearning for high-fat foods
- Difficulties with self-control of attention and positive behavior choices
- Difficulties with focused attention, emotional stability
- Affected regulation and cognitive emotional integration
- Direct effects on learning and memory consolidation, and memory deficits
- Health consequences: illness, poor skin, delayed growth and development.

Researchers are now finding links with other serious challenges. They have discovered that sleep deprivation can result in depression—especially among girls, anxiety, daytime sleepiness, moodiness and hyperactivity. Other problems include a reduction in motivation to initiate long-term or abstract goals, and a decrease in persistence to want to work towards such goals. These motivational changes may, for example, deter students from electing challenging course but not affect their grades (National Sleep Foundation, 2000).

Going to bed earlier protects teenagers against depression and suicidal thoughts, New York research suggests.

Of 15,500 12 to 18-year-olds studied, those who went to bed after midnight were 24% more likely to have depression than those who went before 10pm.

And those who slept fewer than five hours a night had a 71% higher risk of depression than those who slept eight hours, the journal, Sleep reports.

Those who had less than five hours sleep a night were thought to have a 48% higher risk of suicidal thoughts compared with those who had eight hours of sleep.

Late-night teens 'face greater depression risk, [online] http://news.bbc.co.uk/2/hi/health/8435955.stm, BBC News.

Adolescent sleep expert Dr Mary A Carskadon from Stanford University writes about the glut of wakefulness and its impact on adolescents' lives.

Teens may be driven to do things that can wake them up simply because they'll fall asleep if they do not. So we see caffeine, late-night Internet chat rooms, instant messaging, cramming in activity after activity as a means to keep awake necessitating more of the same in an effort to stay awake in the face of declining sleep. This is another way to think of the negative spiral of too little sleep.

These patterns can disguise the extent of their sleep deficit for many teens. It can also be hidden from their parents as well. On the other hand, we see the signs of this deficit emerge in many young people, with each vulnerable in different ways. We see the teenager who falls asleep driving home late at night; another teen has a titanic struggle to wake up in the morning, often failing and resulting in late or missed school; another simply feels sad and moody and blue, lacking initiative or motivation; in another, grades begin to suffer as the teen struggles to keep awake during class and while doing homework; another may turn to heavier drugs to get some positive and arousing sensations; many just struggle along in a kind of haze, never knowing how to feel or do their best.

Mary A Carskadon, PhD, received a doctorate with distinction in neuro- and biobehavioral sciences with a specialty in sleep research from Stanford University.

When I work with adolescents I work through the following list of the effects of poor sleep:

1. Poor sleep can make you sick.
2. Poor sleep can make you dumb.
3. Poor sleep can make you grumpy.
4. Poor sleep can make you negative.
5. Poor sleep can make you fat.
6. Poor sleep can make you become depressed.

The first point is explained by telling an adolescent that their immune system is compromised when they have interrupted or poor sleep. The cell renewal and revitalisation that takes place when we sleep also requires deep sleep—REM sleep.

The second point is explored by discussing the processing and storage of learning—also requiring sound REM sleep. The metaphor of the motel with no vacancies really resonates with today's adolescents. The brain needs to have sound sleep to file away new learning and to make new spaces for learning the following day.

The third item describes everyone. We become more irritable and grumpy when we are sleep deprived. This is of more concern for adolescents because they do not yet have a mature pre-frontal lobe to deal with these effects. Emotional volatility and unpredictability is made much worse by sleep deprivation. The ability to manage the chaos of adolescence is seriously impaired, and often violence and aggression increases with the lack of sleep. I recommend to parents to allow sleepy adolescents to sleep around the clock on the weekend if they can because you will have a calmer and more agreeable adolescent the next day or two.

The fourth point is supported by sleep research that shows sleep deprivation makes people recall unhappy memories rather than pleasant ones. This finding is vital in relation to troubled teens, as well as many people who struggle with deep depression and despair. It adds an additional layer of negativity that adolescents have to fight through to recognise their worth and value in our shallow world.

The fifth point about poor sleep making you fat certainly makes adolescents take note. There is clear research which shows a powerful link between obesity and sleeplessness. Sleep loss elevates the stress hormone cortisol. Cortisol is lipogenic, meaning it stimulates the body to make fat. Human growth hormone is also disrupted. Normally secreted as a pulse at the beginning of sleep, growth hormone is essential for the breakdown of fat (*The Weekend Australian Magazine*, 2007).

The final point about depression is critical. It is a serious mental illness that must be avoided at all costs. Episodes of adolescent depression often lead to more depression as an adult. Getting good sleep, eating healthy food, being physically active, being actively involved in something and having positive human connectedness are the best protective factors against depression.

The influence sleep has on today's adolescents is deep. Too many survive the crippling effects of sleepiness by consuming high caffeine energy drinks, eating high sugar and high fat foods and playing loud music. Adolescents think this is normal behaviour, but they are quite ignorant of the effects these stimulating forces have on their sleep-deprived bodies.

Improving adolescent sleep has always been important, especially for those struggling with stress, emotional overwhelm or anxiety. Now it seems that moods are also very affected by lack of sleep. Research supports the notion that teenagers should start school at a later time, as their brains are not ready for learning early in the morning. The results from the schools trialling later start times—a few Australian schools and many in the USA—definitely supports this approach. These results may be interesting, however it is not practical in every situation, especially in rural areas where sleepy adolescent buses would not be economical.

Things to help build a better sleep pattern for adolescents who are struggling

- Avoid stimulating substances during the day and night.
- Parents to have clear sleep boundary before puberty
- Get plenty of sunlight (where possible).
- Avoid alcohol—especially at night.
- Create a pattern of sleep preparation such as: shower, teeth, toilet.
- Avoid television and screen time at least an hour before bed.
- Turn mobile phones to silent.
- Use some calming music or a relaxation CD to bore the conscious mind.
- Aim to be in bed same time each night; aim for eight to nine hours of sleep each night.
- Create a calming environment in the bedroom by removing clutter and using calming aromatherapy.
- Drink calming teas like chamomile.

- Spend two minutes in bed breathing deeply and relaxing the body before getting in your favourite position for sleep.
- Play Jeff Buckley's version of *Halleluiah* on repeat.

On the *Kit Bag for Adolescents* I have included a track called, Relax and Escape especially for wired individuals. The track begins by asking the individual to imagine unplugging from their busy world by turning off their mobile, computer and other connections to the outside world. They are then asked to imagine going to a beautiful pristine beach. The imaginary process shuts off busy minds and when done frequently over a month, the brain builds a new cognitive map that allows the body to link relaxation and sleep to the same relaxation activity. It becomes like a Pavlov's dog response. The unconscious mind follows patterns of behaviours automatically once they are anchored. This is why people who have always been good sleepers tend to struggle less as they go through both puberty and aging.

Sleep is essential for the physical, mental, emotional, social and spiritual well-being of every individual. It is important for everyone, especially children and adolescents whose brains are still developing. Our wired-up adolescents are struggling with managing their bumpy ride to adulthood, with sleep deprivation being a huge contributing factor.

Invest time and energy to promote healthy sleep patterns and awareness among our adolescents. I believe that if every school, parent and carer could do this then it might lead to less violence, crime, depression and road deaths, and a higher number of happier homes.

We must also educate adolescents about the impact poor sleep has on them and help them get more and better quality sleep. A well-rested adolescent makes a happier home and classroom and ensures they have optimal health and well being on all levels.

Everything Is Possible

Into my life I tread
carefully, gently on a clatter of gangly
limbs, broken voice.
All at once my world is so small, so large,
and...so what?
I am in love.
I love the night, its possibilities
of new faces, places, trends;
the streetlight shadow that stretches
my skin ahead of my step;
ahead of my time, yet pacing with me.
I am in love.
I love the day, it's reality
of home, drowning in my rumpled bed
that's too small now, like my mind—
too many thoughts to contain, they fall to the floor
trying to assemble themselves under everyone's feet;
sometimes they make sense.
Into her arms I succumb, embraced when
no one sees. Mother.
Into his pride I splash, deep, certain,
like him. Father.
Into my life I stumble,
happily, angrily, pushing, pulling this
ravenous body, I am a glutton.
I desire.
Love. Freedom. Me.
I grow into my life. It is loose and folded,
one day it will fit me like
my skin.

August 2009

Key Points:

- Adolescents need more sleep than before or after adolescence.

- An adolescent's circadian rhythm changes to approximately 1.5 hours later at night.

- Adolescents are running in constant sleep debt.

- Broken sleep and poor sleep impacts all levels of an adolescent's life. Poor sleep can make you:
  - sick
  - dumb
  - grumpy
  - negative
  - fat
  - depressed.

- Poor sleep negatively impacts on motivation and hyperactivity.

- School learning improves with later starts for adolescents.

Chapter 8

Adolescent *angst* and the **search** *for* Joy Juice, *Buzz* **Rush** and **Transcendence**

Adolescents of all ages need ecstatic experience to become adult, and if the culture will not provide it they will seek it in any case, often in ways which do them harm

Neville, B. *Educating the Psyche*, (2005).

Adolescents can be so unpredictable in their behaviour due to the collisions of surging hormones, brain reconstructions, functioning from the amygdala rather than the pre-frontal lobe and body changes. Remember, for a time they misread physiology and facial expressions and their sensitivity to threat (mostly perceived and not real) means they are in defensive mode much of the time. The stress they feel because their world is out of control and so confusing translates into a chemical war in their brains and bodies. Before exploring their inner turmoil and the search for feeling good, we should be clear about what they need first:

Five basic tools to ensure adolescents are healthy and avoid depression

1. Loving human connectedness.
2. Good nutrition.
3. Plenty of sleep.
4. Meaningful involvement and physical activity.
5. Laughter and lightness.

The search for transcendence is the search to feel better, 'more' and really alive. Sometimes the urge for transcendence translates into accidents, near death experiences, drugs that alter states of awareness, wildly inappropriate sex and alcohol abuse. In her book, *The Soul of Education,* Rachel Kessler explores the fascination with death among the young and identified that some suicides were not the result of despair and hopelessness, but rather a 'quest for a life-affirming experience of transcendence'. This quest can be fed by poets, songwriters and people of hero status who have died, such as Michael Hutchence or Kurt Cobain.

Kessler defines the term 'to transcend' as:

- to be lost or immersed in a play, dance or creative process
- flashes of intensity against a dull background of ordinary days
- to rise above, or pass beyond, a human limit
- reaching beyond ordinary life and consciousness
- opening to the domain of spirit.

Much of an adolescent's behaviour (and many of their choices) is to change their negative emotional state, and often this drive is unconscious. They are especially sensitive to the state of boredom because that is a brain antagonistic state, and the brain wants to stop being bored so it may learn something new. Certain neurotransmitters are produced when boredom is present, and different ones are produced when an adolescent is excited. Research shows how amazing the neurotransmitters in our brains and bodies are. These brain chemicals whizz around our bodies influencing how we feel at any given moment.

> *So many grown-ups can't manage stress well. Because no-one helped them enough with stress and distress in childhood, they never set up effective stress regulating systems in their brains.*
>
> Sunderland, M., The Science of Parenting: How today's brain research can help you raise happy, emotionally balanced children, (2006).

Children are particularly susceptible to external stressors because they are rushed and hurried unlike previous generations. However, adolescents are also very susceptible to external pressures. Measuring the stress chemical cortisol via a saliva test shows how stressed many of our children are in their everyday lives. It is not a simple case of looking at environments and guessing how our children are managing things. Some children find large group childcare stressful, and yet children from dysfunctional homes have shown to have reduced levels of cortisol, meaning less stress, in the same environment. Adolescents live in an almost constant state of stress because they have so many things happening at the same time and they seldom get to feel genuinely safe in their skin, and are rarely relaxed. Brain changes create states of confusion and uncertainty, and this again creates more stress and more negative feeling states.

In *The Science of Parenting,* Margot Sunderland explores the particular ways of responding to children that helps them establish pathways in their brain to:

- enable them to manage emotions well
- think rationally under pressure
- calm themselves without recourse to angry outbursts, anxiety attacks; or, in later life, alcohol, smoking and drug problems.

We need to know how we can support adolescents to find that place where they feel at peace, transcended or more expanded than they feel. Firstly, lets explore the effects of being stressed.

Stress is the body's response to a perception of a lack of control over an aversive situation. Distress is when there are chronic levels of elevated stress over a longer period of time.

Jensen E., Enriching The Brain: How to Maximize Every Learner's Potential, (2006).

Distress (chronic stress) affects the brain the following ways:

- Neuron development is halved.
- Reduces effectiveness of the dendrites.
- Reduces the brain to survival mode rather than using upper cognitive processing.
- Reduces blood supply to the brain.
- Stimulates emotional meltdowns.
- Impedes the immune system.

These impacts on an adolescent's developing brain can be profound. It means having only half as many spaces for new learning every morning when they get to school. This seriously impedes an adolescent's capacity to learn and they can fail to absorb as much information as an unstressed adolescent. Over time, this leads to a massive cumulative effect of missed learning. Plus, the integration of the learning is negatively affected, which also has a significant cumulative influence.

The toxic teacher in a threatening school environment can have a serious long-term debilitating effect on student learning on all levels—cognitive, social and emotional. Remember, adolescents can create more distress by their inability to manage their negative self-talk and by having poor life management skills. Strive for safer school environments with better informed teachers using a more calming and nurturing focus, rather than better looking buildings.

In *The Biology of Belief: Unleashing the Power of Consciousness, Matter & Miracles* (2008), Bruce H. Lipton PhD shows how the cells in our body can only do one thing: focus on growth or protection, in order to ensure survival. Children (and adolescents) who are experiencing frequent stress will have increased illness because the adrenal hormones will directly suppress the immune system to conserve energy supplies in order to survive their stressful experience.

This is why students of any age who have experienced the distress of a parent's death will feel 'dumber' for ages—sometimes for up to 18 months. The body will preserve its cognitive energy in order to manage the deep challenges of processing the death of a loved one.

The brain adapts to chronic stressors with either of two extremes:

1. Numbness—listless, apathetic, unresponsive: disappearing.
2. Hypervigilance—edgy, suspicious or overactive: acting out.

If a young child gets distressed they tend to cling to an adult who is safe in order to bring down their high body arousal level and high levels of stress chemicals. They try to start the positive brain chemicals that activate feelings of well-being. Given the emotional immaturity and additional stressors today's adolescents face, we need to understand how we can also help them deactivate the high levels of cortisol, adrenaline and noradrenalin.

Soothing and reassuring a distressed baby releases oxytocin and opioids that give a child a sense of well-being, but adolescents are not that keen on being soothed or reassured like a small child! Thus, we can begin to understand their hunt for joy juice and the buzz rush in order to have a taste of transcendence.

> *The biological need for all humans, from pre-birth until old age, is to feel connected and loved.*
>
> Dent, M., *Nurturing kids' hearts and souls: Building emotional, social and spiritual competency*, (2005).

What is transcendence?

We all seek this state of expandedness, where we feel 'more' than we normally feel. It is an opportunity to experience a moment of heightened pleasure and well-being, and sometimes great excitement or a buzz. It can also be a moment after deep profound relaxation or oneness with nature. Some people can slip into a state of bliss when they are surrounded by profound natural beauty. An example is the state most people feel when they see whales or dolphins up close. These mammals have an invisible power to draw us into a state of awe and reverence.

The need for transcendence is part of every human being's journey to awareness and maturity. Some songs, films, plays or dance performances can take us into transcendent states. This is the drive to find the 'joy juice' of deep delight, or the rush of excitement in the 'buzz rush'.

Negative neurotransmitters make it very difficult to feel happy and they also inhibit learning and human relationships. Low dopamine and noradrenalin levels make it more difficult for adolescents to focus and concentrate in any situation, which can lead to learning challenges and a repeating cycle of self-abuse.

> *Low serotonin levels are a key component in many forms of aggression and violent behaviour. Opioids are vital to diminish feelings of fear and stress, so deactivation of opioids in parts of the brain lead to increases in negative feelings and stress, and decreases in positive feelings.*
>
> Sunderland, M. The Science of Parenting, (2005).

These chemical reactions occur all day long for adolescents, randomly and because they do not have a mature, emotional reasoning brain they can be stuck in an emotional state for hours. This is why it's important for parents and teachers to 'lighten up'. When an adolescent perceives less threat they will produce fewer negative neurotransmitters and, in turn, feel better. There is great power in a smile, gestures of kindness and thoughtfulness.

> *When we feel too stressed we are less likely to show exploratory, curious, novelty seeking behaviours.*
>
> Sunderland, M. The Science of Parenting, (2005).

The opposite of stress and feeling threatened is feeling calm or safe and happy. Brain chemicals are responsible for these moods. The good neurotransmitters are called endorphins. Twenty types of endorphins have been discovered; they are a part of the family of neuropeptides that carry information around the body. Candice Pert PhD discovered that these can be discovered anywhere in the body not just the brain.

Endorphins remove stress and pain. Physical and psychological well-being are enhanced by the presence of endorphins.

External stimulus ⇨ perceived as pleasurable ⇨ triggers endorphins

> *The unconscious mind and the psychoneuroimmunological system cannot tell the difference between what is real and what is imagined. So you can evoke endorphins by imagining pleasurable things.*
>
> Bloom, W., *The Endorphin Effect: A breakthrough strategy for holistic health and spiritual wellbeing*, (2001).

Creative visualisations are beneficial for adolescents who are experiencing stress because they flood the body with endorphins and remove the cortisol. This gives the nervous system a break from the stress. This is very helpful if it's done as they go to sleep because it helps the body sleep deeper and more rested, thus giving the immune system time to do vital healing and rejuvenation. Many adolescents have a calming visualisation track on their mp3 players and use them to find a 'chill' place. This is very healthy.

An excellent way to get endorphins flowing is by using the altered state that deep relaxation can bring. The need to create a sense of safety is important; people need to feel they are free of conflict and tension. I use a relaxed state in my counselling work partly because it feels so good. It also allows people, especially adolescents, to realise how good it feels to be calm, safe and free from worry. The body in this state is open to insights and information accessed from a higher place within the personality. This is the inner guidance from our spirit instead of our ego-mask or our shadow.

I began using calming relaxations in my classrooms in 1992 and found that students responded very positively. The benefits were far reaching and surprised me. Students were kinder, calmer, more engaged in their learning and the classroom environment improved.

There are few places where adolescents can have time-out from the modern world, and in those 15 minutes in class they found it. The brain created the serotonin and endorphins that soothed their minds, psyches and bodies. The boys particularly liked the Beach Bliss track off *Just a Little Time Out*. Getting boys to sit still for 15 minutes at an age when they are surging with testosterone meant something good was happening. Calming relaxations improved their creative writing, problem-solving and their capacity to think 'big'. It allowed them to access their full brain, and the absence of stress chemicals allowed them to think and process without being 'on guard'. The latest calming track I have created for adolescents is called Relax and Escape where they have to metaphorically unplug themself from the plugged in and wired world before they relax.

> *There is a circuit of energy in the human body which magnetically attracts and absorbs the benevolent vitality of nature and the universe. This loop functions naturally when you feel relaxed, comfortable and at ease. Your body automatically falls into this loop when it needs rest and revitalization and also when you rest or sleep well.*
>
> Bloom, W. The Endorphin Effect, 2001

Older students preferred the longer 25-minute calming tracks, especially near end of term or near exams. This was in the days before we knew about the brain as we do now, but the benefits were clearly on their faces. They felt better about themselves and life when they were able to use their imaginations to wander off away from the incessant chatter of their negative inner voices[3*]. There is no question that with more silence, stillness and quiet, adolescents can find transcendence in a much healthier form than that provided by alcohol and drugs.

---

3   * For more on the benefits of calmness and relaxation please refer to my book, *Saving Our Children from Our Chaotic World: Teaching Children the Magic of Silence and Stillness*. I cover adolescents and children, as well as what teachers can do to bring more quietness into classrooms, and how parents can bring it into the home.

> *Students who feel deeply connected don't need danger to feel fully alive. They don't need guns to feel powerful. They don't want to hurt others or themselves. Out of connection grows compassion and passion – passion for people, for students' goals and dreams, for life itself.*
>
> Kessler, R. *The Soul of Education*, (2003)

One of the most powerful ways to trigger endorphins and help adolescents change negative emotional states is through safe touch. Touch has been contaminated by our fear-based world. We have let our children down by withdrawing one of the most important ways to offer love and reassurance.

> *Our dilemma, the importance of touch and physical contact, is not fully understood or accepted within our culture. We know that our children need to feel safe and comforted when distressed and yet we live in a society that has gradually pushed physical contact into a negative, unhealthy light, rejecting its importance, so as to make it easier to protect ourselves. As educators, both parents and teachers can do something about this.*
>
> Dewar, D., *Hands on Learning*, (2005).

Many adolescents pull away physically as a normal distancing, but they still have the same needs for safe physical touch. Make your gestures smaller

such as gentle shoulder rubs from behind as they eat their breakfast, the ruffle on the head (be careful of hairdo!), nurse their feet on the couch or just rest your hand on them from time to time. If you can build a positive massage habit BEFORE the hormones arrive you will be able to continue it after the bumpy ride appears. Please trust me, adolescents yearn for safe physical intimacy and less words. Even playing rough when shooting basketball hoops, playing soccer or beach cricket—the touch can feel so amazing to a touch-deprived adolescent.

> *Time spent with a loved one in whose company you feel very safe and at ease can also strongly activate the opioids in the brain, giving you a wonderful feeling of well-being. If it's a physically affectionate relationship, these opioids will have an even deeper effect on you because of the sensitising effects of oxytocins on the opioid system.*
>
> Sunderland, M. *The Science of Parenting*, (2005).

Another simple trigger that many parents already use is the smell of favourite food cooking. Almost everyone enjoys the smell of food, and especially sharing that food together. For some it's bread baking, or maybe a roast dinner, curry, soups, cakes, biscuits, bacon, or onions on a barbeque. We create memory pathways that link positive experiences around food that can trigger endorphins later in life without a thought—it's automatic. Parents should carefully choose the foods they cook when their adolescents have exams or have been dumped by their girlfriend or boyfriend. The automatic endorphin release can give them a break from feeling lousy. Also, try using barbeques at the beach or in a park because the fun memories from childhood can be triggered in adolescence.

> *Studies at the Institute of HeartMath in Boulder Creek, California, indicate that five minutes of anger stays in the muscles and organs of the body for up to six hours. Conversely, five minutes of laughter, humour and joy also biochemically anchor in your body for six hours.*
>
> Goode, C. B., *Nurture Your Child's Gifts: Inspired Parenting*, (2001).

Funny books in the toilet can help shift a grumpy adolescent out of a dark mood. Also, try getting a couple of *Chicken Soup for the Soul* books; there are books for both adolescents and children. They are true stories and easy to read. My boys were never going to read a *Chicken Soup* book if I gave them one, so I left them in the toilet, and before too long they *were* reading them and did so for a long time afterwards. The books lifted bad moods as well as helped build their emotional intelligence and spiritual competence because the stories showed the value of love and kindness, and how people overcame challenge. The right kinds of books have the potential to heal and create uplifting emotional states.

Look in your homes or school and see how many endorphin inducers are present, because we are expecting adolescents with an underdeveloped brain to manage stress and chaos as capably as adults do. Daniel Goleman believes happy, calm children learn best and have healthier bodies. The same applies to adolescents—the calmer and safer they feel, the better they will learn, relate and play.

Research has shown that the following activities can stimulate oxytocin, an anti-stress chemical:

- meditation
- acupuncture
- massage or physical affection
- yoga
- a warm bath
- spending time in daylight.

Sunderland, M. *The Science of Parenting,* (2005).

The reality of the world for today's adolescents is that they have partially been abandoned by busy parents, extended family and teachers. The modern society has become time poor and it has cost our adolescents dearly. Adolescents are biologically wired to overcome boredom in any way they can, so it's important to explore the search for the joy juice and buzz rush.

Joy juice is the state where adolescents are feeling happy and at peace with the world. One of the best ways to lower stress levels is to spend time with emotionally warm adults, but if the adults are absent then they do the next best thing: connect online to friends through social networking sites. This allows adolescents to feel more connected and it tackles the problem of boredom—for a while.

Unfortunately, this is a temporary change of state (except if you are communicating with the one you are madly and deeply in love with this week!). One of the reasons why adolescents spend so much time online or texting is to stimulate the neurotransmitters that make them feel connected and feel better. However, sometimes the opposite happens and they incur more stress and emotional distress when things go wrong, like a nasty message or an email they have misread. Suddenly, they are plunged into an even deeper hole of turmoil. It is sad to know that many adolescents' emotional state is determined by how many friends they have on Facebook any given day.

> *You can survive while under stress from these threats but chronic inhibition of growth mechanisms severely compromises your vitality. In a growth/ protection continuum, eliminating the stressors in your life only puts you in a neutral point in the range. To fully thrive we must not only eliminate the stressors but also actively seek joyful, loving, fulfilling lives that stimulate the growth process.*
>
> Lipton, B. H., PhD. The Biology of Belief: Unleashing the Power of Consciousness, Matter & Miracles *(2008)*

Eliminating as many of the stressors in our adolescents' lives should make a big difference. Ensuring they have safe place to sleep, good food, human connectedness and lots of sleep all helps them find a sense of well-being. However, that only allows them to survive better. We must give them the means to seek out legal, non fattening and affordable ways of making themselves feel good.

Hanging with friends and having fun is the next best thing, and much of the time this is beneficial and helpful. Sometimes groups of adolescents can make dumb decisions about what is fun, like throwing stones at passing cars, shoplifting, fighting, stealing garden ornaments, drag racing, climbing tall trees in the dark or skinny dipping in strange places. What often starts out as innocent fun can have serious and sometimes fatal consequences. If something happens *remember that their original intention was to have fun with friends in order to create the feel-good endorphins.*

Sleepovers can create both joy juice and a buzz rush in a safer environment than the street or at the beach where they can be joined by unsavoury characters. Sleeping near your friends gives adolescents the same feelings that young children get when they sleep near their parents—provided no boundaries are crossed.

Spending long periods of time in nature definitely stimulates the joy juice. Camps that allow adolescents to spend quality time in nature are excellent for helping them learn how their emotional state can change positively while outdoors. Outward Bound and other nature-based adventure businesses offer excellent opportunities for adolescents to unplug and experience the joy juice and buzz rush of life outdoors. Parents can do the same by taking their families, with a few friends or other families, to quiet beachside campsites. Here they can see starry nights, stand beside huge trees, snorkel safely and see water creatures in their natural habitat. I have met adolescents who had been depressed then found a new passion in life after a trip into nature with their families.

As a culture, Australians are depreciatory in their ability to celebrate. Maybe it's the English 'stiff upper lip' that is still present in many of our genes. We tend to hold back on spontaneous joy as though it is something we need to contain. Our children are also conditioned at an early age to 'settle down' when they are too excited; yet they are in the throes of joy or delight. I know that without the laughter and lightness shared with my boys and their many friends in my home, we would all have experienced more pain and challenges as we journeyed through childhood and the teenage years.

> *Experiences of deep connection can bring forth joy. Music, singing, dancing, awesome moments in nature can result in joy. The simple experiences of being remembered, acknowledged, validated or thanked all bring forth a bubbling of joy within us—even if we are alone.*
>
> Dent, M., *Saving our children from our chaotic world: Teaching children the magic of silence and stillness*, (2003).

I encourage adolescents to find their own unique, safe place in nature. It needs to be in a quiet area, preferably near big trees, rocks or water like a lake or beach. This can be the place they go when life gets tough, when they are sick of being annoyed by adults, friends or siblings. The more often they go, the better they build a connection that will allow them to feel safe and centred. This allows their unconscious mind and higher self to meet without the distractions of life— leave mobiles and mp3 players at home, this must be a *silent* and *quiet* safe place! Parents should also encourage adolescents to take some time out and go to their quiet place. This helps empower adolescents to work out pathways to solve their own problems and find the means to do that.

Creating quiet places to sit around home can help too. Park benches in the garden, big rocks and seats that are surrounded by plants all create the same sense of inner calm. Model it for your adolescents by taking your cuppa outside and simply sitting there. Take your time because before you know it, you will find them sitting in your favourite quiet place too.

Girls tend to share more deeply with their friends and are more likely to find their joy juice through emotional intimacy. When I struggled in the area of trusting and sharing my inner self, I tended to follow the boy preferred way of shifting boredom. The boy way is through physical activity, risk-taking behaviour and physical pain. Boys are searching for the excitement neurotransmitter called dopamine, and a bit of adrenalin as well. This gives them a buzz rush that makes them feel really alive.

As a teenager I had a thrill for driving fast and playing very vigorous sport. Thankfully, I survived my two car accidents. Some seeking the same buzz rush are not so lucky. Remember I was an academically capable athletic adolescent experiencing success in my life.

David Oldfield, an American specialist of adolescent rites of passage and the importance of ceremony, wrote the following:

Trying to warn adolescents off rash or suicidal behaviour doesn't work. Adolescence has always been a time for risk-taking and more traditional societies were wiser than ours in that they created fitting tests and challenges for teenagers to face, and turned these into rites of passage.

The Sydney Morning Herald, April 2003.

On the ABC program, *Whatever: The Science of Teens* hosted by Steve Cannane, they examined risk and teenagers. They showed an exercise where a mature man and a 15-year-old boy were asked to look at large pictures of scenes and choose which was safe and which was risky. They had to step on a coloured light as quickly as possible to show their choice. The man chose sensibly by identifying the images of skydiving, dangerous stunts on skateboards and a wild ride on a roller coaster as risky. The adolescent boy chose those same images as safe because he thought they looked like fun.

Everyone likes a thrill but teens take it to the next level. The more dangerous a dare, the more crazy a stunt, teens just can't get enough of risk-taking.

Whatever: The Science of Teens, ABC Television, 2009.

Scientists are now realising that risk-taking is a crucial phase of the bumpy ride to adulthood. By taking risks we force our brains to make decisions that allow them to grow. Often, the painful outcome anchors significantly in our brains and reminds us that we can make a different choice in the future. The final stages of that reasoning brain doesn't take place until the 20s, so it's about a 10-year scary ride for parents of boys.

Adults need to be mindful that they acknowledge the role risky behaviour has in the healthy development of adolescents. The buzz rush is a chemical reaction in the brain that makes them feel transcendent and really alive. The alternative to helping them experience risk and thrills may be to assign them boring lives of misery in their bedrooms where the only risk taking they do is killing people in online games, or illegally downloading hardcore porn. They are wired to break the numbness of feeling dumb, stupid, useless or lonely and if we are not allowing them opportunities to get excited by *real* life, they will use the virtual world to get their thrills.

I have observed in my counselling that overwhelmed adolescents are often ungrounded. This means that an individual is energetically disconnected from their body and their somatic senses as well as the earth. This may sound really fluffy and unimportant, but I know that ungroundedness and emotional overwhelm go together. When I am ungrounded I can get scatty with my thoughts and feel anxious in my stomach. I also know that I give my best presentations when I am grounded and my best writing occurs from the same state.

Simple techniques to help ground an adolescent

- Go for a walk or a run and be aware of pounding your feet on the ground every now and again while taking deep inward breaths.
- Stand still and imagine your feet are glued to the floor or the ground. Imagine roots or tentacles growing out from your feet down into the earth.
- Imagine a ray of bright sunshine flowing down into your head right down your spine and then down into the earth. Imagine that ray circles the core of the earth and returns back up into your body and back out through the top of your head.
- Feel a bright ball of white light in your belly and imagine it is pulsing with energy and power.
- Keep your knees off lock and slightly bent.

Being grounded can help you manage your emotional state, make better choices—first with your thoughts and then with your actions. This is a life skill we all need to master, not just children and adolescents. As we can see by observing adults, getting overwhelmed is a common side effect of stress.

Other areas that can stretch an adolescent's mind and create a sense of expansion in their life include:

- Athletic success—pushing themselves to achieve is healthy and success can give an enormous rush.

- Artistic and creative expression—playing music, being in a band, school performance Rock Eisteddfod, school open days, assemblies.
- Acts of service—especially when they are able to do it over time to see the results of their efforts.
- Discovering new purpose and meaning—becoming involved in a new interest that isn't sport or the arts like Scouts, SES, environmental warriors or animal rescue.
- Celebration activities—opportunities to organise acknowledgement ceremonies like welcomes, farewells and new beginnings for projects or events.

Children throb with a natural connection. But the slings and arrows of outrageous fortune start hitting early. Competitive siblings. Tough schools. Harsh media. Dangerous streets. Social injustice. All the noise of modern life. Hunger and pain. Each of these events, every childhood injury, physical and psychological, creates tension in the physical body. The result is that by the time most of us are teenagers we have lost that bubbling, continuous ability to feel life's natural beauty.

Bloom, W. The Endorphin Effect, (2001).

If we support our adolescents on their bumpy ride to adulthood and help them learn they can change their negative states without resorting to alcohol, drugs or life-threatening experiences, then we show them a doorway to authentic happiness. They are following biological urges to feel better and to escape the mindless misery they witness on many adults' faces. Parents, teachers and lighthouses need to hold the light high and remind adolescents that life can be fun and full of delight—without necessarily reaching for the wine bottle—and that even in the darkest moments we can make ourselves feel better.

Transcendence is a normal human longing, and by providing adolescents with as many experiences as we can while they are evolving rapidly and showing them how to find this place of magic is a huge responsibility we have neglected since the virtual world arrived. Peak human experiences will beat a peak virtual experience any day.

Key Points

- Transcendence is the search to feel better, 'more than...' and really alive.

- Boredom is a brain antagonistic state.

- Stress impacts adolescents deeply and reducing stress helps them manage their lives.

- Transcendence is a normal human yearning.

- Adolescence is a time of massive swings emotionally and is driven by neurotransmitters in the brain.

- Changing emotional states by choice can help adolescents and adults feel better.

- Risk-taking behaviour is normal in adolescents.

- Healthy transcendence can be achieved through many different ways such as dancing, meditation, walking or finding a unique quiet place.

- Being grounded helps adolescents avoid becoming overwhelmed.

- Adults need to create healthy opportunities for adolescents to experience transcendence.

Chapter 9

Parenting *today's* **adolescents:**
Bridging the generation chasm

The best way to inspire your children to develop into the kind of adults you dream of them becoming is to become the kind of adult you want them to be.

Sharma ,R, Family Wisdom from the Monk Who Sold His Ferrari: Nurturing the Leader Within Your Child, Hay House Australia Ltd, NSW, (2000).

Parenting adolescents has always been considered the tough end of the parenting deal. There are physical and emotional changes happening to an adolescent that need to be combined with the balance between protecting and guiding them, and allowing them freedom to develop autonomy and independence. Even with the unique pressures the MilGen Adolescent faces, they still need to have strong healthy connections to their parents.

> *Before long we find ourselves dancing fast to a wild and wooly rumba without knowing any of the correct steps. This can be challenging – not to mention demoralising – when the person we're trying to dance with seems to put the same energy into pushing away when we're trying to connect.*
>
> Feinstein, S. *Parenting the Teenage Brain*, (2007)

A certain parenting style better supports the development of identity and autonomy for adolescents. There are three main styles of parenting:

1. Authoritative
2. Authoritarian
3. Permissive—Indulgent and neglectful

Authoritative

This is a democratic style of parenting. Authoritative parents listen to their adolescents when setting guidelines and making decisions about boundaries. A key part of the bumpy adolescent journey from childhood to adulthood is learning how to take responsibility for decisions. Teenagers struggle with this even up to 25 years of age because the frontal lobe is still growing and they are not yet fully competent. Kids raised in authoritative homes are encouraged to make their own decisions, take responsibility and become autonomous—with age appropriate discretion (Feinstein).

> *Compassion, connection, responsibility, citizenship...this is the cycle we want to start at home. The alternative is selfishness, alienation, exploitation, disenfranchisement. Big words to describe the loud mouthed brats we meet who know nothing of their obligations to anyone else.*
>
> Ungar, M *Turning the Me generation into the We Generation* 2009

The most frequent form of discipline used in these homes is talking about the problem so that adolescents can be shown a more mature perspective. It is important to do this without making them feel stupid, bad or dumb, or merely partially aware or informed.

Adolescents who experience authoritative parenting tend to benefit with more social competence and fewer psychological and behavioural problems. These parents are vigilant without being smothering or over controlling.

I was a very responsible adolescent—no alcohol, drugs or wild sex—and aware of making my choices. But, put me behind the wheel of a car and things were very different. I crashed my first car at 16 when I was racing another boy on a dirt road. I hit a concealed rock and the car rolled three times. I was thrown from the vehicle and it almost rolled back on me after it stopped. Fortunately, I was able to pull myself out of the way, but my right leg was still trapped by the car. When I was pulled free my foot started swelling and my basketball boot split as if a scalpel had sliced it. I did some serious damage to my ankle and was on crutches for six weeks, and unable to play my beloved basketball for over a year. Now, for an intelligent adolescent, you would think I'd have learned to take care when driving because of the consequences of being irresponsible. But, no!

The following year I made an impulse decision to see how fast my Dad's car would go. When it began vibrating, I slowed down—then promptly forgot about the incident. I only remembered it almost 30 years later when I was working with a girl who had done the same with her best friend in the car. She hadn't been so lucky and her best friend was killed.

This shows that even though I was enormously responsible in some areas, I still made big mistakes in other areas. This applies to all adolescents. However, with the guidance offered by the authoritative style of parenting there is a good chance they won't make dumb decisions because they don't have to fight to be heard or have some power.

Every adolescent is still at risk regardless of which style of parenting their parents are using. This style may reduce the need to rebel and make decisions just to spite their parents.

> *Teens need parents who will let them make these decisions in slow increments. Too much freedom will be construed as rejection, not enough as imprisonment.*
>
> Feinstein, S. *Parenting the Teenage Brain: Understanding a Work in Progress, (2007)*

Authoritarian style—My way or the highway

This relationship is based on control and adolescents raised in these homes lack confidence, have more social problems, and have difficulty getting along with their peers and teachers stemming from their sense of insecurity (Feinstein). This confrontational style of parenting creates no feeling of warmth or acceptance in the house, just rigid, and often irrational, adherence to house rules and there is often shaming and harsh criticism involved This type of parenting creates a combination of rebellion and dependency in the teenager. The weaker adolescents remain co-dependent and the strong ones rebel. When this domination is abusive many adolescents simply run away after a time when they feel there is no point to the constant fighting and conflict. Many of our bullies come from this style of parenting as it can be a desperate need to have any power despite the cost.

> *Shame is the name we give to the overwhelming feeling we need to crawl under a rock because we see ourselves as unworthy, unpleasant, dislikeable and reprehensible and because we expect to be judged or rejected accordingly. Shame is like a knife that sharply delineates the limits of love in every culture, the warning signal that something we are doing risks us being ostracised.*
>
> Grille,R *Heart to Heart Parenting.* (2008)

Permissive—Indulgent and neglectful

Indulgent

Overindulgent parents express their love by giving into their kid's every demand—these parents often want friendship from their teens—and act more like peers than parents (Feinstein). You cannot be your adolescent's best friend, that space is reserved for people their own age. They need you to be the adult, and sometimes that means being firm and saying 'no'. Once adolescence is over you can become best friends because the power dynamic has changed and your child is now mature enough to make their own decisions, regardless of your views. If they are still making decisions to please you or trying to meet with your expectations, then that is not healthy.

This type of parent is forever rushing to the school to defend their child, instead of allowing the school to manage inappropriate behaviour or poor school attendance via the school's system. Over-indulgent parents can create co-dependent patterns of attachment that make it difficult for their child to grow into an adult. As adolescents they will never quite mature and stand on their own feet because they still allow their parents to run their lives. These parents even contact their bosses and come between their love partners. Some mothers struggle with letting go. When you are texting your adult children several times every day, you may be holding on too tight.

Neglectful

Neglectful parents send a clear message that they don't care about their children. This could be by neglecting to attend their children's activities or by never being home for dinner. Adolescents receive little guidance in these homes and in their teens will yearn for a sense of belonging, no matter what the risk. Boundaries show you care, even if they cause many heated discussions—just ask an adolescent who didn't have any boundaries.

This style of parenting can trigger the early sexual behaviour of girls as they seek love in all the wrong places to the point where it becomes a pathological yearning for love. Neglectful parenting can feed a deep sense of unworthiness and distrust of love. It can also create patterns of inappropriate behaviour that force the parent to notice their adolescent, especially at school because the school has to contact the parent concerning their child's behaviour.

Our role as parents

Our role as parents includes helping our children to develop cognitively, socially, emotionally and physically. We must guide them into developing an inner locus of control, or a sense of personal responsibility for their actions. This is difficult without a fully developed brain and yet parents still need to keep guiding and encouraging thoughtfulness, kindness, consideration and a growing awareness of feelings and emotions.

Michael Ungar in his inspiring book, *Turning the Me Generation into the We generation*, writes in depth about the role parents play in building a sense of compassion in our children early so that they can take this capacity with them into adulthood. They hunger and long for deep 'genuine flesh and blood, eye-to-eye connections.' Inside every adolescent is a frightened four four-year year-old seeking love, acceptance and reassurance –– no matter what!

> *Parents need to give children the space to explore and a safe harbour to return to so that they may feel secure in the very large room we call our Earth.*
>
> Ungar ,M, Turning the Me generation into the We generation, 2009

Today's adolescents have been influenced more than any previous generation by a moral code from the virtual world of the Internet, and the screen world of television and film. This has made it harder for parents to develop the above competencies and we are paying a price with more violence in the home, in our schools and on our streets. The over-pampered child becomes even more self-absorbed than normal, and the sense that the world owes them something can create a deep layer of resentment and anger towards parents and other figures of authority. The bumpy ride to adulthood is often quite ego-centric anyway without having a pattern of poor boundaries, seldom hearing 'no' and spoilt antics to get one's own way as a learned behaviour. In a 20-year study of parents and children by Professor Marilyn Rossman it showed quite clearly 'that the most likely gauge of how likely kids are to turn out well was whether or not they did chores growing up.'

> *That's the strange thing about providing our children with too much. They lose the advantages of having to take responsibility. They are at risk of never developing a sense of themselves as competent, caring contributors to their communities or families.*
>
> Ungar ,M Turning the Me generation into the We generation 2009

Practical ideas that help with dancing the dance of life with today's adolescents

No matter which parenting style you choose to follow, there are still some things that will not work well with adolescents. They never worked when you were an adolescent and they definitely won't work with the MilGen digital natives of today. Things which won't work with adolescent communication include:

- Lecturing.
- Nagging.
- Poor timing.

- Arguing
- Unkindness.
- Criticism.
- Shouting.
- Manipulation.
- Guilt games.
- Any physical abuse.
- Ignoring them or freezing them out—especially boys.
- Using 'always', 'never', 'It's easy!', or 'It's going to be hard' as a predictor.

The technique of ignoring or freezing adolescents out is an emotional ploy commonly used by females and it must never be used on boys, particularly adolescents. They are badly wounded by this, especially if their mother does it to them. They feel profoundly rejected and abandoned. I have worked with a boy who attempted suicide because he couldn't take the pain of being rejected by his mum one minute longer.

> *Teenagers are perplexing, intriguing and spirited creatures. In an attempt to discover the secrets to their thoughts and actions parents have tried talking, cajoling and nagging them for answers.*
>
> Feinstein, S. *Parenting the Teenage Brain: Understanding a Work in Progress,*2007

Do not beat yourself up if you have done any of the above. Our ability to manage the constant shifts and changes while often struggling with our own levels of over-commitment, work, home and life can be difficult. When we are tired and stressed, we will revert back to our critical parent/reactive parent voice in our head.

At one point I had five boys aged 6–17 years—three of whom were adolescents—and life whizzed by in a blur. They were all playing sport and surfing at every opportunity, so much of my life was as the taxi driver and I had little time to become bored at home. They all had chores and if they had three strikes – there was no ride to football or to the beach! Mostly I aimed to be kind and caring—and often selectively deaf, because I wanted them to feel safe and loved, especially at home. It was especially important that they felt that they mattered and had a valued place on our Earth.

Please avoid arguing with an adolescent. They do not have the prefrontal lobe to be able to construct a logical argument, but they certainly know how to hit the buttons to trigger our darkest emotions. They also have lots of energy and built-up, unexpressed 'aggro' and they will project that onto parents to avoid doing it to teachers at school.

Tips for avoiding the arguing dance:

- Listen to what they are asking.
- Pause and think about it.
- In a **quiet** voice say you will give them an answer soon.
- When they are in their room later, knock, enter.
- Say your piece.
- Turn, leave the room and close the door.

Ignore anything that is thrown at you as you leave the room as it is none of your business.

Remember, ruling with guilt, withholding love and making personal attacks are psychologically damaging to your adolescent. They also inflame the adolescent amygdala and they can reach the 'tipping point' quickly, and unexpectedly. Please do not take this personally—it is better to avoid adding fuel to their already smoking fire.

> *Even if your teenagers use these techniques on you all the time, you shouldn't respond in kind. Comments like 'I hate you,' 'You're the worst mother ever' and 'Everyone else gets to stay out to midnight' are just the frequent mutterings of adolescents.*
>
> Feinstein, S. *Parenting the Teenage Brain: Understanding a Work in Progress,2007*

Many adolescents won't remember these comments in a week's time, yet parents can recall them forever. Remember the emotional barometer and that adolescents need to discharge emotional angst. Mothers tend to get a lot of this verbal discharge, so maybe reframe the discharge experience by thinking:

- Well thankfully he/she will be less likely to hit their tipping point now that they have emptied some muck on me.
- They can discharge this muck at me because they love me the most.
- I'm imagining I have a suit of armour on and all the muck just slides off like water off a duck's back.

Adolescents can interpret some parent behaviours to mean very different things than what you intended.

How adolescents understand an adult's word choice

Adult communication	Adolescent interpretation
Threaten	I don't matter.
Command	I'm inadequate.
Preach	You don't like me.
Advice	You invalidate me.
Lecture	I can't do anything right.
Shout	I am frightened.
Criticism	I am useless and incapable.
Shame	I am bad and hopeless.
Nag	You disrespect me.
Smother	I am trapped.
Withhold love	You make my world unsafe.
Disconnect	There's no one I can trust.
You solve my problems	You crush my search for solutions.
You tell me what I am feeling	You invalidate me and my feelings.
Be unavailable	I am invisible and unlovable.

If we could remember this key aspect of communication, we could better parent our adolescents. Often we assume they will understand what we are saying and why, but quite simply they don't. Because so many of them are experiencing crushing self doubt and self loathing, any act or words that they perceive to be unkind will push them further into the pit of despair. It simply validates their primary negative belief that 'I don't matter.'

> *Parents want to express these perfectly clear and logical thoughts, but trust me, it's not what teens hear. Just listen maybe commiserate and do not trivialise their concerns; at this point in their lives, these are major worries.*
>
> Feinstein, S. *Parenting the Teenage Brain: Understanding a Work in Progress*, 2007

Anyone who lives or works with adolescents needs to fully grasp that they have a unique map of the world with which they are navigating their choices. Our job is to help them to create more helpful maps, or to allow them to see the map of the adult world. Remember, our behaviour is the result of choices we make based on our beliefs and past experiences, and we make assumptions and expectations automatically. Our reality is our reality though—no one else can share our view of reality.

Here is an example of a mother-son conflict that shows how different maps can cause angst:

The son was having difficulty engaging at school and had been wagging occasionally. Mum gets a call to say he has not arrived at school and she was pretty angry because she had dropped him off at school before it started.

She frantically phones his mobile and it's turned off. She goes home to check and then starts to get really worried. Then the school calls to say he has shown up.

She quickly goes to the school and finds her son and confronts him in front of other staff and students. After she has yelled at him and told him how stupid he has been, he then loses the plot and in front of the same group of people tells her to get #&%$#@!

Mum's map of the world told her that he had wagged after she had dropped him off and she was worried the school would expel him because he was on a final warning. Son's map of the world was very different.

When he arrived at school he was told there was a seminar for his year group that cost $10. He didn't have the money, plus he didn't want to go so he went downtown until the seminar was over. He had left his phone in his bag back at school.

Once they were able to have their different maps decoded, they had understanding and were able to appreciate how the conflict was blown out of misunderstanding—not malicious intent.

Totally different maps and different worlds, and neither side could see the other side. A supportive lighthouse or adult ally can help decode each map to the other so they can both understand each other's behaviour. The mother had done something very dangerous in adolescent land: publicly shame an adolescent in their territory. Social inclusion and the biological need to belong is profoundly strong, and she had—unintentionally—made him look stupid in front of his social group. The son had reached a tipping point and exploded; partly to defend his sense of identity and also to retain his place socially.

Decoding maps is my main way of working with adolescents in my counselling work. I avoid blame on either side because that is destructive and unhelpful. Allowing both sides to review the problem without the heat of emotion can dissolve most conflicts. I am solution focused and help create a better view of where families want to be. Most parents and young people tell me everything they *don't* want, instead of what they *do* want. A simple way to move the thinking positive and forwards is to use the symbol of a magic wand. I hand it to either party and say, 'If you could create magic tomorrow, how would it look if the conflict was healed and it had disappeared?'

> *Maggie's Tip: If you start using the magic wand as a metaphor when your children are young, it will work even better in adolescence. It still works when introducing it in adolescence because it shifts the perspective. Strictly use it in a one-on-one situation. Hand a magic wand to an adolescent and ask them to think, 'If I could use magic to fix this how would it look in the morning?'*

Knowing that adolescents see the world quite differently to adults means we can help them by offering feedback from the unique perspective of an adult. Notice the term 'offering' is used; not 'telling' or 'giving' without respecting an adolescent's view.

At times, I offered to give feedback to my sons when it had not been invited, and when they said no I respected that and said nothing. Often, they came back a few days later and then asked me for it. However, saying nothing was hard to do because I was busting to tell them how flawed their choice appeared to me! The occasional, 'I am not sure that is a good idea' did slip out, but the tone with which I said the offending statement was a huge influence on what happened next. When you are able to maintain a calm, loving tone, you can definitely get away with a few small parent cautions without inciting a major reaction.

- Have you thought that through?
- Have you given that much thought?
- I trust you to come up with a positive solution.
- Do you think that will work well for you?

When we ask these four questions and state the encouraging phrase we are respecting adolescents and reminding their inner guidance system, together with their unconscious mind, to review the decision inwardly. These are two of the most useful things parents can say to their children when it appears they're going to make a decision that could result in pain or suffering. Notice that I did not say a *bad* decision. There is no such thing as a bad decision, just some decisions that will cause more suffering and pain than others.

- Maybe sleep on that decision and check how it feels in the morning.

This sentence allows an even deeper review to take place while they are asleep. The higher sense of self and the unconscious work together for the greater good, and with more time, a wiser decision is often made. Some may call this intuition. It is buried deep in adolescents because of the many distractions they are living with, combined with an underdeveloped pre-frontal lobe.

I am deeply concerned that the absence of quietness, stillness and time in nature is weakening the development of adolescent intuition. Every adolescent I work with is required to use a calming CD at night for at least a month. It creates a space where intuition can be heard and is allowed to develop alongside being centred and present. Intuition is the doorway to an adolescent's higher self, inner spirit or God essence—whatever you choose to call it.

Map of the Personality

EGO MASK

Criticism

Blame

Lower Self

Anger

Conflict

Addictions

Spite

Spirit

Distrust

Confusion

Hate

Pleasure

Love

Shame

Spirituality

Compassion

Chronic
Tension

Feelings

Ecstasy

Fear

Intelligence

Hostility

Positive

Rage

Phobias

Disunity

Resentment

Pride

Jealousy

Rationalisation

Self Pity

Negative

This symbolic map of the personality is adapted from John C. Pierrakos.
Sometimes when we communicate we think we are being honest, when in reality we
are speaking from our mask. We have to acknowledge that we have all levels of our
personality and that sometimes we can feel disconnected from our spirit.
The voice of your spirit is much quieter than the voice of your ego.
Sometimes your spirit will try to communicate to you silently through
your senses or your feelings.
ALWAYS listen to your senses and your gut feelings....
Check experiences and choices with your spirit.
IT KNOWS YOU BEST.
Trust yourself.

This map shows the layers of our personality. The ego mask and the shadow are
very strong during adolescence because the prefrontal lobe is incomplete. Once
it has matured the individual can access more emotionally valid decisions and
act less from impulse and irrationality.

However, there are adolescents who can function from a very mature place well before their 20s, so be careful of the generalisations being made in this book. There are no definite markers of when any individual adolescent matures, which is what makes the bumpy ride so interesting.

I have asked many children and teenagers who have hurt themselves, or made a decision that they later regretted, if they had a thought or sense whether they knew it was something they would later regret. Overwhelmingly they have all had an intuitive thought that they chose to ignore. In his research, Andrew Weil (1972) has come up with the hypothesis that the intuitive consciousness (what he calls the non-linear consciousness) is an innate normal drive analogous to hunger or the sex drive (*The Natural Mind*, 2004 [updated]).

I recommend that adolescents try the many ways of strengthening being centred and more present in their bodies. My *Your Stairway to Better Choices* pack contains a DVD of energy techniques that can help lift a person's energy levels. This is useful before exams, job interviews and driving tests. It also contains calming energy techniques to help soothe the mind and body to sleep, be more creative and problem solve better.

> *Each of us has a wise part within, an intuitive part that knows what is best for us. Learning how to contact, listen to, and trust that inner authority are important skills. They are invaluable when life presents us with problems whose answers are not found in the back of the book.*
>
> Moorman, Chick. *The Parent Talk System*, (2003).

A simple shift in focus can strengthen the intuitive voice within all of us, especially confused adolescents. Many young people can find themselves ungrounded and 'stuck' in their heads. Martial arts, yoga, t'ai chi and meditation classes all help to balance mind and body. These practices help adolescents to quieten their inner critic and balance their rational and intuitive thoughts. Creating quiet time and spaces to simply 'be' is enormously important for our homes and classrooms. It strengthens an adolescent's connection to their inner knowing or inner compass.

I have found that children who played freely in the natural world when they were young tend to have a strong intuition, more so than children who have led more confined childhoods. The passive, highly visual world of television and computers starves a child's intuition and makes it harder to find. Our modern world and its shallow preoccupation with fame, entertainment and consumerism may be behind the increasing rates of depression and self-harm in adolescents. Parents can help by encouraging participation in any of the above activities and reassuring their child that they do have an inner compass. Help adolescents learn to trust themselves by using those sentences above; pause and ask within.

> *The words we choose in our interactions with children and adolescents have the power to heal or hurt, to create distance or foster closeness, to shut down feelings or touch the heart and open it, to foster dependency or to empower.*
>
> Aldort, N., *Raising Our Children Raising Ourselves: Transforming parent-child relationships from reaction and struggle to freedom, power and joy*, (2005).

Caring, empowering communication

Good communication leads to:

- Warm relationships.
- Cooperation.
- Feelings of worth.

Poor communication leads to:

- Kids who 'turn off' adults.
- Conflicts and bickering.
- Feelings of worthlessness.

The truth about communication

Communication is done without thinking; it's automatic. It is never taught to us and is largely an unconscious act driven by our past life experiences. We are not always aware of exactly what we are communicating, even though we may know what we are saying. The key to improving communication is having awareness of how we communicate. Neuro-linguistic programming (NLP) explores the art of communication in depth and considers that it consists of:

- 7% words
- 55% physiology
- 38% tonality.

This helps to understand why so much of what we *say* to adolescents is wasted. Physiology is how we stand, move, and silently project when we communicate. Those who have an innate ability to exhibit a physiology that feels safe to an adolescent often wonder why others find it difficult to get on with young people. Those who work with youth, particularly the homeless or those afflicted with addictions, often have this safe physiology. Given that adolescents misread facial expressions and body movements they also misread physiology for a few years.

If you genuinely dislike Aboriginal students, for example, they will know within a few minutes of you walking into a classroom. Generally, Indigenous adolescents are very intuitive at reading physiology and sensing if you are going to be genuine and caring.

The second huge influence on effective communication is tonality. Parents who are able to maintain a non-threatening tone and respectfully communicate in quiet tones tend to have less serious conflict with their adolescents. Then, when something very serious comes along, a loud voice is really taken notice of and the adolescent realises they may have stepped over some line in the sand. If there are a lot of raised voices, the really serious message may be lost among the noise of the usual family dynamics. This is definitely the case with communication between mothers and sons.

If a habit has formed where mum nags, then over time the son's brain has learned to zone out her voice until it reaches a certain decibel. Ensure you have eye contact when you ask your adolescent son to do something, and allow them a timeframe to choose in which to do it. When they are told NOW that can be seen as a threat to their autonomy and they may see a need to fight to hold their ground.

Communication with adult friends and work colleagues can be a good indicator of how to speak with your own family. We should speak respectfully with everyone because we all deserve to be treated well. No one likes being spoken to disrespectfully. Often adolescents sound disrespectful when it's not their intention. They are merely managing their insane world with a body and mind going through major change, while developing emotional and social competence.

Communication that works with adolescents

Adolescents often misunderstand body language and the spoken word. They need to have their feelings validated, be heard and most of all be loved and accepted as they are, not how they could be.

- Conversation—share in a light, non-interrogational way.

- Be a source of support—avoid being a praise junkie, yet offer encouragement, especially about persisting and overcoming setbacks.

- Encourage autonomy—remind them you are helping them build life skills so they can leave home and live with their friends.

- Trust—help them to trust themselves first.

- Monitoring—you are being vigilant because it is your duty as a parent to keep them safe and alive.

- Rules and consequences—even though they have a limited ability to fully understand the why and wherefore, keep explaining, keep the boundaries in place.

- Coping skills—for each adolescent you have, you need to build a comprehensive kit bag full of skills (listed at the end of the chapter).

- School involvement—do everything you can to keep them at school as it's safer to be near friends and in a safe environment, even if they're not doing well academically.

- Lighten up—relax, aim to use laughter and lightness to soothe their negative moods and emotional states and have fun with your adolescents.

> *Telling a joke, particularly one that illuminates a shared experience or problem, increases our sense of belonging and social cohesion.*
>
> Richman, J., Psychiatrist and Professor Emeritus at Albert Einstein Medical Centre in New York.

Adolescents take things very seriously and the brain changes can make it hard for them to understand humour. Homes with laughter and lightness create safety and connectedness that can help diffuse the emotional barometer. I recommend putting funny books in the toilet to help change emotional states. Books such as David Koutsoukis's *366 Fun Facts* and *366 Fun Quotes* are a great way to start[4]*. Families who started with these in the toilet now have a complete library of similar books. They often tell me how a grumpy adolescent can emerge from the toilet quite renewed after a short read. I have had mums tell me that even a dad is less grumpy because of the humour in the toilet. A sense of humour is a life skill that parents need to be encouraging in their children, preferably before adolescence.

Boys who leave school early to do a trade can be the brunt of the practical jokes at the workplace. Many have been sent to get the left-handed screw driver or the striped paint. If a boy does not get the joke he can be laughed at and it can feel like shame. Shame often appears in suicidal young men so it can have lethal consequences. The boy with a healthy sense of humour will not only cope, he will thrive.

Laughter is a powerful tool, it:

- transforms emotional states
- creates endorphins of well-being
- increases the level of serotonin
- is a key coping skill—especially for boys
- is an anti-bullying strategy

- encourages 'lightening up' for serious moments
- is a bonding experience when shared in groups
- builds inclusivity and connectedness
- releases tension and stress

---

4 * Available from my website at maggiedent.com/books.html.

Visual	Auditory	Kinaesthetic
See	Hear	Feel
Look	Listen	Touch
Appear	Sound	Grasp
View	Make music	Get hold of
Show	Harmony	Slip through
Illuminate	Tune in/out	Catch on
Clear	Be all ears	Tap into
Focus	Rings a bell	Make contact
Imagine	Silence	Throw out
Focus	Resonate	Turn around
Catch a glimpse of	Deaf	Hard
Dim view	Overtones	Hand in hand
Get a perspective of	Outspoken	Get a handle on
Eye to eye	Tell	Touch base
In light of	Clear as a bell	Boils down to
Make a scene	Clearly expressed	Come to grips with
Mind's eye	Earful	Connect with
Pretty as a picture	Give me your ear	Cool/calm/collected
Showing off	Word for word	Firm foundations
Well defined	Orchestrate	Get in touch with
Vivid		Slipped my mind
Clarity		

Caring, empowering communication is when you allow an adolescent, with your support, to make positive changes in their thinking and behaviour, and the way they see themselves without telling them how to do it.

It helps if parents work out agreed guidelines and boundaries before adolescence starts so their kids don't try the divide and conquer tactic. There are some things that you need a firm line on and I suggest you keep them to the big things such as no alcohol, drugs, unsupervised parties, driving with friends or sex with others. The next level would need to be around the concept of, 'We can negotiate on a circumstance by circumstance basis'. The final layer is about allowing autonomy where you 'just let it go through to the keeper!' If you try to control too many things you negate your adolescent's opportunity to manage their own world. If you are too controlling there is a good chance you will lose ground on the big issues. Keep expectations age appropriate and update them each year. Family meetings help keep the changing dynamics open and above board as siblings also need to know what's OK and what's not.

More helpful tips about communicating well with your adolescent

Use 'door openers'

'Door openers' are invitations to say more and to share ideas and feelings. They tell your adolescent that you are really listening and interested, that their ideas are important, and that you accept them and respect what he/she is saying— even if you don't agree or completely understand!

Verbal door openers:

> 'I see.'
> 'Tell me more.'
> 'Oh.' (be careful on tone!!)
> 'Say that again. I want to be sure I understand you.'
> 'No kidding!'
> 'How about that!'
> 'Now that's interesting.'
> 'Really?'

Non-verbal door openers:

- eye contact
- posture
- presence
- showing that you're really listening.

Use 'I' messages to communicate your thoughts and feelings, and use the power of suggestion.

- 'I am thinking we need to have a chat about what holiday choices we have for the coming holidays. Let's do that this week sometime.'
- Say, 'What works for you after school tomorrow?' rather than, 'What are you doing tomorrow?' (This shows there needs to be a cooperative approach to family dynamics—give and take.)
- 'John it's your turn to unpack the dishwasher and set the table. Do you want to do it now or just before dinner?'
- 'It's clean up day this Saturday morning and we'll have lunch at a cafe when we finish.'

- 'Someone has left a wet towel on the bathroom floor, please make sure you hang your wet towel up in future.' (Avoid any blame games because this message reinforces to everyone to hang up their towel—including Dad.)
- 'Dad needs someone to help with mowing lawn this weekend. He will leave it until after he has done the sports run on Saturday morning. Any takers?'
- 'Remember, everyone is responsible for changing the toilet roll when it is finished. It's not something only Mum has an ability to do.'
- 'If you drink the last of the milk after school, please let Mum or Dad know before we get ready for bed.'
- 'We are all part of a team around here and each of us helps this home run smoothly.'
- 'Thank you to the person who fed Bert (the dog) last night when I had a late work meeting.'

Sentences that encourage—avoid using 'Why..?' questions

Try choosing just a couple of these communication tools to help adolescents grow in autonomy and ability to make decisions. When you have them as a familiar part of your communication style, choose another couple and start working with them too. This is incredibly empowering and will reduce much of the verbal sparring that happens in homes.

- 'How might we resolve this?'
- 'What do you think needs to happen now?'
- 'Sounds like you have a problem.'
- 'How can we work together to get the best outcome here?'
- 'There is a conflict here. How can I help you sort it out?'
- 'Please make a decision about what you want for dinner' (Choose. Decide. Pick.)
- 'Please consider making a different choice.'
- 'Check it out inside yourself. Does it feel right?'
- 'What's your goal? What's your intention?'
- 'Make a picture in your mind?' (Also known as 'positive picturing'.)
- 'I'm willing to help you complete this task.'
- 'I know you can handle it!'
- 'Every problem has a solution.'
- Avoid sweeping generalisations like 'all of' 'every time' or 'never.'
- Use 'next time' rather than 'don't do this.'
- 'I noticed you cleaned up the bench after having toast—thanks!'
- 'I know you can overcome this.'
- 'There is a part of you that knows the answer—check it out within yourself.'
- 'I have faith in you to make a healthy choice around this decision.'

- 'If I rescue you from this challenging experience I disempower you. Do you want me to do this?'
- 'If I lead you out of this challenge, I am the leader not you. Is this what you really want?'
- 'I will walk beside you, no matter what choice you make.'
- Avoid evaluative praise such as, 'You're a terrific runner!' 'You are so clever!' 'You are so beautiful.'
- Choose descriptive praise such as, 'We have finished dinner and everything looks clean and tidy.' Let your adolescents tell themselves they did a great job.
- Choose appreciative praise such as, 'I appreciate you helping to make the kitchen clean and tidy.'

Adolescents tend to use life-negating language partly because it's cool to speak negatively or monosyllabically. We can help upgrade their language by offering some reminders—very lovingly and gently. This was something I did in my classrooms and I was staggered how the students' language lifted at the same time as their moods and their grades. It makes sense that if they keep repeating 'I can't,' 'I dunno,' 'nup' or 'whatever' then their unconscious is hearing clear directions to sabotage any effort or success. Remember, the unconscious is constantly listening for clues as to what a person wants and if all it hears is negativity, then that's what it delivers.

Life-affirming language

- I choose—Expression of our will and identity moving toward our outcome.
- I can—Expression of our identity, will and potential in choosing our outcome.
- I have—Bring our desired state to now; collapses time from the future to the present.
- I am—Expression of identity, claiming the emotional state of our desire fulfilled.
- I create—Expression of identity, claiming our divine right as co-creators.
- I will—Expression of intention for the future.
- My highest choice—Leaves our highest possibility as a high priority.

Become a coach and not a parent

It can be helpful if you change your parenting style to being more like a coach. However, not all adolescents are going to be happy about that. It has the implication that they need coaching because they are not performing well enough. Treat this style carefully and offer to support them by reminding them of more positive language, ways to lift negative moods or emotional states, organisational tips and life skills they may like to learn. Keep your expectations in check and do not hold the bar too high or you could crush their self-perception and it could backfire badly on you. Try using these words:

> *'Babe (only if you have used this word of endearment often, otherwise use their name), I have been reading a book by Maggie Dent and she said it can be helpful for us parents to act more as a coach while you are on your bumpy ride to adulthood. This means that we can offer you tips to help you manage life and build life skills so that when you leave home to live with your friends you can do so confidently. If this is something I could do to help you grow to be more capable and happier, will you let me know? Then I could get her book out and we might read some of her tips together and you could tell me what I could do that might help you.'*

And then leave it. The unconscious mind has heard it and will mull it over. If they agree then it is a two-way street; they can upgrade your language, and offer you suggestions on how to chill out and calm down too.

Hot tips for parents to teach adolescents

1. Not everyone will agree with you. That's OK.
2. Not everyone will like you. That's OK.
3. Not everyone will be friendly. That's OK.
4. Not everyone will see the world like you. That's OK.

Building life skills and competencies

What skills do adolescents need in their kit bag for life when they venture into the big wide world at 18? Everyone needs life skills to manage life. Life is a journey of continually gaining knowledge, skills and competencies. Every person is unique and every life journey is different. This list is one that many people have contributed to after considering what would help them cope with and conquer life at the age of 18 and what would they need if they were to leave the safety of the home nest. It is the parents' and other significant adults' responsibility to teach life skills so adolescents will be capable.

In 2009 The Kings School in Sydney began addressing the need for their students to have hands-on classes in life skills. The headmaster, Dr Tim Hawkes, said the new program was necessary because students were leaving school without picking up essential life skills. He believed that students should be taught not just basic maintenance tasks, they also needed to be taught how to be resilient and cope with grief, loss, intimacy, relationships and financial skills. This is innovative and will impact on the boys' lives.

Poor social and emotional skills around loss and rejection have been seen as a contributing factor towards suicide. This program is in a way modelling on what traditional kinship communities did with adolescents. They both have accepted that adolescents need to be taught, guided and supported as they gain the life skills needed to be a competent adult. There are still no guarantees they will not make dumb decisions; however, they will have more tools in their toolkit when they leave the safe school environment. I congratulate this school for the initiative and hope that it will flow on to all high schools.

There are so many skills young people need when they leave the safety of home and school. The list below is a starting point only. It is not gender specific, because both girls and boys need these skills to feel capable[5*].

Living with others—essential skills

- Change the toilet roll when it's empty.
- Replace the toothpaste lid after use.
- Know how to clean a bathroom—and how to get rid of mould!
- Avoid using other people's deodorant.
- Don't use other people's towels or use them as a bath mat.
- Wipe the bench down after preparing food or making toast—don't sweep the crumbs onto floor.
- Know how to wash and dry dishes hygienically.
- Never wipe your face or nose on a tea towel.
- Learn basic food preparation skills, especially around raw meat.
- Know how to sweep the floor.
- Know how to wash the floor.
- Cover food left in the refrigerator.
- Don't eat other people's food without asking.
- If you use the last of the milk, bread or butter then replace it.
- Know how to cook at least three main meals that people enjoy.
- Always smell milk before using—if it has lumps, it's off.
- Eat fresh, wholesome meals 80% of the time.

Living in rental properties

- Rental inspections are very serious—do your share of the cleaning.
- Rental inspectors check inside the oven and grill—clean them!
- Know how to mow lawns.
- Know how to weed and make gardens look tidy.
- Never lose your key.

- Any damage after a party will have to be paid for by those who live there—especially the person who signed the lease.

---

5   * A colour pdf poster of these life skills for your home or school is available from this website: **www.maggiedet.com/life_skills.pdf**

- Know the difference between the recycle bin, normal bin and the green waste bin.
- Rent must be paid when due—no matter what.
- Keep doors/windows locked when no one is there.
- Old places will need cockroach baits and mouse traps, and lots of them.
- If you have valuable things, you should have contents insurance.
- Pay gas, power and water bills before they are overdue or they will cut you off and it costs more to reconnect.
- Whoever's name is on the lease is the person held responsible for rental arrears, damage or any other problem. This information will be passed on to other rental agencies for the rest of your life.
- Remember your housemates' birthdays.
- Offer to make your housemates a cuppa occasionally.
- Don't play music loudly after the others are in bed.
- Cook when it's your turn and do it with a smile on your face.
- Have five meals that are tasty and reliable in your kit bag ready to go.
- Keep your clothes, shoes, undies, skateboard, surfboard and wet towels in your room, not all over the house.
- Never throw broken glass into rubbish bins without first wrapping it up.
- Dirty plates will attract ants, cockroaches and rats—wash them after you've used them.

Life skills with cars

- Cars need fuel, oil and water—know where each one goes, and how to check them.
- Never put diesel into a petrol car, or vice versa.
- Know how to change a flat tyre—you need to have a spare tyre to do this.
- Dirty, rusty cars that look poorly maintained are obvious targets for the police.
- Cars with rude stickers are also obvious targets for the police.
- Never, ever drive after you have been drinking or using drugs.
- Never, ever get into a car with someone who has been drinking or doing drugs.
- If you park in a paid parking zone and don't pay, you will get a fine.
- Avoid parking in loading zones or disabled parking spaces—you will get a fine.
- Avoid driving at night with friends—this is proven to be a time of greater risk for adolescents.
- If you do burnouts in public places you will lose your car.

- If you do burnouts, remember how much new tyres cost.
- Cars are expensive to run and maintain—think carefully before buying one.
- A licence is a privilege you can easily lose.
- Drive slowly around schools, even on holidays because children are unpredictable.
- If you can, complete an advanced driving course.
- Brakes and tyres need to be kept in optimal shape.
- Treat trucks with great respect.
- Never, ever overtake on double white lines or on hills.
- Don't lock your keys in your car, especially not in the boot.
- Always keep two litres of water in your car in case of radiator problems.
- Uneaten food left in cars can smell really bad in a short time, and also attracts ants, mice and rats.
- Things like keys, wallets, mp3 players and CDs can slip behind seats and appear lost.
- Never, ever text while driving—pull over and stay alive.
- Get a hands-free kit for your mobile, or pull over and stay alive.
- Avoid any impulses that appear to be a good idea at the time while driving your car.
- Be careful if driving into a setting sun.
- Don't cheat on your driving log—experience is the best teacher for new drivers.

Useful communication and etiquette skills

- Avoid grunting or using monosyllabic answers.
- Say hello to people when you first see them.
- Use manners all the time—people make first judgements about you that last.
- Wait until people on the train get off before you get on.
- Wait until people leave an elevator before you get in.
- Learn how to say 'no' politely.
- Learn to be assertive to ask for what you want, without being aggressive.
- Know how to eat properly while dining in a restaurant.
- Avoid speaking while your mouth is full—or even half full—of food.
- Don't shovel food into your mouth.
- Avoid using your fingers to put food in your mouth, unless it's fruit, on a platter or is an expected cultural custom.
- Make eye contact with people you are speaking to and use their names.
- Avoid burping in public places or during meetings.

- Avoid farting in public places or during meetings.
- Say ' Pardon me,' or 'Excuse me' if you do either of the above.
- Wash your hands after visiting the toilet.
- Wipe skid marks off toilet bowl if you leave any.
- Listen to anyone who is speaking to you.
- Be respectful of older people—they might be your future employer.
- Dress to impress—in situation-appropriate ways.
- Be punctual—on time or up to 10 minutes early.
- Be mindful of people's personal space—this differs from person to person so be aware.
- Avoid telling inappropriate jokes in your workplace, home or any public place.
- Avoid gossip—especially spreading it or, worse still, starting it.
- Learn about appropriate email etiquette.
- Say sorry and apologise when you make a mistake.
- Remember what you put out into the world, comes back to you tenfold.
- Say thank you.
- Be kind rather than right—it's a much easier way to make friends.
- Look after your best friends or you will lose that connection.
- Be there for your friends—the good, the bad and the ugly.
- Be generous—with yourself, your family and your friends.

Life skills around money

- Learn how to save money—keep some for a rainy day.
- Never steal other people's money—you may borrow, but they need to give it to you first.
- If you spend your money on junk food or alcohol, you will eat Vegemite sandwiches for dinner until next payday.
- Accept responsibility for your own bills and debts—pay your own way.
- Never be late with mobile phone payments because this can adversely affect your credit rating for years.
- Credit cards are big traps—check out all the charges and only use it for emergencies.
- Being a broke student or apprentice builds appreciation for having financial freedom later in life.
- Never be afraid to ask banks or financial institutions questions about fees and charges—ask for the best deal they can offer you.
- Cooking food rather than buying fast food is actually cheaper and healthier for you.
- Debit cards are better for young adults than credit cards.

- Shop within your budget.
- Keep an eye on all payslips to make sure you are being paid for the hours you have worked and at the correct rate.
- If you borrow from your parents, pay them back.
- Learn about taxation and how to maximise your return.
- Set clear goals around your financial future.
- Never be afraid to ask successful adults how they became successful.
- Money does not bring you happiness, however it can make living easier and gives you more choices.

Other helpful life skills

- Learn the power of intention through goal setting.
- Complete as much education as you can—if not now, then later.
- Dream your own dreams and don't let anyone steal them.
- Know how to address a letter and where to put the stamp.
- Learn basic First Aid.
- Learn how to laugh at yourself when you muck up.
- Learn to trust your intuition and your instincts.
- Know that everyone makes mistakes—get over it.
- Know how to use a washing machine.
- Know how to remove stains out of clothes.
- Know how to wash delicates and woollens without ruining them.
- Learn organisation skills in your bedroom—especially the difference between dirty and clean. A tidy room can still be dirty!
- Learn simple home remedies to help when someone has a cold or the flu.
- Know how to treat a sprain, splinter and a snake bite.
- Learn how to cheer yourself up.
- Learn basic organisation skills, making reminder lists for important things such as exams, holidays and end-of-year activities.
- Always leave with plenty of time to spare when going somewhere new in case you get lost.
- Keep your mobile charged and have enough credit when travelling long distances.
- Don't drop your laptop.
- Don't drop your mp3 player in water.
- Know that soon you will be old enough to be a 'lighthouse' for someone younger.
- Be good to your mother—always.

I know some parents who keep this list on the fridge and have their adolescents update the skills they have mastered, knowing they need at least 75 per cent before they are allowed out the door to live with their friends. Being capable helps make young people feel confident and happy. Feeling incapable and useless around simple things *can cripple a sensitive adolescent*. Adolescents are all sensitive and vulnerable, no matter how big and strong some may look. It is our job as parents to give them the skills to be adults and not expect them to Google™ the answers to life's big mysteries.

What to look for when you are worried about your adolescent

The following are some signs of mental health problems in children, adolescents and young people. If they last for more than a few weeks, it may be time to seek professional help.

- Inability to get along with others
- Marked fall in school work
- Changes in usual sleeping or eating patterns
- Marked weight gain or loss
- Reluctance to go to school or take part in normal activities
- Fearfulness
- Restlessness, fidgeting and trouble concentrating
- Excessive disobedience or aggression
- Lack of energy or motivation
- Irritability
- Social withdrawal
- Crying a lot
- Feeling hopeless or worthless
- Odd ideas or behaviours

Please err on the side of caution because we know that an adolescent at 'tipping point' can be at serious risk and connecting in a meaningful way with love can reassure them to get some help. Maybe check out some of the help web sites in the appendix and print off some fact sheets that are adolescent friendly. There is also a letter draft that may help give you the language to break the 'ice' without making things worse in the appendix.

It's impossible to include everything in one chapter about what a parent can do to help their adolescent navigate the bumpy road to adulthood. These are some good tips and ideas to start with that can help you better understand your confused and stressed adolescent.

The final suggestion for parents is to use kindness in small ways. It is a very powerful tool to show that you care, even if your adolescent is grounded, has greasy hair or has just had an eyebrow pierced. They are struggling with a negative self-talk that is frightening, and when a parent simply makes them a

Milo, brings them a juice or gives them a small handful of M&Ms without saying a word, they know you care. NB: A shoulder rub and a hug are even better if you can get away with it!

If You Love Something

If you love something, set it free.
If it comes back, it will always be yours.
If it doesn't come back, it was never yours to begin with.
But, if it just sits in your living room,
messes up your stuff, eats your food,
uses your telephone, takes your money,
and doesn't appear to realise that you had set it free,
then you either married it or gave birth to it.

Source Unknown

Key Points

- Parenting adolescents needs to be different from parenting children.

- There are three styles of parenting—the preferred style is authoritative.

- Parents need to help adolescents build emotional intelligence.

- Communication can be improved with more understanding and effort.

- Caring empowering communication helps adolescents better understand themselves and others.

- Laughter and lightness is important in all healthy relationships.

- Have fun times with your adolescents.

- Tonality is a huge influence on adolescent communication.

- Door openers help with communication.

- Parents need to teach adolescents as many life skills as possible before they leave home.

- Kindness reassures adolescents that their parents care for them.

- Model and teach adolescents the value of compassion and caring concern for others

Chapter 10

Personality *matters* on the bumpy road

I felt lucky that I had the tool of the Enneagram to use when I became a parent. I didn't want to have the distance with my son I felt with my father, who was also a Five, so I went out of my way to be engaged and present from the time he was born. I was also very protective since he's a Six-Questioner and he seemed very sensitive and in need of it. Being present for my outer child healed my own inner child.

Michael Gardner

Wagel, E., The Enneagram of Parenting: The 9 Types of Children and How to Raise Them Successfully, (1997).

I often describe children as being roosters or lambs to show that some children are more difficult to parent because of their temperament. A longitudinal study in New Zealand where they studied babies from pre-birth until they were almost 30-years-old came to the conclusion that personality traits are well in place by three years of age, if not before. They suggested that some traits are carried on our genes and some are shaped by nurture and environment. The impact of personality types and the difference in temperaments are worth looking at when supporting adolescents on their way to adulthood.

The New Zealand study has lent scientific weight to the notion that 'the child is father of the man'. Broad personality traits are laid down by the age of three:

- Under-controlled toddlers grow up to be impulsive, unreliable and antisocial.

- Inhibited three-year-olds are more likely to become unassertive and depressed adults.
- Well-adjusted three-year-olds tend to become well-adjusted adults.
- Socially isolated children are more likely to develop health problems as adults.

Macfie, R., 'Show me The Child', *The Listener*, January 19–25, 2008.

Clinical psychologist Andrew Fuller writes about tricky kids to show that some children will display certain temperamental characteristics, which means you may need to alter your parenting style. In other words, parenting is not a level playing field, and some parenting styles in adolescence can simply make things worse. I am going to explore the effects of personality by exploring the nine personality types as presented by the ancient system called the Enneagram.

The Enneagram is a body of knowledge that dates back to ancient times and it is merely a tool to build understanding. I completed an Enneagram course about 15 years ago and was staggered with the insights it gave me as to how other people Interpret the world. It lifted the wool from my eyes about my husband, my sons and people with whom I found it difficult to connect. It also certainly helped me understand myself better.

There is no hierarchy to the numbers; a 9 is no better than a 1. Each number has clearly defined strengths and weaknesses, and when we know that every individual interprets the world through this unique lens it is much easier to avoid conflict. Take the opportunity to do an Enneagram, it will help in every area of your life. But be careful to avoid guessing other people's personality type and understand that you are influenced by at least two other personality types called wings.

> *The Enneagram has the potential to change your life. It is the most helpful tool I've discovered for relationship improvement and self-development. I have studied and taught many personality systems but the Enneagram offers the most clarity and insight into unravelling the intricacies of who we are and how we relate to others and ourselves.*
>
> Brees, K. K. PhD and Pearce, H. MEd, *The Complete Idiot's Guide to the Power of the Enneagram*, (2007).

The confusion of the brain changes, the hormones, the physical changes and the processing through the amygdala makes life interesting for adolescents no matter which personality type they have.

Sites where you can download information on the Enneagram:

- Helen Palmer: www.enneagram.com
- Herb Pearce: www.herbpeace.com
- Janet Levine: www.janetlevine.com

Recommended online Enneagram tests:

- David Daniels and Virginia Price: www.enneagramworldwide.com
- Jerome Wagner : www.enneagramspectrum.com

Following is a brief explanation of each of the nine personality types and possible scenarios that show how we can understand ways of reaching a bridge of understanding with our confused adolescents.

TYPE 1: The Perfectionist/Reformer—I like to do what's right.

Basic Proposition: There is a right way and a wrong way to do everything.

Habitual Focus of Attention: What is right or wrong, correct or incorrect.

What 'Perfectionists' tell us about themselves:

- They live with a powerful inner critic that monitors every thought, word, and deed;
- They worry about getting things right and are unusually sensitive to criticism;
- They strive for perfection and feel responsible;
- 'Perfectionists' also report a focus on being good and repress their impulses/desires for pleasure;
- They can be rigid, overly controlled, seeing virtue as its own reward.
- They appreciate rules and clear guidelines
- They tend to be very responsible and a workaholic

Janet Levine calls this one the Moraliser. They have a very strong inner urge to live virtuously and can come across as self-righteous and morally superior. If a parent is a 1, then they can definitely find adolescence tough going because adolescents will *not* be controlled. Adolescents are also breaking rules and taking risks and when they hear a parent using words like 'should' and 'ought' and 'must' it can inflame them quickly.

The constant driving for perfection for adolescents who are 1s can cause lots of emotional stress as they are excellent at finding faults, and being critical, and they tend to bury their anger until it explodes. Many 1 adolescents struggle with never being 'enough': good enough, smart enough or cool enough. They often compensate by seeking perfection. They can also struggle with deep jealousy and they are often comparing themselves with others, and then attack themselves with lots of guilt because they feel they should be kinder.

The moralistic adolescent who has clear views on how the world should be is often a 1, or has a 1 wing. For adolescents who are 1s, a small misdemeanor can become a mountain very quickly and you need to understand that it's just how they feel about doing the wrong thing.

How to help a 1

Avoid coming down too hard on 1s during adolescence because they are already doing it to themselves. Help them learn how to release anger, frustration and inner turmoil. Encourage yoga, martial arts, meditation or other arts. Ones are particularly sensitive to being angry when the world, and those in it, is not perfect.

TYPE 2: The Giver/Pleaser/Helper—I like to give and be appreciated

Basic Proposition: Love and survival depend on 'giving to get'.

Habitual Focus of Attention: Other people's needs

What 'Givers' observe about themselves:

- A preoccupation with the needs of others;
- Pride in giving and helping;
- Sometimes feel taken advantage of;
- Have a hard time expressing their own needs; Are manipulative; and alter their self-presentation to meet the needs
- Struggle to be aware of their own needs
- Can be manipulative
- Want praise and affection
- Hurt and angry if not appreciated

This type is sometimes called the Helper; essentially, their whole life is wrapped up in helping and pleasing others in the hope they will get love and validation in return. Even though they can be delightful souls who are generous and uplifting, they are often secretly manipulating others into getting their own needs met. They like to be needed and sometimes like to keep others dependent on them so they keep being needed.

> *Two's make you feel special, that you're worth it, you're worth the time. Being helped and considered. Romantic meetings. Sensitive care.*
>
> Palmer, H., *The Enneagram in Love & Work: Understanding Your Intimate & Business Relationships*, (1995).

The 2 parent struggles in adolescence with allowing their adolescent to gain autonomy and independence. They do too much and can get incredibly hurt and upset when told to let go. They also think they know what is best for others and do it for them, thus invalidating the other's ability to choose. This is not appreciated by adolescents who are being driven to become more separated from their parents.

The 2 adolescent has a tendency to be a martyr and needs to have lots of friends who they can be kind to. They are romantics and tend to keep every birthday or

Valentine card. Some 2 adolescents struggle with relationships because they are people pleasers, but adolescents are very perceptive and can sense insincerity. Often they try to please teachers to get them to like them and in a way give them approval.

How to help a 2

Help 2s articulate their own needs and reassure them that you can't please everyone all the time. Twos can struggle with pride because they can develop an inflated sense of self-worth when they help others. This can mask their dependency on their external need for approval. Ensure they have friends and plenty of opportunity to be around people, and maintain healthy boundaries around their giving.

TYPE 3: The Achiever/Success Driver/The Achiever—I like to accomplish and win

Basic Proposition: Love and recognition are only for 'champions'.

Habitual Focus of Attention: Tasks, Roles, & Results

What 'Performers' observe about themselves:

- Their primary identification is with accomplishment and success;
- They seek approval and acceptance based on performance;
- Their attention goes to task;
- Image is important;
- They feel constant pressure to perform; and
- There is an inattention to feelings/'Not now'
- Excelling, driven and image conscious.
- Likes to be number one
- Materialistic and dresses well
- Has a hard time just 'being' prefers 'doing'

Also known as the organiser, this type is a dynamo with drive and energy to keep pushing their own bar higher and higher. The word 'failure' does not exist for 3s, they want to win and be rewarded at all costs. They overcome obstacles with speed and efficiency, and thrive on challenge and are motivated by the dream to achieve the big prizes—the trophy, the degree, the top job. Threes are very image-focused and must have exactly the right outfit for the correct occasion—this applies to both genders.

> *I have a highly energetic 3 son and from a very early age he was very clear about his taste in clothes. As an adolescent he would often have three to four changes of clothes before being comfortable he had exactly the right clothes for the right occasion.*
>
> Maggie Dent

Threes have high energy and are definitely rooster material. They can be very hard to contain when younger, however often by adolescence they are strong goal-focused individuals who aim for success. Their drive to win can often appear mean and they can be selfish, vain, insensitive of others and totally self-consumed—sometimes narcissistic.

A mum told me she had a late born baby and when she asked his pre-school teacher whether it was better to hold him back a year, the teacher replied, 'What? Hold back the social organiser of the whole class? I don't think so!' He was a 3.

For the 3 parent it can be difficult with an adolescent because often they can be more consumed by their own life and dreams than their child's. These are the classic overworkers who resent wasting time; and there can be a lot of time and energy that may appear 'lost' while parenting an adolescent. Sometimes a 3 parent can put too much pressure on their adolescent to share the same approach to life as them, which is to achieve at all cost. They can push too hard, criticise the way their adolescent dresses, criticise their hair and generally demean them for not being 'enough.' The silent disapproval of a 3 parent can crush sensitive adolescents. They need to remember that many excellent personal qualities cannot be tested, such as kindness, loyalty, thoughtfulness, empathy and love.

Threes are natural leaders and as adolescents this can often cause conflict at home and at school. They like to be always doing something and they are serious risk takers.

How to help a 3

Adolescence can be a tough and dangerous time for a 3. They want to stretch their comfort zone and live on the edge, so find activities where they can do this safely with adult supervision like rock climbing, white water rafting, surfing, motor bikes or elite sport. Threes struggle with keeping boundaries, however they need adults to hold firm boundaries most of the time and to allow the 3s to negotiate changes from time to time. Over-controlling adolescent 3s will lead to amazing conflict and often they have to leave or run away because they cannot see any other way to reach their goals and dreams.

TYPE 4: The Romantic/Individualist—I value individuality, creativity and beauty

Basic Proposition: Others enjoy the happiness that I have been denied.

Habitual Focus of Attention: 'Best' is what's absent.

What 'Romantics' observe about themselves:

- There is a constant longing for the missing ingredient for personal happiness;
- Their focus is on the best of what's missing, what's distant, and what's hard to get;

- The 'ordinary' pales by comparison;
- There is a deeply felt abandonment that translates into a belief that 'I am un- loveable': and,
- Romantics' feel special and elite. Their suffering sets them apart from others.
- Sensitive withdrawn, temperamental, melancholic
- Crisis prone
- Sensitive and accepts suffering as a part of life

Also known as the dreamer, 4s are true individualists who often resist being absorbed into group identity in the hope they will be noticed for being unique and different. This results in others being drawn towards them. The 4 is deep on inner exploration, often finding everyday life boring and mundane, so often retreats inside and appears shy, aloof or lonely. They are often convinced 'something is missing' and they are searching for transcendent experiences that allow them to feel alive. In a way 'they are the emotional junkies and emotional roller coasters of the universe seeking experiential, spiritual and relationship thrills and spills to make life worth living' (Pearce, 2007).

The 4 is a creative being with a love of the aesthetics and the arts, and the search for the deeper meaning of life. Often 4s are hypersensitive to criticism and being misunderstood, and often like drama because it makes them feel alive. Be aware that 4s are prone to depression because of the deep intensity and self-exploration. They are particularly sensitive to feeling abandonment and rejection, and when they feel it they can drown in a lack of reality.

Parents who are 4s sometimes are so focused on their own inner searching they may appear to be unavailable for the adolescent, and they can also appear sad, aloof and unhappy. Adolescents misread facial expressions badly, and they can misread a 4 parent as being unloving when that is not the case. The 4 parent can also see things from the glass half filled place, but their emotional ups and downs can simply confuse an already up and down adolescent.

The 4 adolescent is often the non-conformist who will wear weird clothes, or choose to do something to avoid belonging with the pack—they want to be different. They struggle with, 'If only I had Diane's hair,' 'If only my penis was bigger', and this wishing can distract them from reality.

How to help a 4

Adolescent 4s need to have a creative outlet such as music, dance, painting, cooking, landscape gardening or writing because it gives them a voice with which to express their deep inner world. Some famous 4s include Prince, Johnny Depp, Judy Garland, James Dean, Michael Jackson, Angelina Jolie, James Taylor and Judy Collins. Fours are incredibly sensitive souls who may not only get lost in adolescence, they can disappear into depression, addictions and homelessness more easily than other personality types.

TYPE 5: The Thinker/Observer/Investigator—I value knowledge and information

Basic Proposition: Love and respect are gained by practicing self-sufficiency.

Habitual Focus of Attention: What others want from me.

What 'Observers' tell us about themselves:

- They have a marked need for privacy;
- They limit intrusion from a world that wants too much from them;
- As a result, 'Observers' hoard time, space, energy, knowledge and themselves;
- They detach from feelings and observe rather than participate; and,
- They are minimalists
- Secretive and isolated , avoid small talk
- Loves information and knowledge, observes well, analytical,
- Studies in depth
- Likes to know things in advance
- Frugal with money and often socially awkward

Type 5s are known as our knowledge seekers and thinkers. They crave quiet time alone and away from the world and struggle in social settings—unless there is specific purpose to it. They are the minimalists of the Enneagram; they like their sanctuary from the world to have familiar belongings and avoid luxuries just as they avoid extravagance in general.

The 5 loves the process of analysis and especially becomes alive when they discover innovative ways and ideas about how to improve the world, especially ways that are creative and stand up to rigorous logic and even testing. They are objective and independent thinkers who avoid emotional influences from colouring their judgments, and will in fact disengage when there is too much emotion.

The 5 can appear shy, cold, blunt, superior and insensitive and difficult to get close to because they withdraw, often energetically, even when they are physically present. They also like to hoard their stuff and be greedy and are often know for being stingy with money, and hate sharing when they feel it's unbalanced.

A 5 parent needs to explain things logically and avoid conflict at any cost. They often dislike the need to be a disciplinarian and guardian because of the emotional challenge it encourages, and would much rather teach their child about science, books and astronomy. The 5 parent struggles to show their love for their children, and their need to withdraw is seen as being disconnected or sometimes as a form of abandonment.

The 5 adolescent struggles with change because they like their world to stay fixed and predictable. Their need for solo time can become unhealthy and is a way of avoiding life. Some 5s are dreamers and this can be their way of having space away from people—let this be OK. They can struggle with having friends because they like their own company, hate small talk and mainly enjoy talking with people about things they are studying or learning about. Often, they will disappear physically because they are bored or simply disappear into another dreamlike world.

Fives run the risk in adolescence of having few friends or shallow friendships as they can be socially awkward, and they may also struggle with emotional upheaval in the home. Emotions confuse them more than normal adolescents and most of them struggle with that world.

How to help a 5

The good news is if you have a 5 adolescent they probably won't be party animals as they prefer the comforts of the mind because 'they are seduced with new information' (Pearce, 2007). Their bedroom is their sanctuary and must be respected as a private space even more so than other personality types—especially during adolescence.

TYPE 6: The Questioner/Loyalist—I want to know the truth below the surface and prepare for the future

Basic Proposition: Love and protection are gained by vigilance and endurance.

Habitual Focus of Attention: Threat, hazard, difficulties, challenges

What 'Loyal Skeptics' tell us about themselves:

- They are preoccupied with safety and security concerns;
- They greet everything with a doubting mind, and contrary thinking;
- 'Loyal Skeptics' report active imaginations that amplify questionable areas;
- They question people and authority;
- They procrastinate because of fearing the outcome, failing to complete projects
- Responsible, anxious and suspicious
- Once they have built trust they are very loyal
- Highly values groups, friendships and social causes

The motto for the type 6 is: Be prepared. I saw a video of a 15-year-old who was a 6 and he said where ever he went and whatever he was about to do, he had to work out first 'What is the worst thing that can happen, and can I deal with that?' and then I was happy.' This perfectly captures the 6 and their need to question, often being the Devil's advocate.

The 6 is hyper-vigilant as to possible dangers and is often seen as the guardian and protector; they are loyal and love to be team players who can be relied on. The 6 also sees that the glass is half full but can still be a pessimist and a worrier.

There are 6s who often ask, 'Yes but...', 'What if...', 'This may not work because...' and they struggle with making decisions and become paralysed by cowardice.

The 6 parent can be too over-protective of their adolescent and also be 'doomsayers' to some of the adolescent's ideas and requests. Adolescents are already negative, so they can drown if they have a 6 parent who is very negative. An adolescent can struggle with a 6 parent who wants them to take endless steps to stay safe or to follow rules; their brain is not at that point yet and this conflict alone can cause some serious emotional challenge.

The 6 adolescent can become an irrational worrier and struggle with decision making; they need careful reassurance when they need to make important decisions. They can feel they are the underdog and can adopt a victim persona of 'poor me.'

How to help a 6

Parents can help the 6 adolescent to develop competence and strengths. They can benefit from learning how to manage their stress and anxiety because they will always tend to do these things later in life. Remind them of their gifts of being prepared, very loyal and great friends and they can be a 'rock' of dependability who helps others.

TYPE 7: The Optimist/Epicure/The Enthusiast—I just want to have fun, cut the heavy stuff

Basic Proposition: Pain and frustration can be avoided and the good life assured by inventing options, opportunities, and adventures.

Habitual Focus of Attention: The positive in all things

What 'Epicures' tell us about themselves:

- Life is an adventure!
- 'Epicures' are pleasure-seeking and gluttons for experience and enjoyment;
- They are optimistic, active, and energetic;
- See multiple options, but have difficulty with commitment; and
- Do not want limits on themselves
- Spontaneous, versatile, scattered
- Loves change, newness
- Hates negativity, starter but not necessarily finisher
- Highly social and humourous

Type 7s are the fun lovers, the optimists and the adventurers. To them it's always party time. This type brightens every home, classroom and workplace. Famous 7s include Goldie Hawn, Robin Williams, Jim Carrey, Jack Nicholson, Lily Tomlin, Steven Spielberg and Carol Burnett.

The 7 tends to be extroverted, social, engaging and loves to entertain and be entertained. They love freedom and they have tons of energy, and the glass is *always* half full. They are highly adaptable to change and are full of resourceful ideas. They can struggle with challenge or emotional pain and often bury it by planning another project or party.

The 7 parent can make it hard for adolescents to explore their struggles and angst because they will distract them with glib comments like, 'build a bridge', or simply give them something delicious to eat. Also, the 7 parent may be too busy with their social calendar to have time to support their adolescent on their bumpy road to adulthood. They can get frustrated by an adolescent's indecision, inactivity or inertia, and invalidate the introvert or thinker and the ways which make them feel safer.

The 7 adolescent will have to be at every party—all three in one night if necessary. They will do anything to have a good time and can be easily led in the hunt for more fun. They will struggle with boundaries and simply avoid studying, working or doing chores because they are no fun. They also tend to burn out and get sick because they do too much, too fast and too often.

The adolescent 7 can also make bad decisions because they are unable to consider possible risks in the way a 6 can. They hate being inactive and can have problems managing friendship groups because they think more is better.

How to help a 7

Parents of 7s need to make sure they know how to give feedback 'sandwiches' so they can hear constructive criticism to help them better manage their chaotic life, without it appearing like criticism.(Feedback sandwiches mean you give constructive criticism by prefacing and finishing with positives) The 7 adolescent can have difficulty finishing things like projects or school assessments because the need to have fun is so strong; encourage the 7 to finish what they have started. Another challenge is the 7s need to be funny or make people laugh, but sometimes they can choose badly and offend people; remind them about appropriate language and sensitivity to others. Sevens can also be intolerant to those who are slow to act and appear unhappy, and as parents we need to help them be more empathetic and tolerant.

TYPE 8: Director/Challenge—I'm in charge and in control of the situation

Basic Proposition: Protection and respect are gained by becoming strong and powerful and by hiding vulnerability.

Habitual Focus of Attention: Power, Injustices and Control.

What 'Protectors' tell us about themselves:
- They want stimulation and excitement;
- They are concerned with strength and protecting the weak;

- 'Protectors' are direct, confrontational and express their anger immediately;
- They are aggressive, intimidating and impulsive; but
- Deny their own vulnerability and weakness
- Impulsive, impatient, excessive, very energetic
- Generous to those they care about,
- Intense bravado but softer underneath
- Confronted parents as children

You will certainly know if you have an 8 in your house! This type is also known as the boss and they have a huge sense of needing the truth and to right injustices, even from an early age. Their presence is easily noticed as they take charge quickly. When they are healthy they are excellent leaders as they are protective of everyone, not just themselves. They like action and can be driven by impulse.

They are very short on patience and get angry quickly if people don't take action quick enough or to cover any sense of being vulnerable. They work very hard to achieve goals and prefer their own way of getting there, so they can be rebellious. The 8 is very decisive as a decision maker and can have problems when making decisions for others, in fact they can be known to bully others who are indecisive. They hate wasting time and if anything gets between them and their goal, watch out.

Some powerful 8s include Dr Martin Luther King, Winston Churchill, Lyndon Johnson, Mikhail Gorbachev, Muhammad Ali, Donald Trump and Richard Burton. They are another rooster personality type, which can cause problems on the home front.

The 8 parent will most likely be very busy conquering some mountain outside the home, however when at home they can be the authoritarian parent of 'my way or the highway'. They can be too strong, use fear and threats to get their way, and find it hard to listen to their adolescent; they are definitely not open to negotiation.

The 8 adolescent will rebel against too much control, they will argue like mad and can bully parents if they're allowed to. They have lots of confidence in their own ability and will run away if the battle gets too frustrating and annoying. Power games are something the 8 adolescent wants to win in order to feel a sense of value and worth. They are at risk of suicide if they fail a big goal because they prefer to die if they cannot win.

The 8 adolescent can fight for underdogs, good causes and can be influenced by more power. They can be charismatic leaders while they are still young and impressionable—this can be positive and negative. They often shoot off at the mouth impulsively—often at figures of authority as they never lack courage.

I am an 8 and my oldest is an 8 and it was helpful for him that I recognised his need at 12 to take charge of his own choices. He felt I was trying to manipulate him (uh-oh), and with me being an 8, of course I had been—although quite subtly. I valued my freedom as an adolescent and with that understanding, there was little confrontation with his bumpy ride. When confrontation did arise, it was when he tried to bully and dominate his brothers. Interestingly, he is now a lawyer who works in personal injury compensation helping others rebuild their lives and receive justice.

How to help an 8

Always help them find the positive intention under their outburst at a later time so they can save face. Help 8 adolescents avoid pushing themselves too hard to achieve too much, too soon because they put enormous pressure on themselves. They are very strong-willed and can be very stubborn and rigid in how they see things.

Despite their strong exterior, 8s are soft on the inside and will always fight for justice no matter what. An 8 will respond well to kindness and laughter and lightness. When they feel safe and free to be themselves they can be very intuitive and insightful. To better parent an 8 adolescent read the chapter about How to Build an Optimistic Adolescent as some of the unconscious language will help avoid confrontation and help you both not sweat the small stuff.

TYPE 9: The Peacemaker/Mediator—I like to create peace and harmony

Basic Proposition: Belonging and comfort are gained by attending to and merging with others and by dispersing energy into substitute objects.

Habitual Focus of Attention: The inessential and the agenda of others.

What 'Mediators' tell us about themselves:

- They see all sides to every issue as peacemakers and harmonizers;
- They avoid conflict and want the comfortable solution;
- They have difficulty saying 'no';
- They are ambivalent about their own needs and wants;
- Like comfort and repetitive habits
- Gets along with people easily
- They 'go along to get along';

The final personality is the 9, also known as the mediator or the accommodator. They are our peacekeepers who value peace and harmony more than any other type. Most people want to know 9s because they are trustworthy, thoughtful and forgiving. They enjoy life and look for the best in others. But they prefer to avoid conflict and dealing with problems and often do this by sleeping and disappearing energetically. They can be indecisive, confused and too agreeable, and unable to say 'no.' They can feel used and struggle with working out who they really are because they can mould themselves to fit whoever they are with.

The 9 parent can get walked over by rooster children, particularly adolescents, so they must have clear boundaries. They yearn for a peaceful home, however struggle with dealing with anything that is not peaceful, and then feel guilty that they have failed in some way. Ignoring or denying conflict does not help adolescents learn how to manage it in their lives.

The 9 adolescent can find it hard to stand up for themselves and they can be easily led by more powerful peers—they are very susceptible to peer

pressure. They can struggle with being organised to meet goals and find it even harder to set any, preferring to drift along to see what happens.

Adolescents already have difficulty with planning and motivation, so 9s have an additional challenge. Be careful of them wanting to sleep too much or hide in their rooms with faked illnesses. They also will want to spend as much time as possible with their friends and will often be the mediator trying to fix their problems while avoiding their own at any cost.

How to help a 9

Avoid confronting the 9 adolescent as they can react by avoiding life by hiding and becoming lazy, slothful or full of inertia. They need lots of reassurance and nurturing to grow stronger and more balanced, and need to learn to say no at the right times. Outline their strengths of being loving, considerate, thoughtful and supportive and make sure they are out in the world stretching and growing and being more assertive. The 9 adolescent hates being rushed or pushed and parents have to sometimes do this to get them to step forward and grow. If you have a 9 your house will be full of adolescents for years.

And finally...

This explanation of the Enneagram personality types is not an attempt to take you on a personal discovery journey, but rather to show you that you may be struggling with an adolescent whose personality type is resistant to the parenting choices you are making. We have one or two dominant types that we will generally behave like, or a single dominant type with influences coming from two wings.

The more exhausted, stressed and overwhelmed we are—adolescents included—the more likely we will function from our compulsive or wounded state where we exhibit our more negative traits instead of our more healed states. Remember that adolescents still have an immature brain with which to process their chaotic world, so understand that this is why there's so much angst at times.

I firmly believe that helping adolescents understand the strengths and weaknesses of their unique personality type will help them on many levels. But be warned, this is a two-way street and they will be able to inform *you* when you are out of balance. It would be wonderful if schools could also help adolescents understand how personality and temperaments can influence school performance, behaviour and engagement.

Key Points

- Temperament and personality can influence relationships with family.
- There are strong and sensitive personality types.
- There are nine personality types according to the Enneagram.
- Every personality type has strengths and challenges
- Understanding personality influences can help with communication and building connectedness.
- Exploring personality types builds empathy

Chapter 11

Secret *girls'* business *on the* bumpy road to adulthood

I am not saying that all adolescent girls or even most are overwhelmed by emotions or circumstances. But girls are incredibly complicated. I am generally a happy and healthy adolescent girl but I was very depressed at one point in my life. I still smiled a lot, did better in school than I ever had, worked out and ate well. But inside I felt like I was dying.

Shandler, S., Ophelia Speaks: Adolescent Girls Write About Their Search for Self, (1999).

My experiences in the classroom and in counselling have shown that girls are much more complicated and difficult to support. The emotional roller coaster of adolescence seems to go much higher and lower for them than for boys; and the emotional game playing, especially the destructive game playing, can be much crueller than that of boys.

A disturbing trend that has emerged in recent years is the increase in violence among girls. It used to be that roughly one in four assaults was by a girl, but now it's equal to the boys. The police are concerned that the violence from girls is very much premeditated and planned, whereas boys just tend to lose control more spontaneously. Another shift that has been created by media, particularly movies, is the glorification of female violence, usually by beautiful women.

Let's explore some of the concerns today's adolescent girls are struggling with and consider suggestions of how we can better support them. You may need to reframe how you see the adolescent girl's journey down the bumpy road.

Many people speak about 'surviving' and dreading the adolescent years, but I know things can be better and more enjoyable for both girls and their parents. Adolescence is a shared journey where both sides will grow and change. We all want the same things: to be loved, valued, respected and accepted by those who love us—no matter what. When we accept that mistakes will happen, and that conflict is a sign that something is missing, then it means new choices need to be considered and made. In the words of Danielle Miller, an expert on adolescent girls in Australia:

> *I believe the key is empathy. Instead of viewing adolescence as a stage in which fights between mothers and daughters are inevitable, try viewing it as a stage when a new connection can be found and a new level in your relationship reached.*
>
> Miller, D., *The Butterfly Effect: A Positive New Approach to Raising Happy, Confident Teen Girls,* (2009).

Boys and girls interpret the world differently, and many of the differences are deeply biological and driven by the brain. The female brain is wired to ensure they have a capacity to nurture and care so that they have a high chance of continuing to breed and ensure the survival of the human race. If females do not have this drive then babies will not thrive and the species will be threatened. This innate need to bond and develop attachments to babies and children drives much of adolescent behaviour. If girls received poor emotional attachment as babies and children, they can form a deep irrational yearning for love and affection when adolescence arrives. This can manifest in emotional neediness and can be seen by early sexual activity, highly manipulative games within female relationships and destructive patterns of abuse to themself, or towards others.

Girls who have a best friend who is stable, reliable and trustworthy have a huge protective factor that increases their chances of surviving adolescence much better than those who don't. I explain to all adolescents that 'good friends' are more than being a good-time friend. Good friends also turn up when things are tough, especially when their friends get hurt, their friend's parents divorce, they get expelled, or they lose someone they love through death or social relocation. A healthy friendship must allow adolescents to be able to share their vulnerabilities and fears safely. Even having sound friendships is no guarantee an adolescent will be able to drown their overwhelming sense of self-criticism, self-loathing or even self-hatred—especially with girls.

How Can a Person be Lonely

How can a person be lonely
When surrounded by friends?
How can a person be lonely
When taking and making calls?
How can a girl be lonely
When their parents are near?
I am lonely.
I am alone.
Because no one sees my thoughts
No one understands them
I am lonely
I am alone
I am dead.

Melanie Woss

Giles, F., [ed], *Melanie*, (1992).

The writer of these words was an intelligent, caring and healthy 18-year-old who took her life the night she wrote these words. Melanie came from a loving family, achieved well at school and was well liked among her friends. This is the terrifying potential of the negative thinking patterns of the adolescent brain in a world that has become too busy, too shallow and too confusing for many to cope with. Melanie lived in the days before the Internet, social networking sites and cyber-bullying. Depression can be overwhelming for adolescents who are already struggling with their massive changes and uncertainty.

Same-sex friendships can also be the cause of much of the angst that girls experience. An unhealthy side to modern friendships has emerged from the constant barrage of television soapies, films and some modern books. The barrage has created serious competition among our girls to be the prettiest, thinnest or one most noticed by the boys. The negative influence of popular culture has changed the way our girls shape their identity and sense of self.

Because of the technological advances and forces of globalisation never before have television, film, magazines, advertising, music and other cultural influences such as food and fashion had the power to persuade, seduce, shape, control and manufacture imaginations and identities: not just of children, but of adults as well.

Brooks, K., *Consuming Innocence: Popular Culture and Our Children*, (2008).

Dr Brooks writes about how we are now dressing children like adults 'instead of in fashions that acknowledge or celebrate childhood'. This weakening of the boundaries around childhood and adolescence puts enormous pressure on girls to dress to please. With sexual overtones present in many of the clothing lines for girls, we are also suggesting that pleasing and appealing to men is an important part of being a girl. The airbrushed and digitally altered images of famous models and actors just makes our girls cringe secretly in their bedrooms and bathrooms.

> Around my mirror are women Nadia Anerman, Kate Moss, Amber Valetta, Shalom Harlow
> I get to see them as I look at myself
> And then I wonder why I hate myself
> When I am alone in my room, I look at myself
> And I am disgusted.
> After seeing what I should look like around the mirror
> I hate my body and self.
> Charlotte Cooper aged 18
> Shandler, S.

I remember clearly my appalling sense of hatred towards my body, and that was *before* television and magazines glorifying celebrities. This negativity appears in most adolescent girls regardless of the popular cultural influences that we blame today. Maggie Hamilton in her book, *What's Happening to Our Girls: Too Much, Too Soon. How our kids are overstimulated, oversold and oversexed* explores this influence in great depth. I often hear about 5-year-old girls who won't go out their front door without full make-up on, and who refuse to wear clothes that don't match their shoes. Parents need to work hard to preserve childhood and 'tweenhood' so that adolescence occurs when it's meant to.

Little girls are meant to be playing and being free to develop their own unique sense of self without worrying about meeting some invisible high-bar of feminine approval.

This stage of a girl's life is the latency period where girls are meant to be forming deep female friendships before they form relationships with boys. Many girls are skipping this important developmental stage of adolescence.

> *By not addicting their little girls to consumerism and shopping, and by taking things more slowly, parents give girls a chance to grow up at a more leisurely pace, and to have many wonderful possibilities to look forward to.*
>
> Hamilton, M., *What's Happening to Our Girls: Too Much, Too Soon. How our kids are overstimulated, oversold and oversexed*, (2009).

Disturbing trends in our modern world have definitely been influenced by the sexualisation of our girls, which in turn has weakened the boundary between being a girl and a maiden (before becoming a woman). One is the increase in the incidence of sexual behaviour in girls aged under 12 years. Anecdotally we are told of girls who give oral sex to boys on school buses and behind school gymnasiums just for fun. There are also sexually driven wristbands which girls wear to show what kinds of sexual activity they partake in. And we hear about adolescent girls having anal sex because it allows them to stay a virgin. Do everything you can to support the anti-sexualisation of girls through monitoring advertising, not buying *Bratz* dolls, and not buying sexually suggestive clothes for girls and tweens.

It is normal for girls aged 12 and up to begin to want to dress differently to young girls. Some will start to wind their skirts up higher and reach for the mascara—just as we did at that age! Yes, mums worry just the same as they have with every generation. Kathy Lette captures it humorously:

> *I'd conveniently forgotten that at 13, I too had been taken hostage by my hormones [...] My dresses were so short [Mum] wasn't worried about people being able to see my pants; she was worried they'd see me ovulating.*
>
> Kathy Lette, 'Living with the enemy', *The Weekend Australian*, (3 October 2008).

Fathers or father figures have a huge role to play in protecting girls from the modern, popular sexualised way of being a female. I encourage dads to step back into the role they used to have as the protector of their daughter's name and character. He needs to be tough and sometimes say, 'You are not going our dressed like that, so go change your clothes or stay home'. Dads know what looks cheap or slutty and they need to speak up. Boys and men read impressions about girls from what they wear despite what fashion says is 'cool'.

A daughter may be angry at her dad until her pre-frontal lobe finishes growing at about 22 years of age, then she will realise why her dad stood up and protected her. I would like to see a return to dads advising the boys who come to take their daughter out that if they mess with her, then he has a 'shot gun' all ready to sort him out. This metaphor is very helpful in man-talk because it means the boy will be held accountable should *anything* happen to his daughter—whether it's the boy's action or not.

When girls develop their sense of self via external means, such as physical appearance, what kind of mobile phone they have and how many friends they have on Facebook, they begin to skate on the thin ice of insecurity that can plague them for life. It is very disturbing to hear about the high numbers of adolescent girls in America who are having breast augmentations before they are 18 years of age. Even more disturbing are the stories of adolescents who are having Botox to remove small lines. This quest for perfection that the airbrushed images of models have set up is dangerous. There is no perfect person, and certainly no perfect adolescent. The pressure to be flawless and behave in a socially accepted way at all times is impossible.

> *You are not alone. Many hundreds of thousands of girls all around the world are, right at this moment, going through similar changes, emotions and feelings that you are presently feeling. Girls similar to you are asking the same questions, thoughts and experiences as you.*
>
> Witt, S., *Teen Talk: Girl Talk*, (2008).

Girls need to accept that they are an artwork in progress, that they are unique and not like any other, even their sisters (if they have any). I have two sisters who have smaller feet and hands than me and for much of my life I have compared myself to their slighter builds. I felt like a large elephant when I was near my sisters during my bumpy ride to adulthood, and it took years for me to accept that I am not meant to be the same build and size as them. My generous bum is also very much me. Even when I starved myself in my late teen years, I not only became more miserable and bony, but my bum essentially stayed the same size. Being able to accept our unique body type and learning how to dress to take the best advantage of our unique shape can be very helpful during adolescence.

If you have a daughter, help her discover her body shape by using the book, *The Body Shape Bible: Forget Your Size, Discover Your Shape and Transform Yourself* by Trinny Woodall and Susannah Constantine. These two body shape specialists have done a great job at helping women the world over get to know the strengths and weaknesses of their body shapes and how to dress to take advantage of their best assets.

I was a very late developer in terms of what-not-to-wear and am very grateful to my niece Leanne and Laura, a non-biological daughter, who (at about age 17) took me shopping and taught me how to hide my bum, and show off my waist. I wore brown for years throughout my university days in a desperate bid to appear invisible. I was rebelling against beautiful women because my mum was very beautiful and she wore make up and dressed carefully. I didn't wear lipstick until my thirties when a girlfriend fronted me and told me I had great lips and that a little bit of lipstick would look good. I have been a very reluctant woman, and of course having four sons meant I stayed well away from the influences of women's business, spending most of my life dressed in a tracksuit chasing boys.

Help your daughter dress in a way that celebrates her body without over-exposing flesh or resorting to surgery, Botox, starvation or looking for love in all the wrong places. Help her dress to suit her own unique shape and style by working out which colours suit her best. This is a simple thing, yet it can make a big difference. Colour has many other helpful benefits such as lifting flagging spirits, building confidence and expressing individuality.

> *It can be scary. Don't worry. It can also be FUN. Mood swings, confrontations with parents, thinking that you're not attractive enough, being sexually attracted to others, having crushes on people. It's all normal. Relax.*
>
> Hobbs, A., *Getting real about growing up*, (2003)

A daughter embarking on her bumpy ride through adolescence brings up lots of concerns for a mother when it comes to helping them avoid repeating the same mistakes they made as a young person. Those who had eating issues want to work hard to help their daughter avoid doing the same. Those who were sexually active early in adolescence often try to 'lock up' their daughters to avoid them doing the same.

From my experience in counselling adolescent girls I have found that daughters often repeat the mistakes of their mums. I worked with a 13-year-old who had become sexually active, and when I asked her mother about her story at the same age, she became distressed and said she had done the same. This happens often, including with runaways, rebellious behaviour, being expelled from school, drug abuse and binge drinking. My best advice to mums is to find a professional to help you process or decode your story about what happened on your bumpy ride to adulthood. The invisible patterns tend to weaken when exposed to light or honest exploration, and the chances of your daughter repeating your worst disasters will diminish. There is no guarantee they will not repeat them, but if it happens then mums are better able to support their daughters overcome any adverse experiences.

Girls learn more from what you *do* than what you *say*. If you tell your daughter to eat healthy food, and avoid alcohol and drugs, and yet you choose to never eat dessert, stress about how many carbs you're eating, smoke and occasionally drink to excess, then you're giving her tacit permission to follow your lead. The same goes with how you manage conflict within the family. If you yell and shout to deal with conflict then you have normalised this behaviour for when she becomes a partner one day. If you go silent and freeze everyone out for weeks, then you are teaching her this is how to deal with emotional conflict. Consider the following questions:

- What am I teaching my daughter to behave like in a loving, committed relationship?
- What am I teaching my daughter to behave like as a solo mum?
- What am I teaching my daughter to behave like as a working mum?

Many women run themselves ragged trying to be everything—mother, career woman with an amazing body, having a *Home Beautiful* home, being a perfect partner. And they wonder why they struggle with their daughters when they become adolescents?

Adolescents benefit from positive parental involvement; this takes time to build from early childhood. The ability to be positively involved in your daughter's life while trying to do everything else as well can create the 'empty cup' syndrome. This occurs when women have given more than they had to give and they begin to struggle with poor health, exhaustion, depression and sometimes profound resentment at feeling unappreciated. The absence of a healthy connection to your daughter will suddenly loom like a nasty monster, and you won't know how to fix it.

Relationships are organic and grow and evolve over time. An unhealthy relationship is not something you will be able to fix in a day. Your own relationship with yourself is the best place to start. The unexpected venom coming out of your mouth may very well be stuff from your own unresolved adolescent wound, or maybe just unexpressed frustration that you can no longer control your adolescent daughter like you used to. There are the cascading emotional turmoils of being terrified that your daughter will publicly embarrass you or mess up her life badly. You know what? Welcome to the parent hell of uncertainty, of not knowing how to help fix what's not working.

I have been telling parents for a long time to stop 'Skippying' about other parent's choices—tsk, tsk tsk, look at the Mohawk that boy has; tsk, tsk, tsk, did you hear so and so's daughter was taken to hospital after she passed out from binge drinking; tsk, tsk, tsk, look at those jeans so low you can see that girl's underwear. If there is one thing I know from working with adolescents is that the next public 'disaster' could be *your* adolescent. No matter how fabulous and committed your parenting is, how big your house is or what school your adolescent attends, they can all make really dumb decisions while on the bumpy road to adulthood.

> *Alongside the many issues our girls currently face are a wealth of opportunities. It is our job to help our girls recognise these opportunities and give them the confidence and resources they need to lead lives that are richer and fuller than our own, and to find solutions to problems we can but dream of.*
>
> Hamilton, M. *What's Happening to Our Girls* (2008)

For this to happen our girls need to have responsible parents. I have worked with many adolescent girls who have been spoiled as children and drowned with endless praise and have become part of the most coddled generation ever. Michael Carr-Gregg calls them 'Princess Bitchfaces'. These are the chore-dodging girls who manipulate their parents, divide the family, make outrageous requests to reach well-orchestrated 'compromises' and who threaten self-harm to get what they want. These girls are often the product of over-parenting from overprotective parents who have not allowed their children to learn from life experiences and realise that life is not a bed of roses. Many of these girls have been raised on Disney films where the traditional fairy tales have been sweetened by taking out the suffering, moments of revenge, nastiness of bad people and reality that life sometimes sucks badly. These girls are scary to work with because they believe they know everything and they have the power. This is a sign of ineffective parenting and the parents have failed to teach these girls some very important things about life. Not only are these girls wreaking havoc in homes and schools, they are going to have a tough time in committed relationships in the adult years.

> *Some girls I meet now have a sense of entitlement more suited to a 30-year-old executive. I meet girls who can't see why they should have to start out at the bottom and work their way up [...] Girls with a sense of entitlement believe they shouldn't need to do such gritty starter jobs because it's beneath them.*
>
> Miller, D., *The Butterfly Effect: A positive new approach to raising happy, confident teen girls*, (2009).

Maintain healthy boundaries for both children and adolescents and adhere to the tough love philosophy that 'No' means 'No'. This is one of the greatest gifts parents can give their children.

> *If we're overindulging our kids and couching useful advice and criticism in such saccharine sweet and politically correct language that it has become detrimental to their sense of self, then we need to be talking about this, as individuals, as families and as a society.*
>
> Brooks, K. *Consuming Innocence: Popular Culture and Our Children* (2008)

The role of fathers

Many dads get confused when their daughters begin puberty and start the bumpy ride to adulthood. Often in my counselling I hear about girls who were upset at their dad because he has disappeared out of their life. Good dads step back from certain spaces of intimacy knowing that their little girl is now becoming a woman, and they are careful not to cross that line of sexual inappropriateness. Some stop hugging their adolescent daughters, stop tickling them and become wary of how their ridiculousness may embarrass their daughters. Stepping back, even as respectful disappearing, is really painful and confusing to an already confused adolescent girl.

We undervalue the role of dads in girls' lives. I wonder about the irrational need for young girls to become sexually active as young as 12 or 13 years of age. Just as I wonder about the confident girls who appeared in my classroom, yet were not the prettiest or the smartest. How did that happen? I wonder how some girls have a healthy sense of humour that allows them to move through challenging moments easily, while others simply drown in the negativity. I believe dads may be the clue in each of these instances.

Dads, or caring men, who appear consistently in a girl's life shape her perception of herself, particularly her sense of self-acceptance and self-esteem. Dr Bruce Robinson explores the importance of dads and positive, caring men in his book, *Daughters and their Dads: Tips for fathers, adult daughters, husbands and father-figures*. He explains that dads need to be aware of the ways a daughter's future is peculiarly influenced by her relationship with him. These include:

- Approval of her attractiveness as a person, her beauty including acceptance of her body shape.
- Encouragement to make her feel confident in the world, including the confidence to say no to drugs and to think and learn for herself.
- Understanding what she should expect in her relationships with men, including a healthy view of sexuality.

Robinson, B., *Daughters and their Dads: Tips for fathers, adult daughters, husbands and father-figures*, (2008).

One of the common mistakes that dads make is to treat their daughters the same as their sons. From the three key areas of importance listed above, it can be seen that girls need different nurturing from their dads. We need to honour the value of dads in our world, and I have noticed an increase in the number of dads coming to my seminars. Not only are they learning about how to be better fathers, they are learning how important they are in the shaping of the children's future relationships. Dad's matter, and if there is no Dad, a significant loving Dad figure can definitely help.

> *Most husbands and wives aren't aware of how much their marital relationship is influenced by the relationship the wife had with her father.*
>
> Robinson, B. *Dad's and Daughters* (2009)

Developing a sense of strong connectedness between dads and daughters that is not reinforced by material things is one of the ways that we strengthen a girl's sense of self and personal value. Many girls strive to fill the ache of the distance they feel from their dad with the pursuit of shallow temporary relief like gossiping, shopping, make-up, online chatting or self-medicating with alcohol and drugs. Many girls also strive to get approval from other men in their lives and this can create unhealthy patterns of dependence on bosses, colleagues or figures of authority. Girls who have experienced abuse and constant criticism and shaming from their dads will tend to find partners in their life who treat them the same. Much of the early promiscuity is considered to stem from poor relationships with dads rather than a poor relationships with mums.

It is important to show our daughters that we love them unconditionally, even when they fail, have acne, put on weight or recognise that they are gay. This shows them how to be loving and thoughtful, as well as non-judgemental—even if it may not be obvious until that damn pre-frontal lobe has finished growing.

Dads have a big responsibility to teach their daughters how to do things like fix a puncture, maintain a car, change washers on taps, mow lawns and to do general maintenance. Girls who have these competencies often feel more confident and resilient when they leave home. Having self-efficacy is seen as a key attribute to having a healthy sense of self; the more tools in an adolescent's toolkit for life, the better.

Dr Robinson writes in depth about ways in which dads can build healthy connections to their daughters and help them communicate more effectively. Men tend to be problem-solvers and function from the left side of the brain; girls, especially adolescent girls, seldom function from there, meaning that dads often fail to connect with how their daughter may be feeling. The result is they are unable to validate their daughter's feelings first before exploring how they can best support them.

When a dad asks me how to connect with his daughter and find out what she wants, I tell him: 'Ask her!' The way and timing of how you do that is very important due to the massive hormonal swings girls have, and also due to the complete unpredictability of their emotional world. Dr Robinson suggests that dads have 'dad dates' with their daughters—especially before puberty happens—so that they are showing that time with her has some priority.

Most men are wired to be warriors and to provide and protect their family, they are often poor at communicating about deeply personal things.

> *Maggie's Tip: If a dad wants to find out how to be a better parent to his 14-year-old daughter, go find a card that says it for you. Then simply write, 'Please tell me how to be a great dad because you deserve a great dad. I have never been a girl, so I would really appreciate some tips! I want to be the kind of dad who you will be proud of when, one day, I walk you down the aisle to marry the person of your dreams.'*

I have a strong drive and passion for what I believe in. There is no question that even though I struggled with adolescence emotionally, I have never questioned my ability to achieve, persist at things or take risks. All these qualities came from the strong relationship I had with my dad. My dad taught me how to be a humanitarian who cared for her family, community and physical world. His rich and often naughty sense of humour lightened many moments, and his respect for women and children certainly shaped the person I have become.

If you are reading this and wondering how to heal a fractured relationship with your father (or with a daughter if you are a man), do it now! Sit down and write a letter and say you regret whatever was not enough, for the hurt and for letting someone down. Better still, if you are feeling brave go and say it to their face.

But if this is all too hard then seek some professional help and resolve it. Do not leave it for a moment longer because healing an old wound can allow people to bring more love and joy into their lives. It can affect not only that immediate relationship, it can heal your future children and your children's children's relationships.

> *Fathers, if we accept that we can improve as dads we need to get on with it. We ought not to be distracted from improving our fathering by anything. We especially need to avoid the notion that work is more important than our children. One of the main purposes in life as fathers is parenting our children well—for most of us they will outlast the results of our work.*
>
> Robinson, B. *Dad's and Daughters* (2009)

The role of stepdads and grandfathers

The role of being a 'good dad' sometimes ends up as being the job of a stepdad, grandfather or uncle. It is vital that a girl gets to have a deep, loving connection with a male who acts like a protective figure. Many stepdads are unsure of their role in a stepdaughter's life. Be aware that how you treat her mother, and how you treat her will be shaping her belief in how she will expect men to treat her as an adult. You can build her sense of confidence, and her sense of being attractive through love and respect.

I have seen many stepdads who have been asked to walk their stepdaughters down the aisle and shed tears of joy, and everyone present has felt the authentic love between them. Profound human connection has such a powerful healing potential for all concerned regardless of biological bloodlines.

> *Don't forget to show your daughter that you love her. And if she seems unlovable at times, remember that it is often those who are hardest to love who need our love the most.*
>
> Miller, D. *The butterfly effect: A new positive approach to raising happy confident teen girls,(2009)*

Key Points

- Girls can struggle with more intense emotional highs and lows than boys.

- Violence among today's adolescent girls has risen.

- We must be careful to avoid sexualising our girls in both childhood and adolescence.

- Strong friendships can protect adolescent girls.

- Girls can be very nasty and cruel to other girls.

- Mums can help girls dress to suit their body types rather than to suit fashion trends.

- Mums teach girls how to be women more by what they *do* than by what they *say*.

- Dads are very important in their daughter's lives.

- Dads help build confidence, acceptance of beauty and an understanding of what to expect from men in her future relationships.

- Dads can step back in their daughter's life at times, but never disappear.

- Dads need to teach their daughter how to care for their car, mow lawns and fix things.

- It's never too late to fix a poor connection to your daughter.

- Show and tell your daughter that you love her.

Recommended reading

Here are some recommend books for parents of adolescent girls. In Australia we have some excellent experts on the healthy raising of girls and I highly recommend books by Dannielle Miller, Karen Brooks, Maggie Hamilton, Sharon Witt, Kaz Cook and Amrita Hobbs.

For daughters[6]*

10–12-year-olds

Secret Girls' Business by Fay Angelo, Heather Pritchard and Rose Stewart, (2003).

10–14-year-olds

More Secret Girls' Business by Fay Angelo, Heather Pritchard and Rose Stewart, (2008).

13–18-year-olds

Teen Talk: Girl Talk by Sharon Witt, (2008).

15-year-olds +

Girl Stuff: Your full-on guide to the teen years by Kaz Cook, (2007).

For parents

The Butterfly Effect: A Positive New Approach to Raising Happy, Confident Teen Girls by Dannielle Miller, (2009).

What's Happening to Our Girls: Too Much, Too Soon, How our kids are overstimulated, oversold and oversexed, Maggie Hamilton, (2009).

Daughters and their Dads: Tips for fathers, adult daughters, husbands and father-figures by Bruce Robinson, (2008).

Growing Great Girls by Ian and Mary Grant, (2008).

What Teenage Girls Don't Tell Their Parents by Michelle Mitchell (2011)

---

6   * Please read the book first and see if it is suitable for your daughter's emotional and physical maturity. Read any book you ask your daughter to read.

Chapter 12

Secret *boys'* business *on the* **bumpy road** to adulthood

Emotional literacy is the most valuable gift we can offer our students, and urging parents and educators to recognise the price boys pay when we hold them to an impossible standard of manhood is important in today's modern world.

Clark Wight, Former Principal, Christ Church Grammar Junior School, Western Australia.

Dent, M. Nurturing Kids Hearts and Souls, (2005).

I am a proud mum of four sons and I write this chapter with a deep sense of urgency. Our adolescent boys are struggling with the modern world and its massively stimulating environments full of distractions and mixed messages about how to be a man. The biological drives in adolescent boys to become warriors whose primary purpose in life is to provide and protect, have had their ride to adulthood stripped of purposeful risk-taking, strong guidance and mentoring by men, and replaced with mind-numbing passive activity in classrooms—which is brain antagonistic for most boys.

> *More and more boys in our schools are becoming aggressive, violent, inattentive and hyperactive. This is happening at younger and younger ages. Many boys are in emotionally charged situations that challenge and confuse them. Many boys are frustrated in school systems that are conditioned against boys, or that have teachers inadequately trained to meet the learning needs and styles of most boys.*
>
> Dent, M. *Nurturing Kids Hearts and Souls,* (2005).

There are gender differences regardless of those who hate to look at adolescents through different lenses. Those who have taught high-school students know that boys and girls are different to teach. Adolescents are motivated by different things, and boys often struggle with the dilemma of looking strong and brave when their inner world is in turmoil with massive surges in testosterone. They guard their vulnerability with masks of indifference, defensiveness, arrogance or inappropriate humour. They struggle to understand their volatile emotional world and spend much of the time in confusion.

> *Growing up is tough, especially the bit between being a boy and a man. It's tough because so much is changing at once. Your body, your emotions, your interests, and the way other people see you. The way you look at girls and the way they look at you. Plus there are those dreams.*
>
> Roy, J., *The 'S' Word : A Boy's Guide to Sex, Puberty and Growing Up*, (2006).

Boys get confused and lost in the chaos of adolescent changes. When girls feel the same way they tend to share it with their friends, which helps diffuse their emotional angst. Boys rarely share their emotional vulnerability, and when it reaches their tipping point their emotional barometer explodes.

> *From a young age boys are systematically steered away from their emotional lives towards solitude, silence and distrust. This is also done...but also at more undetected levels, such as the 'culture of cruelty' that exists among adolescents, in which anything a boy says or does can and will be used against him.*
>
> Kindlon, D. and Thompson, M., *Raising Cain: Protecting the Emotional Life of Boys*, (2000).

The author of *The Wonder of Boys* and *The Good Son*, Michael Gurian explains how the male amygdala—the primary aggression centre in the brain—is larger than that of females and creates more aggression in males. When this is linked to the massive surges of testosterone it gives us a clue as to why boys are more wired to like risky behaviour.

It seems that a boy's natural impulsiveness could also be rooted in his biology. Boys tend to have lower levels of serotonin, the calming neurotransmitter, and thus their heightened state means it is more difficult for them to manage impulses. Boys definitely benefit from clear rules and boundaries, but not too many. With strong emotional support and bonding, boys can grow into men who are able to manage the uniquely special qualities of being a man.

I am still concerned that adolescent boys are yelled at, ridiculed, shamed, hit or constantly punished for things they have little understanding of and no help to resolve. I worked with a 15-year-old boy who was still doing extra duties at his boarding house for things he had done when he was 13! The following is an adolescent's take on mucking up:

A perfect example is how to deal with something like ur son getting done for drink driving. In the eyes of the parent, it sounds like the most stupid and irresponsible thing they could possibly do, and absolutely lose there nana over it.

I agree it is very stupid, but boys are boys, we all have done it, and at the time, you have been drinking and it seems like an ok idea at the time, and you have the thought process, oh im just going down the road, she'll be right.

That doesn't make ur son a bad irresponsible person, it just means that he made an error of judgment in that instance, and trust me, they know they have stuffed up, and the punishment of losing ur license, copping a big fine, and possible getting a crim record is punishment enough. It doesn't help anyone is you go off ur tree and punish them more.

This is the same as a lot of the mistakes boys make, they know they have done wrong, but wen ur young, you just don't think things through all the time ... and the classic line 'seemed like a good idea at the time' comes into it.

Anyway... food for thought

I am continually surprised with how open and forthcoming adolescent boys can be about the things that concern them. There were many times when a mother told me she was making her son come and see me for counselling, and that the son had said he wouldn't say anything. I made sure she agreed to take her son to McDonald's afterwards, so that he could have at least one win for the day. When the boy arrived, albeit reluctantly, it took only a few minutes and he was an open book. Boys ask me questions that they had wanted to ask someone, but hadn't been able to find a person safe enough. When I help them with a few skills to better decode the adult and adolescent worlds, they leave so relieved, and often they are very hard to shut up!

> *Our boys are nothing if not morally fragile, from the inside out. And there are ways in which our boys are simply more vulnerable than girls to moral instability. To neglect this fact is to neglect our boys.*
>
> Gurian, M, *The Good Son: Shaping the Moral Development of our Boys and Young Men*, (1999).

Boys are more resistant to getting help than girls which is why we must build support structures, especially lighthouses, around them before adolescence. Boys are very vulnerable, especially to being shamed, criticised, ridiculed and ignored. They also struggle with stress and relationships. They often wear a tough mask that covers this vulnerability, and their behaviour often masks their confusion and emotional turmoil.

> *Often we place boys in the most terrible situations because we genuinely believe it will be the making of them, not realising how much of them we might be destroying in the process.*
>
> Hamilton, M., *What Men Don't Talk About*, (2007).

I have worked with many men still deeply scarred from hideous experiences at boarding school. It wasn't just the bullying that scarred them, it was the massive sense of abandonment they felt from both their mums and dads, and often their beloved home as well. They had to find a way to make sense of the chaos of adolescence while feeling like a ship without a rudder. They are much younger emotionally at 12 and 13 than girls, and this is when many go to boarding school.

The search for identity can be even more confusing for boys than for girls. Some boys want to avoid becoming 'macho dickheads' like those they see on television, in the movies and on the news. I believe much of the drunken violence on our streets by young men is a sign of deep personal shame, emotional illiteracy, and a profound anger and resentment at the absence of love and intimacy in their lives.

> *As a result of the classroom discussions I had with boys I came to believe that adolescent boys are less resilient than girls of the same age. There were moments when their vulnerability washed over me and I was wondering how we actually manage to get so many of them safely through to adulthood...Their childlike naivety...their dependence on their peers to define their behaviour, their desire to live in the moment and their associated unwillingness to plan all combine at a time when male hormones are raging through their bodies and the blood appears to be going down rather than up.*
>
> Lashlie, C., *He'll Be OK: Growing Gorgeous Boys into Good Men*, (2007).

Computers have created a new area of risk-taking behaviour for boys that was normally found out of doors. The addiction to online games, especially those where individuals are rewarded for senseless violence, has been shown to be changing personalities in some boys. There are also risky chatrooms and hardcore porn. The risk of doing something illegal in your bedroom has created a new unhealthy activity for boys who would normally be out running or playing sport. Remember, boys are hunting dopamine, the excitement brain chemical (also known as the reward transmitter), and they will chase it irrationally, especially if it's free and they can do it in the comfort of their own bedroom. The effect of viewing hardcore porn, especially during the window of sensitivity at under 16 years of age, can transform a boy who has been raised to respect women into an adolescent who wants to dominate and use women. Norman Doidge MD wrote about the effect of viewing pornography on the adult male brain:

> *Pornography's influence is more profound now because it is no longer hidden, it influences young people with little sexual experience and especially plastic minds in the process of forming their sexual tastes and desires. All addiction involves long term, sometimes life long, neuroplasticitic changes in the brain.*
>
> Doidge, N. MD., *The Brain that Changes Itself Stories of Personal Triumph from the Frontiers of Brain Science*, (2007).

Doidge explains how mature men can become hopelessly addicted to online porn and masturbation, and yet become impotent in their intimate lives. Adolescent boys' brains are highly plastic due to the massive increase in dendrites, so they can have massive brain changes quite quickly compared to a mature brain. They can become addicted to shutting the world out by using their PC. They can lose all track of time and become extremely angry when asked to stop. I am including a letter written by a 16-year-old via email to his parents explaining why he preferred his computer to his family. You can clearly see how they see the world when they're addicted to being online.

Why I like my computer over people

This is a list of reasons as to why i prefer my computer over people:

1. a computer is a controlled environment
2. if there is an error its more than likely because the user typed something wrong more than the computer
3. a computer doesn't argue or get angry at you
4. a computer can't get sick or damaged easily
5. the computer is easier to get along with and the people i talk to through it i can relate to and they respect me for what i can do
6. if i don't feel well or anything the computer wont yell at me
7. there is always something new to do on a computer
8. a computer wont yell at you for being on it to long
9. the computer wont become angry at me if i choose to stay on it late
10. the computer will not call me names if i choose to do something on it some one else doesn't agree with
11. computers are not irrational in their behaviour-everything that happens is because you made it happen
12. the computer will not refuse to do something if it chooses to
13. a computer wont start meaningless arguments or repeat the same statement continuously
14. a computer will not choose to go on rants about things or bring up old topics i don't wish to talk about

there are of course more reasons but that is a few as to why i prefer my laptop over you people. now maybe you will learn to accept that i prefer to be on my computer rather than be with people, as i am in fact with people just people that also like computers as much as me.

Printed with permission

There are other illegal activities that adolescent boys get a kick out of while online. One is the illegal downloading of anything—software, movies or television shows. This is like a game to them, and yet if they're caught the consequences are quite serious. Another appealing past time is to go phishing, which involves surfing the Internet and copying people's email addresses and selling them to illegal spamming groups. I know of a 15-year-old boy who was making about $150 a week doing this. Remember, the adolescent boy has great difficulty understanding moral choices, especially when he is having fun and taking risks.

We must be very vigilant to protect an adolescent boy's developing sense of self from the unhealthy influences that are available online, and restrict their use of computers.

Keep computers and televisions out of a boy's bedroom

They will still be able to access this same material via mobile phones or on an mp3 player, but it will be in a more public domain, which is an inhibiting influence.

About mothers

I often remind mums that they have to ensure their boys are loved tenderly as babies, toddlers and children so they will know they are valued and that they matter. Gradually, boys step back from their mums as they begin the journey to manhood. The bumpy ride to manhood is a journey mums cannot take them on. If you didn't have brothers, or if you had a distant relationship with your father, you may find boys incredibly difficult to understand. Boys need the following:

- Boys like to explore the natural world in a much more physical way than girls.
- They need to investigate how things work.
- They need balls to kick, things to climb and to pit themselves against a challenge.
- They need structure and boundaries.
- They need goals and coaching in how to persist.
- They need a safe environment and a zero tolerance towards ridicule.

Grant, I., *Growing Great Boys: How to bring out the best in your son*, (2008).

Some mums struggle with the massive physicality of boys. Boys love to be active and hate sitting still, and when they reach about 13 years of age this physicality, especially with other boys, often gets *stronger*. Boys of this age simply need to punch and shove each other, and without understanding that this was a biological need and not a deliberate act to piss off their teacher, it can be seen as something they do with intention. They are often oblivious to how they look or how they are expected to behave.

> *The boys' entry into school halls also made me laugh. They appeared to have no real sense of their bodies and no awareness of the world around them. With shirts hanging out, socks down around their ankles, sandals or shoes flapping loosely, they lumbered around or over chairs, jostled one another and in what appeared to be a totally unfocused way, they eventually found their way to their allotted seats.*
>
> Lashlie, C. *He'll be OK*, (2005).

This robust way of experiencing the world is normal for boys and they need to be better supported to allow their bodies to move around as they work with their energy. Boredom and disengagement threaten the brain and they must break that cycle, we must either acknowledge this reality and create opportunities for them to discharge energy in a non-destructive way, or wait until they find some other way to do the same discharge. The best way to engage boys is by using more movement in learning environments. Co-education schools at times struggle with boys' excess energy, and the same happens in our homes.

Celia also found in her work that adolescent boys struggle with long-term planning and often delay doing major assessments until the last minute. If we remember that boys are still primarily wired to be warriors with the same genes that made them able to hunt ferocious animals, then it's possible that life is not presenting them with enough challenge.

> *Is it possible that the inertia frequently displayed by adolescent boys occurs because the challenges being put in front of them aren't of sufficient depth to merit a real response?*
>
> Lashlie, C. *He'll be OK*, (2005).

I have worked with boys who leave major assessments, even 5000 word university papers, until the last 24 hours because then it's a challenge. They then pull an 'all nighter' and work at an intensity never normally seen and they feel enormously exhilarated when they reach the deadline. Maybe the same thing is happening when some men leave Christmas shopping until the day before Christmas because then it's a challenge to meet a tight deadline—it's so much more exciting than buying them early.

As a celebrant I have conducted many funeral ceremonies, and over time have heard many stories from Australia's early pioneering days. Many men were working in remote places or on shearing teams by the age of 13 or 14, and they stepped up to the challenges of this hard work in tough conditions, often living in tents. Maybe it's the need for adventure that is missing in our boys' lives today, which may partially explain why they spend so much time playing violent online games. They miss the challenges of *real* life.

Mums need to remember that although her son is growing taller, hairier and hornier, her 4-year-old son is still present. Boys particularly have times when they seriously don't want to be an adolescent because it's too hard. They want you to make their lunch, help them find their socks and to come and cuddle them at night. Relax, this is normal. They only do this in the privacy of home, never in public. This may be the same son who has asked to be dropped off a few streets from school now that he's 15 just in case you embarrass him.

Adolescent boys have difficulty finding things, even when it's right in front of them. Please be careful to avoid shaming or ridiculing them when this happens. We have a saying in our house, 'Have you had a *Ben* look or a *Mum* look?' Ben had great difficulty finding anything during adolescence no matter how prominent it was in his view, even though he was very intelligent. Fortunately, as an adult he finds this family expression amusing.

All adolescents have problems with short-term memory and organisational skills, especially boys. Help them make some key lists to remember things such as when they have to play football, go to Scouts or go to a music lesson. Make a memory card or a poster as a reminder to check if they have everything—it will save your voice and sanity! List-making is a valuable life skill that boys can benefit from.

Boys get very frustrated when mums nags and repeats herself. If a boy of any age does not have eye contact with you, they cannot hear you. When you have their eye contact, ask them *one* thing only as politely as possible. Double check that they heard it by asking them to give a thumbs up to say, 'Got it.' As soon as there are too many words or commands, a boy's brain 'zones out' the information.

A lot of male communication is non-verbal. I have watched a dad with his sons at a park; few words of guidance passed between them and yet they all had a great time. This dad also made some strange grunts that meant quite different things and his sons knew exactly what he was communicating. When a mum is there, a lot more words are used. Avoid drowning your son in too many words with too much explanation and too many requests, and remember this is a female code of communicating.

Here are some innovative ways to get reluctant adolescents to do things. These ideas especially work with mums and sons:

- Steve, as I make your toasted sandwich will you please take the bin out for me?
- Brian, when you've finished feeding the dog will you come over here and help me for a minute get dessert ready?

- Alex, as I get dinner ready would it be OK if you cleaned away your bike tyre from the dining table?
- James, we will get the Milo and cake ready once you finish your homework.
- Billy, we can pick you up from the library after you finish your assignment, and then we'll go to the beach.
- Michael, it will be OK for your girlfriend to come and watch a DVD once you have mowed the lawn.

Boys are less complicated to live with if you are able to keep things consistent— rules, meals, discipline and fun opportunities. Mums need to lighten up because when those adolescent hormones come racing through the door, a boy's sensitivity level rises.

Maggie's Tip: Please appear as comfortable as possible with the presence of erect penises—especially in the morning. Boys have little control over them and need you to be able to act as though they aren't there. Some mornings I had to weave among four erect penises in a narrow kitchen without a murmur!

Your son will like to have more privacy as he starts his bumpy ride to manhood. So this means the bathroom door gets locked and the bedroom door is shut. If you need to go into their room, knock and wait respectfully. There is some serious boy's business they prefer to do without a mum knowing, and that is very healthy. You may find they still like walking in while you are having a bath or a shower, and that's healthy too.

Boys have a need for secrecy that many women find very challenging. Boys do not see it as secrecy, they see it as part of the natural stepping back from their mum in preparation for manhood. In some Indigenous cultures the boys are ceremonially 'stolen' from their mothers at some point so that the ties with their mums are clearly cut. In our Western world, there can be some murky confusion on both parts about the healthy separation from a mum's apron strings.

In the woman's world there is deep sharing between family and friends about almost anything depending on the level of trust. Boys and men seldom share as deeply, especially when it's about really sensitive areas such as failure, loss, relationship breakdown, death and shame. They struggle with their deep emotional pain alone, and it's one of the reasons why we have such a high suicide rate in men and boys. Some men have likened it to being a warrior, which means that you are wired to win, and when they lose sometimes it feels better to die than to be a loser. This ancient archetype is slowly being pulled apart with the excellent work being done by men across Australia.

Mums need to be aware that adolescent boys may be reluctant to share what has happened at school, on the weekend or on the football trip. This is healthy and very normal and a mum needs to allow their son to share only what they want without pulling a guilt trip on them. The pressure to interrogate your son may make them want to pull away even faster. They are wired differently to girls and you must respect that.

Every mother of a son needs to read Celia Lashlie's book, *He'll Be OK: Growing Gorgeous Boys into Good Men*. She has spoken with hundreds of boys and has heard from them what matters, especially what they need on their bumpy ride to adulthood: They need their mum to get off the bridge to manhood and they need their dad to get on with as many other good men as possible. Stepping back is essential for boys to mature healthily. I have worked with adolescent boys whose mums have stayed on the bridge—and even kept their dad off the bridge—and many of these boys have quite child-like faces in enormous bodies. Much like the body has been able to grow, but somehow the boy is trapped inside. Unfortunately, there is also a deep layer of rage within these boys, as well as a deep sense of being trapped and crushed.

> *My mother wanted to know everything about me, especially how I thought about things. It drove me mad and I felt sort of invaded. One day I screamed 'Stop trying to get inside my head.'*
>
> Hartley-Brewer, E., *Self-Esteem for Boys: 100 Tips for Raising Happy and Confident Children*, (2000).

Maggie Hamilton in her book, *What's Happening to Our Girls,* writes that mothers shape boys' values and selfhood by the narratives they use both verbally and internally. It's a subtle and often unintended influence that can shape how boys see themselves. This could be a problem for mums who have been scarred by a negative relationship with a disrespectful man.

> *'Mothers play a central role in the family narrative because they are generally the main story tellers.'*
>
> Hamilton, M. *What's Happening to Our Girls*, (2008).

Dear Boys

| Frozen heart – cold bitch or emotionally & physically absent | Smother mother – invasion on all levels |

Seeking mother during
Adulthood
Punishing mother

Avoiding mother during
Adulthood
Punishing mother

Healthy Mothering

On the mothering journey with sons there is a continuum where the degree of mothering can go from unhealthy at either end, to healthy in the middle. Healthy mothering in adolescence requires mothers to step back and allow them to become who they are biologically wired to be. You may wonder where your loving, considerate son has vanished to and may want to try even harder to instil in him good morals and values. The work you have done up to 12 years of age is what matters, but after that it will look like you have failed—relax, this is normal! Know that when the pre-frontal lobe finally grows the son you have invested so heavily in will return. If a boy has not been given lots of love and guidance before 12, it's a challenge to create it, however it is still possible. The brain changes when it receives consistent loving care, so we must never give up on young people no matter what.

> *Yes your boy's going away for a time, but he's coming back; he knows you're his mother, and he knows you're there. Trust that process, trust your intuition and trust his.*
>
> Lashlie, C. *He'll Be OK*, (2005).

Mums need to let their sons know that they have to step back, but they won't be disappearing. Have the conversation about the bridge to manhood and reassure your son that you will be there if they need you for the big stuff—then step back.

Michael Currie explains that studies show some adolescent boys struggle deeply from their perceived loss of their mother because they can feel a deep sense of emptiness. The sense of loss can cause some boys to seek some form of unconscious restitution for this loss.

> *Self-destructiveness and depression are so often associated with anger and aggression. There is a strong link between anger and sadness and a boy's maternal bond.*
>
> Currie, M., *Doing Anger Differently*, (2008).

When there has been a marriage separation and the children have stayed with Mum, be mindful of a need to review the above information when your son gets to adolescence. Celia Lashlie writes of her son's desire to get to know his father when he was 11-years-old, and of *his choice* to do that. She had been a sole mum and it was very important for her son to get to know his dad and a part of himself.

I had a similar experience. When I moved from the town where the boys had been raised, the only son left at home came with me. Just before he was due to start school in this new town he had two good mates come and spend a week. I heard these good friends playing cards in the triangular bath for about two hours with much laughter and joking. Suddenly, it occurred to me that I should reconsider moving my son away from his best mates and a community where he had such strong connections. Then I pondered about whether his dad, from whom I was divorced, would like to have his son full-time. It was obvious in a flash that my son needed to stay and finish schooling in his familiar town and spend his last years of schooling with his dad.

In some way my moving town appeared more about creating a space for this new direction to happen than about the original reasons. When I called his dad, he was a bit surprised and then very delighted. The next few years were very successful and worthwhile for all of us and the relationship between son and father became very strong. It wasn't easy for me to let go of my baby, there were times I found it really hard; every holiday was spent with me and school terms were spent with his dad. The solid base that my son had was an enormously stabilising influence on his life—same friends, schools, football teams and surfing friends. Also, the mums of his friends took over and made sure my son was 'mothered' in my absence. I am deeply grateful for their love and support. I often had their sons with me during holidays; this is collective parenting at its best.

Women are much bigger worriers than men. For some mums, in the 10 minutes that her son is late for his curfew, she will have imagined him dead in a nasty car accident with blood and guts everywhere. Be aware that fear-based thinking can impact on our loved ones. To help yourself relax and go to sleep until the curfew time try any of the following:

- Set an alarm clock inside the front door. If it rings, your son is late and you will wake up.
- As you prepare to go to sleep imagine seeing your son already asleep in his bed, safe and sound.
- Imagine sending very large guardian angles to watch over him until he gets home.
- Pray that he gets home safe.
- Take three deep breaths and go to sleep.

In my work around death and dying I have supported parents who have turned off life support for their adolescent son, others who lost their son to a tumour, another pair who lost a son in a multiple death car accident, and a mum and dad who lost their son to drowning. Nothing can prepare you for the death of your child. One mother shared with me the last words she had said to her son: 'Have fun, know that I love you and may God go with you'. She told me that while she was struggling with her grief she said, 'I have a strange sense of peace that if I had known that they were the last words I would ever speak to him, I would have said exactly those same words.'

> *Maggie's Tip: Ensure the words that you say to your adolescent—girl or boy— as they go out the door are words you would want to exchange if they were going to be the last words you ever get to say.(This actually isn't a bad strategy to use with all the people in your lives).*

Top tips for mums of sons

- Use less words and more focused attention.
- Never shame, guilt or freeze out your sons.
- Avoid overreacting when they bugger up.
- Provide support when it's needed.
- Be there when they need you and not before.
- Feed them well and keep your fridge stocked with good food.
- Lighten up where possible.
- Leave the small stuff—it's the big stuff that really matters.
- Be consistent in all areas.
- Allow them the freedom to make their own choices.
- Trust your boys and avoid suspicious thoughts.
- Show you love them often—a touch, a word, a treat.
- Be kind, generous and gentle.
- Don't restrict them in achieving goals, support them.
- Teach them the life skills they need to be even more competent than their dad.
- Avoid catastrophising.
- Keep them active and involved in life.
- Welcome their friends around to the house.
- Enjoy your boys.

About dads

I begin this section by acknowledging I do not have a penis and I have no right to sound like I know what adolescent boys need from their dad. My knowledge is from what boys have told me in my counselling room. I have a special affinity for boys and I enjoy the way men 'are'. I was a tomboy for many years and spent a lot of time with my dad on our farm. My boys have told me that I am 'part-bloke', meaning I recognise how men think.

In many ways our modern world has devalued men, which is something Celia Lashlie agrees with. Our education system has a lot to answer for in the shaping of the image that boys are a waste of space in many classrooms. I feel that schooling has failed thousands of boys and men, not the other way around. There are good men out there and we need to stop generalising when we speak about men. Women's business often confuses me and I shop like a man—I drop before I shop, not shop until I drop! The more positive involvement men have in the lives of our children, the better our world will be. However, there are men who have not had the parenting to allow them to grow into good men, and if they're struggling, they need to take note of the following:

> *Men need to stop beating their wives and killing their kids and their step-kids; men need to confront other men about selling drugs to children, about taking money that should be used to feed their children to feed their alcohol and drug addictions; men need to stand up and be more accountable as fathers.*
>
> Lashlie, C. *He'll Be OK*, (2005).

There are some excellent books written by men, for men, about how to be a good dad. But the main problem I hear from men is that they can't seem to get around to reading them. A farmer came up to me after a seminar and said he only read the *Farmer's Weekly*, yet he still wanted to know how to be a better dad. He suggested I put the information on an audio CD so he could listen in his tractor or truck[7*]. This shows the natural pragmatism of boys and men—find a simple solution to fix the problem.

> *There's something about it when a man doesn't get along with his father. It makes him mean; it makes him dangerous; it makes him angry.*
>
> Bill Glass, former NFL player/prison guard.

A personal development facilitator said something once to a man at a seminar that had a profound affect on him. He said every boy and man wanted three things from his father:

---

7   [*] I have done that with my *About Kids* pack. I will also create a CD of this book for dads and those who do not have time to read.

1. Respect.
2. Acceptance.
3. Love.

That may not be *everything* a boy needs from his dad, but it's an excellent starting point. Boys often tell me what they don't want from their dad—cruelty, sarcasm, grumpiness, silence, absence, drunkenness, rudeness to their mother, violence, constant criticism, or being made fun of.

Ian Grant in his book, *Growing Great Boys,* writes that boys need their dads to 'download the software' about how to be a man.

> *This is the greatest privilege given to a father and the greatest gift that a father can give his son. What a boy needs is an 'effective father' – a backbone father – loving and firm fair and friendly.*
>
> Grant, I. *Growing Great Boys,* (2006).

Steve Biddulph says that at about four years of age, a boy becomes a male-role-model-seeking missile and he will long to be around men. This is a great age to start sharing with a boy the enjoyment of male activities like cars, fishing, woodwork, golf, surfing, swimming and camping. This male connection and bondedness helps grow good boys into good men. If there is no dad, then positive and stable men who care can build the same inner foundations and sense of being supported and guided.

In adolescence the yearning for dad, or deep male connectedness, appears to rise again. Biologically it makes sense because boys are seeking men to walk beside them on their journey to manhood. If there is a profound absence of a father figure who can show them respect, acceptance and love, then it can create a deep sense of resentment, worthlessness and despair.

Many adolescent boys who have attempted suicide have had no man they could turn to, or feel safe enough to just turn up and spend time with. They are hungry for belonging with peers and friends, and they hunger for positive family connectedness.

Adolescent boys need to be surrounded by reliable adults in order to create a positive environment for them to help shape their sense of identity. If this does not happen they can use aggression and violence simply to defend their fragile sense of self that needs some shaping.

> *These developing abilities of thought in adolescence can be shaped, and used to question the utility of boys' thinking and beliefs, including automatic judgments, inferences and attributions.*
>
> Currie, M. *Doing Anger Differently,* (2008).

There is an enormous scope for helping boys shape themselves into someone they would like to be. When I was teaching, I was staggered at times with how an adolescent boy changed in a matter of weeks when he was able to pull off a mask of indifference or aggression simply because it was no longer valid in the environment we, as a group, had created in the classroom. They may put that mask on when they go home or to another class, however, they were able to glimpse another identity that felt safe and comfortable.

Something important that dads and safe male mentors need to affirm to boys, especially adolescents, is summed up perfectly by Ian Grant:

Your son has to hear from you, his parent, in a thousand different ways the words 'You've got what it takes, mate'. Every problem he faces, every difficulty you help him to own, can be supported by this message:

'You can solve this because you have what it takes.'

This is the most important message to give adolescent boys and show that you love them no matter what.

There is inherent wisdom in acknowledging that the ride to adulthood is bumpy and there will be moments of challenge. For boys to grow into healthy men they need to stretch and scare themselves, hurt themselves and hopefully come to the realisation that they are not invincible—they are human, life is precious and it needs to be respected. When adolescent boys bugger up it shows they have taken some action to explore themselves and to find where the edges of their being exist. They learn how lousy it can feel when things don't always go to plan. They also get to experience 'peak' moments when something risky is successfully achieved. Allow your adolescent boy to stretch himself and go to the edge of his physical, psychological and mental reality. Without allowing this freedom we may keep losing today's boys to senseless violence, depression and suicide as they search for themselves in a world that often fails to honour the ancient knowledge of life.

When adolescent boys have been stretched to the very edge of their being and face death, they may glimpse the mysterious, the sacred or that which cannot be measured or taught. This is the place where truth will appear like never before, and the opening to something far greater than being a mere mortal can occur. This is where they may find their life's purpose, divine mission or sacred contract, and suddenly they have found their path. This is what happened when I almost committed suicide. I went to this sacred place and ever since I have had a reason to be here, and that awareness has helped me overcome every challenge I have met.

One 15-year-old, almost six-foot lad asked for a job to do for his Mum so he could earn some extra money to repair his skateboard. She asked him to use the vacuum cleaner to remove webs and Daddy long legs spiders around the house.

When the Mum returned later she noticed the job had not been done. When she questioned her son he said he just couldn't do it because he didn't want to hurt the spiders!

Top tips for dads of sons

- Be firm, fair and friendly.
- Believe in him.
- Coach him how to be a good man.
- Model healthy restraint around alcohol.
- Have fun with him.
- Make him feel he is part of a team at home.
- Stay physically connected to him.
- Tell him clearly the dos and don'ts of life.
- Show him how to do stuff.
- Have dad-son times regularly.
- Connect him to nature.
- Show him how a loving relationship can be.
- Show him how to say sorry.
- Stay involved in his adolescent ride.
- Never be afraid to cry.
- Take him on a symbolic journey of challenge.
- Be consistent.
- Show him respect.
- Accept him as he is, not how he could be or how you want him to be.
- Show and tell him you love him.

> *Teens need to know that they can rely on their parents when the going gets rough. They are naturally drawn to risky behaviour and are unable to make good decisions, so you are guaranteed they will need a safety net at some point.*
>
> Feinstein, S. *Parenting the Teenage Brain*, (2007).

Key Points

- Boys are really struggling in today's chaotic world.

- Boys can get easily addicted online.

- Boys are wired to be warriors and need opportunities to conquer 'things'.

- Boys brains are wired differently

- Boys have special needs of their Mums and Dads.

- Boys need healthy men to guide them on the road to manhood.

- Boys are vulnerable even though they often look big and strong.

- We must stop shouting, shaming, hitting and being verbally and physically abusive to our boys.

- Schools need to keep addressing the unique needs of boys.

Chapter 13

Sex, *drugs,* Rock'n'Roll *and* Cyberspace

Oestrogen sashays down the hallway and testosterone thunders towards her. Puberty has ambushed the sexually dormant child.

Feinstein, S. Parenting the Teenage Brain, (2007).

Some sobering information from the Australian Bureau of Statistics:

- 39 per cent of Australian boys and 34 per cent of girls had used alcohol, tobacco or cannabis, compared with 25 per cent of American boys and girls (high school).
- 25.9 per cent of all sexually active students report that they have had unwanted sex at some time.
- The most common reasons cited for having unwanted sex were being too drunk (15.9 per cent) and pressure from a sexual partner (12.6 per cent).
- In relation to the most recent sexual encounter, 22.7 per cent indicated that they were drunk or high at the time.
- In 2004–5, 10 per cent of children aged 10–14 years were reported to have some form of mental or behavioural problem as a long-term health condition.
- 26 per cent of people aged 16–24 years—about 650,000 people— suffered mental illness in 2008; 14 per cent of Year 8s in Australia self-harmed in 2008.

The best support parents and lighthouses can give adolescents is the preventive sort. It is easier to prevent problems from occurring by using vigilance and caring communication, especially in the areas of alcohol use, sexual behaviour, drug use and social freedom.

Once the horse has bolted it's very hard to get it back in the yard. Keep it locked away from the world for as long as you can!

Sex and physical urges

There is a high degree of 'cringe factor' when parents step into the domain of adolescent sexuality. Secretly, we would love our children to be locked up until the brain finishes developing so that this part of the bumpy ride to adulthood could be smooth, with no sex with anyone—including themselves! The biggest potholes, roadblocks and major accidents on the ride to adulthood are triggered by the risky things adolescents yearn to do in order to make themselves feel good, or release their primitive urges. This chapter will aim to give you guidelines on to how to parent responsibly—not perfectly—as your adolescent gets sexually aroused and just plain horny.

> *We do not know when teenagers are meant to have sex. We do not know what is healthiest and we do not know what is best. All we know for sure about teenage sex is that it varies a great deal between individuals and it has changed over the course of human history.*
>
> Bainbridge, D. *Teenagers: A Natural History,* (2009).

Bainbridge writes that puberty, which normally was the trigger for adolescents to become sexually active, has moved forward over time. In previous decades, boys' voices usually broke around their 18th birthday, which is much later than today. The same earlier onset of puberty is happening for girls, yet in both cases the brain still lags behind.

We cannot ignore the hormonal shifts that occur without an adolescent's permission (or often knowledge), that suddenly make them open to infatuation, lusting and sexual experimentation. This is normal and must not be shamed. This is another biological drive to ensure the survival of the human species! Positive parental influence with clear, certain boundaries around sex, alcohol, drugs and other risky behaviour definitely helps adolescents stay chaste and safe longer.

> *It is important to realize that a preoccupation, bordering on obsession, with the opposite sex is normal: be tolerant but vigilant. Monitoring is vital.*
>
> Feinstein, S., *Parenting the Teenage Brain,* (2007).

Parents *must* have the sex conversation. Yes, it is difficult. It helps to have some good books to get the facts right, especially the body parts. I recommend the following books to help with THE talk:

- *Secret Girls' Business;. Secret Boys' Business; More Secret Girls' Business; More Secret Boy Business* by Fay Angelo, Heather Prichard and Rose Stewart. These make a good starting base.
- *Teen Talk: Girl Talk, Teen Talk: Gut Talk* by Sharon Witt. These are good because they're not too sexually adult-like.
- *Ten Talks That Parents Must Have with their Teenagers about Sex and Character*, by Pepper Schwartz PhD and Dominic Capello.

It is also helpful for parents to follow up any school-based sex education programs. It is useful for anchoring the parents' expectations of, 'We expect you not to have sex with anyone else until you are much older'.

When adolescent girls do not have the chance to have important and meaningful conversations about sex with their parents, it's hard for them to be clear about boundaries they are comfortable with. They may end up doing what their peers expect or what they think everyone else is doing.

> *Often these girls are desperate to be accepted. Boys say, 'You've got to give us head to be accepted,' so they do and then they are shunned. This was a frequent story.*
>
> Hamilton, M., *What's Happening to Our Girls*, (2009).

We must step up as parents, families, lighthouses and teachers to push back the mixed messages that permeate our sexualised world where girls have to 'put out' to be acceptable. It is possible that much of the binge drinking culture and early drug taking is linked to the deep shame felt by many adolescent girls who have been pressured into being sexually active well before they were ready. They are seeking to numb the negative feelings and allow themselves to lose their sense of better judgement so they can do it again and again, desperately trying to convince themselves it's fun and it's what everyone's doing. There's every chance they are seeking love and intimacy that they cannot find elsewhere in their lives.

> *It is of course tempting to suspect that boys over-report their number of sexual partners and under-estimate the age of first intercourse, whereas girls may do the opposite.*
>
> Bainbridge, D., *Teenagers: A Natural History*, (2009).

Shelley's story: A cautionary truth

Shelley was a 17-year-old Perth girl from a loving home. When I met her she had just returned from living on the streets in Sydney and she had a heroin addiction. I was intrigued as to how a girl with loving parents had ended up in such a painful place on her bumpy ride to adulthood.

When she was 14, Shelley and her friend made themselves look much older and escaped out a bedroom window to go to Scarborough beach—a hangout for young people in Perth. They wanted to have fun, unfortunately having an immature and naïve mind and being made up to look older was a disaster waiting to happen.

A group of older boys offered them alcohol—lots of it. They were soon very drunk; Shelley described to me that they were 'out of it'. The eight boys took them to an underground car park and pack-raped them, vaginally and anally, then to finish the nightmare they urinated on them. Both girls had been virgins.

Neither of them shared their story with anyone and Shelly spiralled out of control. She said the shame and disgust made her feel physically sick, and the only way to feel better was to be drunk or stoned. She was too embarrassed to have her parents see her like that so she fled to Sydney to get as far away from the pain as possible, and life went from bad to worse.

Shelley had to prostitute herself to survive and she lived in squats and slept on the streets. She said she had been raped several more times, beaten up and used and abused by so many others that she simply lost count. The heroin was her only release and it took all her pain away—even if only for a short time.

She could not tell anyone about what had happened, especially not her parents. She was so ashamed and felt so stupid and could not face the pain it would cause her caring parents. This is how naïve young girls can be deeply wounded when they play with the fire of the dark side of the adolescent world. The saddest thing with Shelly was that her parents thought she and her friend were home under their safe care the night of the pack rape.

It's not just girls who are raped and abused. Equally, naïve boys who make dumb choices to look tough, or who run away from home, or flee conflict at school are used and abused as well.

A male friend of mine told me how he was groomed by a paedophile in a Timezone while he was wagging school. School was not working for him and he was feeling like a failure. He was sick of the physical abuse from his Catholic school, so when this older man offered work in another state and tempted him with a good job and a chance to buy his own car, he was gone. It took a few days to realise that things were not as they seemed. The first time the man raped him he remembered how stupid he felt and how he desperately wished he was back home. He felt obligated to stay because the man fed him and he had no money to escape. It wasn't until the older man offered to share him with his paedophile mates that he found the courage to run.

> *Teens will have surfed the net, talked to friends and seen or tried many things such as mutual masturbation and oral sex long before you get around to talking about sex with them, but that doesn't mean you don't have to have the conversation.*
>
> Brooks, K., *Consuming Innocence: Popular Culture and Our Children*, (2008).

Tell your adolescents about their need to have knowledge about protective behaviours and their rights. No one has the right to touch their private parts without their permission—even their parents. Teach them to learn how to trust their inner instincts by asking, 'Does this place or person feel OK in my stomach?' Warn them that there are people who are sick and want to sexually abuse children and adolescents, and frequently these abusers (around 92 per cent) are people they know.

Tell them never to keep silent about abuse and that it's never their fault.

Reassure them they can tell someone who is not family like a doctor, nurse, police officer or teacher. I recommend Holly-ann Martin and her protective behaviours seminars for adults and children. She teaches two main themes:

1. We all have the right to feel safe all of the time.
2. We can talk with someone about anything.

Adolescence is the time when young people start to explore their sexual orientation, as well as everything else sexual. Slowly they may be changing and accepting that being heterosexual is not something they simply 'choose'. Being gay is a bumpy ride on an already bumpy road to adulthood, and parents and lighthouses play an enormous role in supporting adolescents to accept and embrace their unique individuality—no matter how challenging that may be. We may save a lot of adolescent suffering if we choose to focus on supporting adolescents, rather than judging, over-controlling and changing them.

> *Homosexual teenagers are more likely to become depressed, to be victims of violence or to become homeless. It has been claimed as many as 10 per cent attempt suicide. Because of this parental support can be essential at this time, since there may not be much support coming from elsewhere.*
>
> Bainbridge, D. *Teenagers: A Natural History*, (2009).

At times, sexuality can be tricky for mature adults to work out, so it's easy to see why it can be confusing for horny adolescents. They need to know that a fulfilling sexual intimacy between two consenting post-puberty individuals is one of life's delights. They must also understand that having sex by coercion, force or with little regard for the other person is NEVER acceptable, and that blaming alcohol or drugs is pathetic and never a valid reason.

Everyone Matters

no matter what

> *Grab, grope and grunt is where the person is eager for sexual release and doesn't care how he or she gets it. You are literally grabbed, sometimes against your wishes, your genital area is touched, you are banged a few times, the 'person' comes and collapses. Bad sex is like eating cold fish and chips. Unappealing, it's tasteless with the fat solidified and sticking to your mouth leaving a yukky taste afterwards.*
>
> Hobbs, A., *Getting Real about Growing Up*, (2003).

The emptiness or sense of loss that follows poor sexual encounters can create more negative emotional pain for adolescents. Again, the emotional barometer rises with the pain of disconnection, sense of personal shame, resentment and anger and this can help adolescents reach their tipping point quicker. They can be in trouble emotionally and spiritually. Sex can be a fast track to the adolescent dark side, even though it is often driven by a profound need for intimacy and love. Adolescents who have strong positive relationships with family, friends and especially themselves are less likely to indulge in sexual encounters that are not based on love and affection. Emotional intimacy can be a healthy substitute for the physical intimacy many adolescents yearn, and it is one of the reasons why adolescents need to have people who really care as a regular part of their lives.

Some people may be offended by this next piece of information and be mindful I am not recommending this. Adolescents over 16 years of age can have very positive, loving, respectful, sexually active love lives. If these qualities are present, it can stabilise the bumpy ride because their needs for human connectedness, love and intimacy are constantly being met. It's like having an additional ally and someone to hang out with while their peers are off searching for that missing 'something'. The young relationship can fill the empty cup of loneliness. There is nothing like having someone who loves you, especially when you have zits, small boobs, can't do maths, and forget to shower and use deodorant—or all of the above!

Adolescents need lots of guidance and information they can trust to help them navigate this part of the bumpy ride. The more adults try to frighten them, lecture them or imply they are disgusting for being sexual beings, the more problems they will have. Be brave, have a one-on-one conversation with your adolescent. In the appendix to this book there is a suggested letter with possible language to use that may help you. *Please avoid telling them your disasters until after they turn 30!*

Mistakes or poor decisions based around sex can damage the deepest layers of the sensitive adolescent sense of self, and can invisibly affect their relationships with their own body and those they love forever.

Drugs and alcohol

Most young people have never tried illegal drugs, they have no interest in these substances and they never will. Study after study confirms this, yet try to get this fact reported in the media and you hit a brick wall.

Dillon, P., *Teenagers, Alcohol and Drugs: What your kids really want and need to know about alcohol and drugs*, (2009).

The best book for in-depth information about adolescents and alcohol and drugs is Paul Dillon's book, *Teenagers, Alcohol and Drugs*. Every parent of pre-teens and adolescents needs to read it. He writes that the minority of adolescents tend to be giving the rest a very bad name in terms of alcohol and drug use in Australia. This noisy, badly behaving group of adolescents is drinking heavier and earlier. Remember, if you read in the paper that one in 10 adolescents are binge drinkers, then that means that nine out of 10 aren't.

Between Year 6 and Year 8:

The proportion of students who had ever consumed alcohol increased for both boys and girls—from 39.4 per cent to 57.4 per cent for boys, and from 22.9 per cent to 48.2 per cent for girls.

ARACY-commissioned report produced by the Murdoch Children's Research Institute (2009), *Violent and antisocial behaviours among young adolescents in Australian communities: an analysis of risk and protective factors*, [online] http://www.aracy.org.au.

Research shows that the earlier adolescents start drinking, the more chances there are they will have problems with binge drinking and future health and alcohol addiction problems later in life. In Australia, the provision of alcohol to teenagers has now become a cultural problem. Parents should avoid the little tastes that were once thought to be a sensible way to show adolescents responsible drinking. Avoid getting adolescents used to the taste of alcohol— especially the sweet alco-pops, because they disguise the often bitter or sour taste of alcohol.

Early adolescence is window of sensitivity where the massive over-production of dendrites means they can learn things fast, and learning to become addicted is definitely one of those things. The 14–16-year-old brain is unable to process the sensible management of alcohol, which is possible after 16–17 years of age due to the myelination of some of the frontal lobes. The binge drinking culture is doing serious damage to the developing brain and is impeding the growth of an individual's true potential. Girls get drunker quicker than boys, and have been shown to have more neural abnormalities than boys after drinking.

> *A generation of Victorian teenagers are drinking themselves into oblivion, with more than a quarter of 15-year-olds bingeing until they black out—the point at which brain damage is likely to occur.*
>
> *Research has also found that more than a third of 11-year-old boys have consumed alcohol.*
>
> *The figures, contained in a study by the Murdoch Children's Research Institute, have alarmed brain development experts who say a generation of young people are destroying their chances of reaching their full potential.*
>
> Jennifer Sheridan, 'Booze putting teen brains at risk, *The Age*, 1 November 2009.

It is normal for adolescents to want to experiment, however binge drinking is not experimental when it becomes a daily or weekly activity. There is a very serious difference in how the adult and adolescent brain process alcohol. Adults will tend to get sleepy and tired after drinking a certain amount of alcohol, but adolescents appear less drunk and more alert after similar amounts.

The television program, *Whatever: The Science of Teens* showed this difference. In one test it showed how an adolescent boy became more 'pumped' and 'confident' the more he drank, while the adult male became more drowsy, and slower to react.

> *If teenagers are less sleepy and less wobbly they will tend to carry on drinking. Also teenagers who drink seem to experience more 'social loosening' than adults and their memory is more affected too. These two findings mean that drunk teenagers are more likely to do things they do not really want to do, and not remember it afterwards—and we know that teenage girls are more likely to experience non-consensual sex if they drink.*
>
> Bainbridge, D. Teenagers: A Natural History, (2009).

This shows why alcohol is so important to adolescents. It makes them feel socially more acceptable and confident, they can drink more and feel quite invincible, and it can wipe away those crushing feelings of insecurity, inadequacy and self-doubt. Alcohol supplies adolescents with a dopamine rush which makes them feel good and relaxed. However, over time with more and more dopamine being delivered from regular drinking the brain is fooled into believing it does not have to produce its own. This is how addictions can occur and why people need to have more alcohol to feel good. It means the individual will not have the same highs or transcendent states of joy like they did before they began binge drinking. It is a clear example of how the cycle of binge drinking can happen so easily.

> *The hippocampus shrinks with excessive drinking which limits short term memory. It is thought that one binge drinking episode can impair a teen's memory for up to 30 days.*
>
> Feinstein, S. *Parenting the Teenage Brain,* (2007).

Parental guidance from early adolescence can prevent excessive binge drinking – and it can be a challenging time of monitoring and holding boundaries. The long term consequences are certainly worth being unpopular with your adolescents for a few years.

> *Research shows that adolescents with serious addiction problems with alcohol and drugs have had more family problems before they began using. Teenage drug users often have more family problems, mental illness and psychological abnormalities than adult users and they more often use multiple addictive substances. Social stress and poor self-esteem are other factors which have been claimed to be important and perhaps crucial in teenage drug taking.*
>
> Bainbridge, D. *Teenagers: A Natural History,* (2009).

Self-medicating with alcohol and drugs to numb pain and relieve stress is common. Many teens believe they can manage their use without it becoming a problem, unfortunately they are unaware of the higher risk during the window of sensitivity in adolescence. There are many who simply stumble into an addiction because of what their friends and peers are doing. The same goes for tobacco. If they are surrounded by friends who smoke, this increases their chances of becoming addicted as well.

Drug use and alcohol misuse is linked to educational failure, impulsive violence, eating disorders and self-harm. The links to mental illness are now overwhelming. Cannabis has been shown to be particularly dangerous because it is a fat-loving substance and the layering of myelin in the developing brain is impaired as the cannabis eats it up. More use means more myelin is lost, and the final stages of brain development will be much more impaired. Cannabis slows down the brain's processing and strips motivation—which is already in short supply during adolescence! It can have a massive paralysing effect on regular cannabis users. Impaired mental processing and depression, psychotic symptoms and subsequent schizophrenia have all been linked to cannabis use. Do everything you can to paint this drug in as dangerous light as possible, especially for adolescents. Tell them if they want to experiment with cannabis wait until their brain has finished growing in their mid 20s.

What parents can do to help adolescents on their bumpy ride around alcohol and drugs

> *Research confirms the benefits of parents providing consistent rules and discipline, talking to children about drugs, monitoring their activities, getting to know their friends, understanding their problems and concerns, and being involved in their learning. The importance of the parent-child relationship continues through adolescence and beyond.*
>
> National Institute on Drug Abuse, *Preventing Drug Use Among Children and Adolescents: Research-Based Guide for Parents, Educators and Community Leaders*, (2nd ed.), [online] http://www.drugabuse.gov/drugpages/prevention.html.

Research shows that families with clear boundaries, who inform their adolescents of the facts and use negotiation styles of communication appear to be able to delay the age their child starts to drink and other experimental behaviour.

> *Maggie's Tip: Keep your 13–15-year-old adolescent as financially challenged as possible. If they have money to spend, it increases the chance of excessive use of alcohol or drugs. Otherwise they have to rely on friends and other people's generosity.*

Be as firm as possible about no alcohol before 16 years of age and explain about the higher risks because of the sensitive stages of adolescent brain development. I recommend the same for sex and parties, where it's better to encourage regular supervised sleepovers at friends' homes with lots of fun—it is possible. The later exposure is better for the following reasons:

- The brain is a bit more mature.
- The window of sensitivity has closed.
- Stronger friendships are more protective.
- It's a safe mixing environment with older individuals.
- There is less chance of being addicted.
- Adolescents can take responsibility more easily.
- Messages about what to do are kept simple and clear.

The better adolescents feel about themselves, the less likely they will adopt destructive patterns of alcohol and drug use during adolescence or adulthood. Positive family relationships, involvement in healthy pursuits like school, sport, hobbies or music are huge protective factors in an adolescent's life. If they can find dopamine from other natural sources it will reduce their yearning to get it artificially. If they feel valued, loved and know that they matter, they will make better choices around the scary things like sex and drugs.

Parent tips

- Never buy alcohol for your adolescents even when they are of legal age.
- Model responsible drinking of alcohol.
- Insist they never ride in a car with any young person who has drunk <u>any</u> alcohol—even if it was only one beer.
- Actively discourage any spirits or other alcohol in the house and keep it locked, or away from a highly visible place.
- Avoid using shock tactics to scare adolescents about the effects of alcohol and drugs—this is not necessary.
- Never use shame if there is an incident about inappropriate use of alcohol or drugs.
- Remind them to watch out for their friends.
- Be careful of drink spiking—never leave a glass unattended, taste anyone else's drink or accept a drink from anyone.
- Reassure your adolescent that you can be called if ever they are worried, frightened, drunk or hurt—no matter what.
- Reassure them that having them alive and safe is your number one priority—no matter what.

Adolescents are more receptive to important information if it's given in the context of respect and caring, and usually when it's more about their friends than themselves. Paul Dillon says that overwhelmingly, adolescents want to look after their friends and so the message parents need to reinforce is: 'Be careful, and if something goes wrong here is what you need to know to help your friends'.

How to help friends who have drunk too much

1. Never ever leave them alone—stay with them.
2. Keep checking on them—are they getting worse?
3. Reassure your friend.
4. Keep them out of harm's way and comfortable.
5. Keep them hydrated with water—avoid force-feeding them water as this is dangerous.
6. Giving them coffee will not sober them up.
7. Putting under a cold shower in a bathroom could be more hazardous that just throwing a bucket of cold water on them—neither action will reverse the effects of being very drunk.
8. Never feed them bread or any food.
9. If in <u>any</u> doubt call for help.
10. If you need to call an ambulance, work out the exact address and nearest cross street before you call.
11. Better to be safe than sorry.

> *Alcohol is a powerful depressant and can cause death directly by 'turning off' the brain areas that control consciousness, respiration and heart rate, resulting in unconsciousness, coma and death.*
>
> Dillon, P., Teenagers, *Alcohol and Drugs: What your kids really want and need to know about alcohol and drugs*, (2009).

The reason you vomit when you get drunk is because you have poisoned yourself and your body is trying to rid itself of any remaining poison in the system. Encouraging a friend to vomit can help reduce the level of poison in their system, but vomiting for long periods of time can be a clear sign something's not right and medical help is a good idea.

Never leave adolescents to sleep off being drunk. They can roll over on their back and drown in their own vomit or simply have a complete shut down and die. Always keep monitoring them or get them home and have their parents take care of them. NEVER LEAVE THEM ALONE.

Other drug use and misuse

Parents need to monitor adolescent behaviour and be mindful of any changes, because they can be an indicator of drug or alcohol misuse—but not always. Be careful to avoid accusing adolescents because this is a fast way to ruin a healthy relationship with them.

Warning signs and symptoms of drug use/misuse may include:

- Decline in schoolwork or after school sporting activities.
- Changes in attendance and being unwilling to take part in school or other group activities.
- Unusual outbreaks of temper, mood swings, restlessness or irritability.
- More time being spent away from home, possibly with new friends or with friends in older age groups.
- Excessive spending or borrowing of money.
- Stealing money or goods.
- Excessive tiredness without obvious cause.
- No interest in physical appearance.
- Sores or rashes—especially on the mouth or nose.
- Lack of appetite.
- Bloodshot eyes.
- Wearing sunglasses at inappropriate times—usually to hide dilated or constricted pupils.
- Use of drug-takers slang.
- Being the subject of rumours about drug taking.
- Having friends who use drugs.

http://www.laneworksafe.com.au

Many of the above mentioned signs and symptoms can also be signs of normal adolescent behaviour. They can all be result of something other than drug use. If there is a combination of symptoms, maybe start by asking other family members or friends if they have noticed any changes. Other things to be aware of about drug use with adolescents:

- The same drug can produce different effects in different people.
- The same drug can produce different effects in the same person at different times.
- The 'signs' of drug use may be nothing more than an unconfirmed rumour and your worst imagination.

> *No matter how much you prepare yourself for the day that you discover your child has used an illegal drug, the impact is still devastating. So many thoughts are likely to go through your head but inevitably the fear of progression to other drugs is one of the greatest fears that parents have.*
>
> Dillon, P., Teenagers, *Alcohol and Drugs: What your kids really want and need to know about alcohol and drugs*, (2009).

Many parents mistakenly believe that by the time their children reach 20 years of age they are safe from illicit drug use. This is a common mistake because of the illusion they only have to worry during the teenage years.

> *I never have the heart to tell them that if their children are ever likely to experiment will illicit drugs it is most likely to be in their twenties, after they have left home and not in their teens.*
>
> Dillon, P., Teenagers, *Alcohol and Drugs: What your kids really want and need to know about alcohol and drugs*, (2009).

Any drug can have lethal or dangerous consequences, whether it's taken at dangerous levels or quite innocently. The nature of the risk is partly what drives an adolescent's need to take drugs, illegal or otherwise. Smoking cigarettes has a huge price which costs our health system an enormous amount of money and many lives. Just because it's legal does not mean it is a lesser evil.

> *Tobacco is deceptively harmful. If you start smoking at an early age it can inhibit physical growth. It also causes damage to the brain, the respiratory system, the lungs and other vital organs in the body. One result of smoking is cancer.*
>
> Hobbs, A. *Getting Real about Growing Up*, (2003).

Be informed about the effects of drugs and have a conversation with your children well before adolescence about the 'not negotiable' boundary around alcohol and drugs. To monitor this boundary you need to be present in their lives. Avoid the rumours and the urban myths about alcohol and drugs and download the latest information from *government* web sites and talk about it. The risk of a parent not doing this is they will learn about it from other adolescents—and they do not always have the correct information! I recommend every parent reads Paul Dillon's book to get an accurate picture of the scene.

Rock 'n' Roll and the Party Scene

From the age of 13 adolescents want to have fun in groups. They want to hang out and usually want loud music, and that's how it has been for years. When communities have nowhere for adolescents to party, they are creating a pattern of high risk for their adolescents. Instead of having a safe place to socialise, they will find another party, often one without adult supervision, and that's where trouble can happen. They may end up at parties with much older unsupervised adolescents who can take advantage of younger teens, or worse still, adult parties where the same can happen.

Alcohol-free events help adolescents learn they can have fun without being drunk, and if they're held regularly, there's a good chance the adolescents in that community will feel valued and that their needs matter. This often means they will respect their community, and there will be less vandalism and violence towards community members. Drop-in centres and recreation centres where adolescents can play pool, watch DVDs and hang out should be a compulsory part of a community. When a centre like this has a skate park or basketball court nearby, there is a gathering point that can be loosely supervised by community members.

Boredom is a potential disaster for adolescents because that's when they start hunting dopamine. If it's not available in a healthy way then they are biologically wired to find it in another risk-taking way—drinking, drugs, sex and violence, or the Internet.

CyberSpace, Cyberia and The Internet

Many parents of today's adolescents are walking in uncharted territory on a whole new invisible world that has both wonderful and dangerous components to it. How can you protect your adolescent from something that changes and evolves almost daily that you cannot see? The massive amount of time adolescents are spending online is reshaping their brains in ways we can only guess.

> *On the one hand it has been described as 'Cyberia', a virtual wasteland that young people navigate without rules or regulations: a catalyst for bullying, suicide and anti-social behaviour including Internet addiction. On the other it has been touted as a new community with the potential to prevent mental health difficulties like depression and anxiety, an online setting with potential to connect those experiencing isolation and marginalisation—Cytopia*
>
> Burns, J. *Young People and Technology: Cyberia or Cytopia?*, (2009).

Two of the main drivers of adolescence are the need to belong, and the push towards independence and autonomy—the Internet gives teens both. If we add the hunt for dopamine into the mix we really understand why adolescents are hungry for more time online. Adolescents can now stay wired and plugged in almost 24/7 through mobile phones and mp3 players.

Video games, especially violent ones, require reflexive reactions not reflective responses. This means that the games tend to stimulate the amygdala and neutralise the pre-frontal lobe, which can delay the healthy development of the adult brain. This means that logical, reasonable thinking can be impaired, while fast, reactive thinking is stimulated. This can play out quite clearly in an adolescent's life:

> *Instead of carefully deciding that they should get all of their equipment ready for band and leave for practice with an appropriate amount of time to park and get inside teens find themselves shopping at the mall until ten minutes before band rehearsal, driving like a maniac through the traffic; and then get surprised when they get an expensive speeding ticket.*
>
> Feinstein, S. *Parenting the Teenage Brain*, (2007).

Violent games also trigger testosterone into the system which further agitates the over-worked amygdala. There are some who commend the use of video games because it speeds up hand-eye coordination and improves concentration. Scientists have since found that the only part of the brain that is being stimulated are the parts associated with vision and movement, and the only positive benefits that gives them is the ability to play video games well. The parts of the brain associated with learning, memory and emotion remain under developed.

> *Every time a child goes online they run the risk of viewing material that is unsuitable, frightening, distasteful or illegal. Most parents are aware of the online prevalence of pornography, but children may also come across material that is intolerably violent, gory, hate-filled, prejudiced, propagandist or inflammatory.*
>
> Carr-Gregg, M., *Real Wired Child: What parents need to know about kids online*, (2007).

Adolescents have difficulty managing impulses, making accurate decisions, being mindful of other people's feelings and keeping healthy boundaries, and these levels of emotional illiteracy wreak havoc online. Another area of concern is what adolescents are *not* fitting into their world due to the arrival of the Internet—what *was* filling their lives before going online? Adolescents believe they are more connected, but I argue that it is shallower communication and the perception of having lots of friends is an illusion. Parents must be informed about what information they need to allow adolescents and younger children stay safe online.

12 steps to keep kids and adolescents safe while using the Internet

1. ABSOLUTELY NO PERSONAL DETAILS TO BE REVEALED.
2. Create anonymous usernames that are impossible to trace.
3. Strictly limit time online—it can easily become addictive and a huge distraction in your lives. AVOID bad habits from forming!
4. NEVER give passwords to anyone, (except your parents) even your best friend!
5. NO meeting people you meet online—even if you have become 'friends!'
6. Be prepared to hit delete often! No cyber-bully can have power if the message is deleted BEFORE it's read in its entirety.
7. Tell trustworthy adults of any cyber-bullying immediately.
8. NEVER download free stuff because it often comes with nasty spyware that corrupts your computer and your security system.
9. Google searches are NOT research! Many sites are completely fabricated. Don't trust everything you read online and question everything you read.
10. Warn your friends of the dangers in case their parents have not warned them.
11. It's better to stay connected via mobile because you can do that anywhere, not just indoors. It's harder to get distracted for hours. Be careful—there is little filter protection for mobiles that can access the Internet.
12. Online games can be highly addictive—especially those that need you to become a character. AVOID those that reward killing.

Michael Carr-Gregg, *Real Wired Child: What parents need to know about kids online.*(Printed with permission)

I would add the suggestion that no computers or laptops with access to the Internet should ever be in kids' or adolescents' bedrooms. Keep them in a family friendly area where they can be supervised—and breeze by from time to time.

Once they disappear into their bedroom it is very hard to monitor and homework wars will take on a whole new dimension. I would get into habit of having a 'mobile bucket' after dinner where kids' mobiles have a little rest so that study can get done without distractions. (Make sure they are on silent too or the constant beeping will drive you mad!)

Norman Doidge MD writes of the massive plasticity of the human brain, especially during early childhood and adolescence. He describes a significant study with over 2,600 children that showed early exposure to television between the ages of one and three correlates with problems of paying attention and controlling impulses later in childhood. This is because the brain changes itself in response to the environmental influences (2007). The same is happening to our wired-up, plugged-in adolescents. The constant bombardment of the visually rapid changes of images like cuts, edits, zooms, pans and sudden noises, alters the brain over time to be acutely sensitive to such high-speed transitions.

> *No wonder people report feeling drained from watching TV. Yet we acquire a taste for it and find slower changes boring. The cost is that such activities like reading, complex conversation and listening to lectures become more difficult [....] All electronic devices rewire the brain.*
>
> Doidge, N. MD. *The Brain that Changes Itself,* (2007).

Multitasking may appear to be a positive thing for our wired-up adolescents, but that is not what research is showing. They are finding that the brain is simply going through the motions at a more superficial level, and that deep cognitive and creating abilities are being impaired. We must keep a balance in an adolescent's life so that they may realise their full potential.

While there are warnings about the possible negative effects of the modern preoccupation with electronics, there are some programs that are helpful, exciting and innovative. Check out the Fast Forward program and what it has been achieving in terms of rewiring the brain using a specific program of mass stimulation. Dr Jane Burns from the Orygen Institute argues that interactive websites around mental health are improving the lives of many young depression sufferers because they can connect and get information and support from the anonymity of their own bedroom. The test on Lyn Worsley's Resilience Doughnut website is another example of helpful IT material that can help adolescents better understand themselves and our world. Some 'serious' games created to improve conditions such as obesity, diabetes and asthma that have also been shown to be successful.

Any game that uses rewards of any kind can become addictive, and the greatest threat is still the violent games where adolescents are rewarded for senseless violence—monitor these carefully.

Anecdotal evidence suggests that older adolescents are moving away from the Internet, especially social networking sites, in favour of real human connection and experiences. Many are cancelling their Facebook pages and are choosing to meet face-to-face to hang out together. This is a sign that shows the final growth of the pre-frontal lobes is happening, and the shallow virtual world does not meet the needs of real human relationships.

Adolescents absolutely benefit from having healthy parental and adult guidance during their bumpy ride to adulthood, and it's an area where tough rules and guidelines are essential. Relax about their bedrooms, the unwashed clothes, their mumblings and forgetfulness around the chores and stay tough and firm on the rules around sex, drugs, alcohol and rock'n'roll.

Many adolescents tell me that they fight about the rules, but they also know they exist because their parents care. Many admitted that they wished they had boundaries, but their parents had not bothered or cared enough. Remind adolescents that you are doing this to keep them safe and that when their pre-frontal lobe finally grows they will be set free.

No one is ever completely safe in our modern world. The ability to take better risks should increase with age, but we know this doesn't always happen, and accidents can also happen to any mature adult.

The main message is that many of the problems that happen around sex, drugs and rock'n'roll occur more often and sooner to adolescents who feel unsupported, struggle with challenging home and school environments, and feel stressed and overwhelmed with their bumpy ride to adulthood. They tend to have a low self-concept and will seek external means to build it up. With more support from parents, family, friends and lighthouses there could be less pain and suffering—and maybe less fatalities.

Finally, the best prevention for abuse in any of the areas of sex, drugs, alcohol and partying is by consciously building social and emotional competence in our children through positive parenting at a community level. To develop a sense of positive identity and character that is based on the values of respect, trust and a sense of purpose is the best way to turn a drunken culture on its head. We may very well keep more young people alive, un-maimed and unscarred.

Adolescence Unplugged

Human Needs

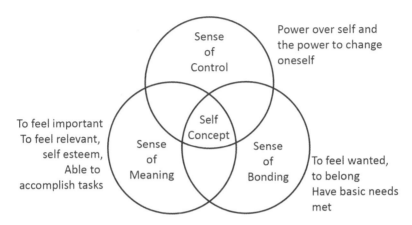

Nancy Phillips 'Wellness During Adolescent Development' July 1990

Key Points:

- Positive parental influence with clear, certain boundaries around sex, alcohol, drugs and other risky behaviour definitely helps adolescents stay chaste and safe longer.

- The best support parents and lighthouses can give is the preventative sort.

- Parents must talk to kids about sex and help negotiate the mixed messages of the media and society.

- Discourage *any* experimentation with consumption of alcohol or sexual activity until adolescents are 16, when they are better able to navigate the challenges alcohol and sex present.

- Emphasise that NO MATTER WHAT, your adolescents can talk to someone, and hopefully you.

- Talk to your adolescents and their friends about how to look after each other when they are out, particularly if alcohol and drugs are in the mix.

- Provide safe spaces for your adolescent to gather with his or her friends and be prepared to have some loud music some of the time.

- Establish firm guidelines around cyberspace and mobile usage.

- Parents must model responsible drinking if they hope to teach their adolescents to be responsible.

Chapter 14

How *to build* Optimistic adolescents *who* thrive *(most of the time)*

If we consider that adolescents can be measured along a continuum from optimistic and thriving at one end to dis-engaged and delinquent at the other, then we need to view the characteristics of disengagement in order to better appreciate the preferred reality.

> *Despite the different approaches to studying the experience of youth, the evidence on the impact of disengagement and exclusion is clear: young people who are disengaged or excluded from their peers, schools, families and communities experience poorer health and mental health. They are at increased risk of long term unemployment, chronic alcohol and drug use, homelessness, mental illness and suicide. The subsequent social, health and mental health problems experienced by young people who are disengaged or excluded impact significantly on the broader community including increased health, justice and welfare system expenditure, lower social cohesion and loss of economic productivity.*
>
> Preventing Youth Disengagement and Promoting Engagement, Australian Research Alliance for Children & Youth, (2008).

Delinquency occurs when there is a crime committed like truancy, alcohol or drug possession, theft of property or possession of illegal weapons. There are many studies that indicate a strong link between delinquency and maltreatment as a child, but a significant study by Stewart, Dennison and Waterson (2002) found that maltreatment during adolescence was a much more accurate indicator.

> *[...] peer pressure. Associating with a circle of friends who exhibit delinquent behaviours and perform delinquent acts increases the risk of non-conformity to social norms as well as deviant and delinquent behaviours.*
>
> Bahr, N. et al *The Millennial Adolescent* (2008)

School failure is another contributing factor towards delinquency. Truancy is considered a way of dealing with school failure and the feelings of worthlessness and alienation that can occur with repeated failure. During the brain pruning window 12-15 adolescents are particularly vulnerable as many feel confused, less competent and are often disengaged in the classroom!

> *Reducing disengagement and promoting engagement is important for young people now and in the future. Young people who feel engaged and who are provided with opportunities to participate will experience a better quality of life and contribute to creating and building better communities. In the long term, young people who are valued and feel connected have better health and mental health as adults.*
>
> Australian Research Alliance for Children & Youth, (2008).

Every adolescent will make a dumb decision at some point during their bumpy ride to adulthood—sometimes the mistake will be serious. Here are five steps that can help parents support their adolescent overcome a negative experience and help them recognize:

1. It was not an OK thing to do—ownership of poor choice.
2. They are sorry it happened—apologise to all who have been hurt.
3. Repair the wrong and make it right—restitution and restoration.
4. Forgiveness—for self and others.
5. Acknowledge the valuable learning experience—growth and awareness.

And leave it at that. This must be the end of that story and adults must let it go because unfinished business from adolescence can cause emotional angst for the rest of a person's life. If you help adolescents 'learn' from their experiences you will be giving them a big gift. This helps them to avoid becoming 'victims' and supports them to develop a resilient mind set.

The role of significant adults—family and non-family—is vital. Lighthouses are critical because they offer support to reduce the crippling effects of alienation and disconnectedness. The basics adolescents need to be healthy are:

- Loving human connectedness.
- Good nutrition.
- Plenty of sleep.
- Meaningful involvement and physical activity.

- Laughter and lightness
- Deep connectedness with nature

What else you can do to help adolescents manage their chaotic ride to adulthood?

You can start by helping adolescents with how they see the themselves, others and the world.

In our achievement driven world we must be careful that adolescents don't come to believe that they are only worthwhile when they reach clear goals like passing exams or reaching a parental expectation. This can set up thinking that can lead them to having problems later in life.

Rather have them accept:

- Everyone matters
- Your true value and worth is never attached to your goals
- Everyone is contributing to how others grow and learn
- Growing and learning is what life is about, especially the unexpected
- We can *never* control our lives however we can guide our life

There is no such thing as:

1. The wrong way to go in life – so avoid having regrets
2. You have missed something – again have no regrets
3. You should've, could've – that means you are judging, rather than accepting that where you are is perfect for now.
4. You have no worth or value – everyone has value

Acknowledgement to Greg Neville, Melbourne

These last four patterns of thinking can help create the type of mental foundation that supports depression. Think carefully about someone you know who has depression, and see if any of the above thought patterns is present.

Parents can help an adolescent's mind follow more optimistic pathways when they struggle with their world. Here are two simple formulae to help them learn that they can influence the outcomes of an event or experience by changing their response.

Even adults frighten themselves with their imagination at times and so we all need to remember this simple anagram: FEAR.

Fantasized

Experience

Appearing

Real

Complete this statement when you are afraid of anything, especially change: 'I am afraid to.............'

Now change the statement to: 'I would really like to ....and I scare myself by imagining ....'

Use your imagination to grow, not to limit yourself.

The second tip is: E + R = O. It is the **E**vent plus my **R**esponse that creates the **O**utcome.

Ask yourself:

'What am I doing to deal with this situation or change it in a productive manner?'

Take for example someone saying something inappropriate to an adolescent. The adolescent can choose to think 'that is their stuff – and their problem!' and ignore the comment. Or they can choose to agree with the comment and then allow themself to feel hurt or wounded. There is always a choice to be made.

No one can MAKE you feel anything without your agreement.

Think about ways you can respond to a challenging moment rather than the ways that others are not responding to your needs. We need to teach our adolescents that they are the ones controlling their own thoughts and feelings, not others.

Have you heard of the story of two boys at Christmas, an optimist and a pessimist? When they looked under the Christmas tree to see what Santa had left they found a big pile of pony poo. The pessimist was very unhappy and was thinking how bad is that; just getting pony poo for Christmas! The optimist was running around very excited happily searching everywhere. His brother asked him what he was doing. The optimist replied, 'By the size of that pile of poo there must be a pony hiding here somewhere.'

Dr Martin E. P. Seligman in his book, *The Optimistic Child: A Proven Program to Safeguard Children Against Depression and Build Lifelong Resilience* (2007) explains that optimism is not just positive thinking, it's more about the way you think about *causes.*

There are three main dimensions that individuals use to explain any good or bad event that happens to them: permanence, pervasiveness and personalisation.

Permanence

Individuals who are more at risk of depression and disengagement often believe the causes of bad events that happen are permanent. What they say is not always the reality:

- 'It always happens to me that I get picked last.'
  (Occasionally I get picked last)

- 'Everyone hates me and no one will ever want to be my friend.'
  (It takes time to make good friends and I need to be a good friend to myself first.)
- 'My mum is the moodiest mum in the entire world.'
  (My mum is in a bad mood today.)

If your adolescent tends to think of things like 'always' or 'never' that can be a sign that they have adopted a pessimistic style of viewing the world, or adolescence has given them a temporary pair of dark glasses.

It's funny, yet sad, that when good things happen the optimist will believe the causes are permanent and the pessimist will believe the causes are temporary. Remember they have 'wired' themselves to this way of viewing the world and the pessimist, or the adolescent with dark glasses, will see that bad events are their fault because of some deep abiding flaw in their personality.

Our thoughts not only create our own version of reality and our map of the world, they create our emotions as well. When adolescents keep running a story that simply is not true, they keep triggering their own misery. We can help them by pausing their thinking with questions, it interrupts their mind from looping a familiar negative story. Try asking:

- 'Is that really true?'
- 'How do you know that is true?'

When I am working with adolescents with negative maladaptive thinking loops, I teach them a technique how to cancel negative words and thoughts, and also give their parents' permission to spot negative words. This works best when adolescents can do the same for their parents and if it's done in a lighthearted way. It can be an excellent way to interrupt the negative pattern for everyone. If an adolescent comes home from school complaining that they have had the worst day of their life, we ask, 'How do you know that is true?' Or we say, 'Cancel, Cancel!', and then maybe acknowledge, 'Today was a little bit bad.' When we add quantative measures like 'a little', 'a bit' or 'a tad' and limit it to just one day, the unconscious mind downplays the emotional intensity that follows the statement.

This is why I suggest that we use the term 'Now that's interesting!' instead of 'Oh My God!' when anything goes wrong. The words are less explosive as a message to the nervous system and less cortisol and adrenalin will be released into the blood steam, which means we can behave in a calmer manner. If an adolescent reverses the car over their $500 bicycle, or into the letterbox just say, 'Now that's interesting!' You will definitely help your adolescent and yourself avoid a complete melt down. And then say *'and what do you think you can learn from this event?'*

There are two other fun and powerful ways of interrupting these thinking patterns. The first is called Provocative Energy Therapy (PET) and is taught by Dr

John Lake and psychologist Steve Wells. This involves the adolescent tapping on the acupressure points that release emotions (see Appendix 2) at the same time as provoking their negative thoughts. This only works with adolescents who have a have a sense of humour and who are keen to try something quite weird.

The second is a state interruption technique that involves adolescents stepping into three different places on the floor connecting to different states: negative, neutral and a highly suggestive pleasant state. After just a few rotations, the pattern collapses and they are unable to run their old story and its accompanying feelings.

We can also teach adolescents easy ways to break their negative thinking patterns by using a trigger, or circuit breaker. This can be a phrase, a word or even a physical gesture.

Circuit breakers for negative self-talk

- I am enough exactly as I am.
- I am, I can, I will.
- Everybody matters—no matter what.
- I am so much more than this experience.
- Stretching my comfort zone will make me grow stronger.
- I can deal positively with anything that happens in my life.
- No matter what happens I am still a worthwhile person.
- I matter in this world.
- I make a positive difference every day.
- Cancel, cancel. cancel

Pervasiveness

The second dimension that individuals use to explain the good and bad events of their life is pervasiveness. If you believe a cause is pervasive, you tend to project its effect across many different situations in your life.

If an adolescent failed an essay they may think thoughts like, 'I'm useless and dumb', 'I am crap at everything', 'Nothing ever goes right for me', and 'I will always end up doing badly anyway.' This is the pattern of the 'catastrophiser'.

A more optimistic adolescent will still feel bad when they fail an essay and yet come to the conclusion that it was just the essay on the day that failed, not every thing else in their life—or maybe they needed to spend more time on the next essay.

Some children can put their troubles neatly into a box and go about their lives even when one important part crumbles. Others catastrophise. When one thread in their life snaps, the whole fabric unravels.

Seligman, M. E. P.

Personal

The third dimension is the 'personal' where individuals decide 'Who is at fault?' When bad things happen individuals can blame themselves (internal) or they can blame other people or circumstances (external).

Adolescents are brilliant at blaming others for things that go wrong especially siblings and parents! Accepting responsibility for your own choices and actions is the sign of an emotionally mature person, which is something adolescents are still working on achieving. Too much of either way of thinking is unhealthy— always blaming the self, or always blaming others.

> *Depressed children and adults are forever blaming themselves and feeling guilty over things that are not at all their fault, and being a self blamer increases a child's chances for depression.*
>
> Seligman, M. E. P. The Optimistic Child

Parents need to be mindful when using an explanatory style of communication with children, particularly adolescents, that it avoids doing the permanent, the pervasive and personal.

10 tips when correcting your adolescent's behaviour to help avoid developing pessimistic thinking

1. Be accurate with blame—guide them to decide where their blame lies, if there is any.
2. Use optimistic explanatory style—avoid any hint of permanent (always, never) and stick *to just one incident, on one day.*
3. Avoid any criticism that hints they are flawed in other ways—avoid global statements like, 'All teachers are bad', 'Alcohol sucks' or 'Every time you come home you leave your stuff everywhere'; stick to specifics like, 'Mr Jones can be unreasonable', or 'You enjoy parts of school', or 'Sometimes I get annoyed when you find it hard to take your things to your room and you leave them on the kitchen floor.'
4. Their thinking patterns are seeking further validation—avoid minimalising their communication.
5. Avoid adding to their catastrophising, making fun of their view of the world or correcting how they see the world—just interrupt their story with as much love as possible.
6. Avoid making judgements on events and happenings—things are not necessarily good or bad, they just 'are.'; this is when we place a judgement on an event and our thoughts then create a perception that then creates emotions; remember, 'This too will pass...'
7. Learn to say sorry when there has been a genuine error on an individual's part—model this as adults.

8. Avoid using non literal words like 'don't'—consider the effect when someone says, 'Don't think of a blue elephant.'
9. Conclude any communication with your adolescent with the question, 'What can you learn from what this experience?'
10. Reassure them that no matter what, you will love them—the good, the bad and the ugly.

It is helpful to guide both children and adolescents to focus on what they can learn from each happening or experience, rather than waste time judging it. If someone is mean to them, they can learn how that feels and so they can learn to be more empathetic and understanding. Also focus more on what you want, rather than what you don't want!

> ..... *teens need to know that they can rely on their parents when the going gets rough. They are naturally drawn to risky behaviour and are unable to make good decisions, so you are guaranteed they will need a safety net at some point.*
>
> Feinstein, S *Parenting The Teenage Brain*, (2007)

If you are concerned about an adolescent who has strong pessimistic tendencies I suggest you get Martin Seligman's book *The Optimistic Child* because he explores indepth ways to help change the automatic choices they make with their thoughts. There is also a test you may give your child or adolescent to see how they rank[1]*.

Dr Seligman describes four skills that are helpful in building optimism:

1. Thought catching—being mindful of the thoughts that flit across your mind.
2. Evaluating—acknowledging that the things you say to yourself are not necessarily accurate.
3. Generating more accurate explanations—easier said than done, especially for adolescents.
4. Decatastrophising—the art of taming the terror our imaginations can create.

When I was teaching I often began the year teaching my students some thinking strategies from Edward de Bono. I found that they helped adolescents manage their own thoughts, as well as help them write better essays.

The first technique was the simple PMI process where students were given some issue to ponder and they needed to write down the pluses, minuses and the things that didn't fit in either of those boxes but were still interesting. If an adolescent is in a highly charged emotional state they are unable to access their

---

1   * You need to have a very positive relationship with your adolescent for this to be accepted in the spirit for which it's intended.

thinking skills because they have been hijacked by their lower brain. Given time and a place to calm down, they can do this process to better resolve any conflict.

The second process that helped to build empathy was the OPV, which means Other People's Viewpoint. This stretched their ability to see their story not quite so accurately and often gave them fresh insights that they found quite surprising. In neuro-linguistic programming, being able to shift perspective while in a trance or deeply relaxed state can be an incredibly powerful way of moving blocked emotional pain.

Before explaining how we can influence our adolescents by using unusual techniques and sentence styles, remember that you can use your toilet to be more than just a potential laughter centre with funny books.

Georgi Lozanov was considered the father of 'suggestopedia' and he found that the unconscious mind processes information without us being aware of it. Those of you who slip into a trance on a long trip that is familiar to you may have had the experience where you couldn't remember driving through a town that's on the route. The unconscious competency mechanism of the brain has simply taken over.

There are some fascinating studies out now that show how that our brain can do preconscious processing. This means that we are already observing and learning before we think we are. One of the key ways of doing this is through our peripheral vision. Our unconscious can absorb every word from signs and posters and also the sense of meaning without you being aware. With repetition the mind will retain the message.

Therefore, my suggestion in the family toilet is to hang inspirational posters filled with values and messages that show how to be loving, caring human beings. My favourite posters are the Native American Commandments, How to Love a Child, Life's Little Instructions, The Serenity Prayer, The Desiderata and Footprints. Over time these positive messages are absorbed by those who frequent the toilet. One of my sons suggested one day that he thought it was time to change the posters because he could recite the entire 10 Native American Commandments without looking—and he proceeded to do so!

Milton Erikson was an experimental and clinical hypnotist whose work in the Sixties set much of the groundwork for neuro-linguistic programming when it was initially explored by Richard Bandler and John Grinder. Erikson found that people move in and out of trances all the time and that you did not need to have people in a formally induced trance to be open to the power of suggestion. The unconscious mind responds to symbols, metaphors, stories and directives that come from subtle suggestions, or by distracting the conscious mind by making it bored, confused or distracted.

Essentially, he aimed at creating change though suggestions made to the unconscious. The tips I have already given to help allow adolescents to become more optimistic have some implicit messages for the unconscious mind.

Erickson emphasised the futility of trying to change behaviour by telling or advising people how to behave. Instead his strategy was to influence his patients through indirect suggestion so that they freely chose to change, often without any awareness that they had been influenced.

Neville, B., *Educating Psyche: Emotion, Imagination and the Unconscious in Learning*, (1989).

This explains why the well intentioned lecture or constructive criticism that parents give their adolescents is mainly a waste of time for both parties. The more you challenge an adolescent's belief that they are useless, or damaged and how they should behave, the more you may be strengthening the unhelpful behaviour. Let's start with the subtle art of embedded commands.

Embedded Commands

This is a technique that many excellent teachers and some parents do without noticing. They are commands that the unconscious mind follows because it has been distracted by non-literal language. It is easy to mark such commands using tonality, by lowering your voice for the command, or by pausing in your communication before of after the command. Aim to say at least three to five commands over a day or two in an unremarkable tone, and get competent at the pause. The unconscious pays attention to what's different and is more attentive when the conscious is bored or distracted. Because an adolescent is biologically driven to create autonomy and independence, they unconsciously must resist anything that challenges that, and being told what to do is a call to resist.

> *Maggie's Tip: When parents ask respectfully, while allowing adolescents a time frame with which they can choose the when, it will increase the chances of getting things done.*

For example, to help overcome reluctance at doing English assignment try saying the following:

- How surprised would I be Johnny to know that **you had completed your English assignment early?**
- I am curious to know how you would feel Johnny if **you completed your English assignment early** for the first time ever?
- Wouldn't it be wonderful Johnny if you could feel excited when **you completed your English assignment early?**

To improve their organisational skills for getting homework started earlier before playing games online, try saying:

- I was wondering if you would know how it felt to **get your homework done before you played games on your PC?**

- Is there absolutely no reason why you couldn't **get your homework done before you played games on your PC?**
- How surprised would I be to see you **get your homework done before you played games on your PC?**

To get adolescents to help with chores without being nagged, try saying:
- I am quite curious to know how it may be to live in a place where **you would willingly do your chores without being asked.**
- Given that today is just another day and life goes on, maybe **you would willingly do your chores without being asked?**
- How surprised and delighted would I be when **you would willingly do your chores without being asked?**

Some non-literal headings to include at the beginning of your embedded command can include:
- I was wondering…
- How surprised will I/you be when…
- I'm curious to know…
- I wouldn't try to suggest to you…
- I wouldn't pressure myself to…
- Have I /you realised that…
- Given that today is another day…
- In the event that there is no reason why…
- It would be a joke…

Embedded suggestions are helpful, especially ones that use images rather than indepth wordy descriptions. Try the following:
- I need us to work as a team so that so that we help each other, and no one is alone unless they are on the bench taking a rest.
- School is just a part of the journey of life, and becoming a decent person matters more to your mother and I than getting the prize in Biology.
- You are all gifts to your mother and I/we value the privilege we have been gifted with.
- The bumpy ride to adulthood is a part of life's bigger picture and we want you to ride into the rest of your life happy to be yourself.
- Our home is a harbour for when it's windy and wild out in the real world, you will always be safe here.

Another possible way of influencing resistant adolescents is directing by suggestion. Try the following phrases:
- You don't need to talk now (instead of 'Be quiet!').
- You don't have to move (instead of 'Be still!').
- You can get the dishwasher unpacked (instead of 'Unpack the dishwasher!').
- You may not understand what I am suggesting first up (implies that you will understand later).

- You may not want to listen to what I am saying now (implies that they will listen later).
- I don't know when you will be more focused on your school work (implies that that they will be more focused at some point).

Here is a technique of giving multiple tasks that makes the conscious mind drop attention and allow the unconscious to follow, even though sometimes reluctantly:

- David, when you've finished feeding the dog will you come over here and help me for a minute get dessert ready?
- Karen, when you've finished talking to Sarah on your mobile can you come down stairs and help me sort out some clothes to give away?
- I guess you are not interested in taking the bin out before you feed the dog and eat the banana split I just made you?

Erickson also used the bind, or the double bind, technique to great effect. The bind gives someone an illusion of choice between comparable alternatives. Examples include:

- Do you want to go to bed now or after this program?
- Do you want to get your laundry now or after dinner or do you need me to help you?
- Do you want to do this the easy way or the hard way?
- Which of your chores do you want to do first?

The double bind gives the rational mind no way out even with reflection, it just causes more confusion. It was very helpful in inducing a trance in resistant people like adolescents. Examples include:

- Would you like to have your hands on your thigh or by your side as you wait to hear what I am saying next?
- If your unconscious is ready to go into a trance your left hand will rise. If not, your right hand will rise.

Erickson's technique may simply be more effective than persuasion, command or mindless violence. Perhaps it's like a bit of reverse psychology, such as:

- I want you to keep banging your head on the desk until I tell you to stop.
- I'd like you to keep doing that until you start to feel silly.
- As a response to abusive language, from now on I insist that you call me a %#&@$$ every time you talk to me.
- You will probably learn how to do this in spite of yourself.
- Try very hard not to remember what I am about to say to you.

Neville, B. *Educating The Psyche* (2005)

The ability to build rapport with the adolescent and the underlying intention of the parent or adult determines the success of these techniques. We must acknowledge that an adolescent's view of the world which is creating the resistance and hostility is totally valid to them.

Giving Feedback to Adolescents

There is an art to giving feedback to adolescents that allows them to embrace feedback enthusiastically and avoid being crippled emotionally. The adolescent psyche is so sensitive to criticism that often the amygdala sets up an emotional hijacking so quickly that they freeze their auditory channel and they never hear a word of anything that sounds like criticism. We need to be able to give them feedback at times to help them grow in their ability to make better choices and to overcome failure or less than optimal results.

A study was done that showed that when a teacher began a debrief with a class with 'what went wrong' it rarely saw student outcomes improve on a similar assessment. However, if the teacher began with the words, 'I am really pleased to say that the assessment was done well (even if some did poorly), and if you want to get a higher mark next time you need to do these three things' and proceeded to give them three tips that would improve the grades. Something wonderful happened form this; the results of the next assessment were higher for everyone, especially those who had done poorly.

If you check that statement, you will notice it has an embedded command and an indirect suggestion that the unconscious was able to hear because their system was not in emotional hijack mode. The non-literal beginning of the sentence zoned out the conscious mind, and the suggestion went straight to home base.

Parents can do the same. Here are some examples:
- John I have been observing you lately and I have noticed that you are making an effort to improve your school grades. You still need to focus on using your time more efficiently at night, and bring your homework diary home more often. However, it's a terrific turn around and I am really happy for you to see this change. Well done.
- Karen, things have been moving along really well lately and you know that you are a strong willed young lady with lots of energy and drive. At times this can appear to others to be pushy and bossy and I need you to keep this in mind when you are with your friends because they really value your friendship and I know how special they are to you.
- Billy, I need to share something with you, if that's OK? You are such a handsome spunk and you have lots of charm and personality that sometimes I think you forget about your personal hygiene and you neglect to use deodorant and clean your teeth. To be the awesome chick magnet that you are it may be helpful to keep this in mind in future.
- Chelsea, with the end of term coming I want to tell you how focused you have been in your studies. However, I have noticed that you are getting tired and more unsettled emotionally and at times a wee bit crabby with your sister. Please make sure you get lots of sleep in the coming weeks so that the beautiful loving soul we know can be around a bit more.

This is what we call a feedback sandwich where you put a great affirming message (top and bottom) around a piece of constructive criticism. This gives the adolescent mind a chance to hear it without shutting down into survival mode.

Parents can also use a metaphor from childhood if they have a favourite teddy, doll or super hero. If you come out with the metaphor and say something like, *'Teddy is worried about you. He thinks that you have been unhappy and crabby and that makes him very, very sad.'* The use of a well-loved character from childhood will trigger deep seated feelings of being loved and special and it's a bit like 'a teaspoon of sugar helps the medicine go down.'

Consider: Do you have a symbol that you need when having a serious chat so that it shows it is coming from love? Maybe a cup of *Milo* and a *Tim Tam* is a sign that we need to chat somewhere away from the flappy ears of the rest of the family. The softening effect of the act of kindness and the chocolate biscuit allows them to also avoid emotional hijack in their brain. Remember, keep your tone as quiet and secretive as possible.

If you are unable to trust your tone because you are too angry, disappointed, upset or hurt then please consider the mum or dad letter (see the Appendix pages for examples).

Finally some suggestions for optimistic circuit breakers that can help diffuse a huge disappointment or setback. These work for anyone—with or without an adolescent unfinished brain.

- That's a 'bugger' moment!
- Mustn't be my lucky day today.
- In five years time will this matter?
- Someone else needed it more than me.
- Now this is really interesting!
- My time wasn't right—it's still coming.
- My 'great things' bucket was already full for today.
- Tomorrow is another day.
- This won't go down in history as my finest hour!
- Now I know how Custer felt at the Battle of Little Big Horn.
- I must have needed to learn this lesson now.
- What a gift this will be in a few days.
- I wouldn't wish this on my worst enemy.
- Thank goodness I have clean undies on.
- Must have forgotten my lucky undies .
- When all else fails, there's always chocolate.
- This too will pass.

Adults need to be creative in how they help adolescents broaden their perspective and loosen the grip of their story. Remember what worked for you when you were on the bumpy road to adulthood, and offer unconditional positive regard and consideration. We hate to have adolescents waste the precious years of their youth, and yet we all know lots of adults who are wasting the precious years of their life being grumpy, unhappy and full of blame.

The Bank of Life

Imagine there is a bank that credits your account each morning with $86,400. It carries over no balance from day to day.

Every evening deletes whatever part of the balance you failed to use during the day. What would you do? Draw out ALL OF IT, of course!

Each of us has such a bank. Its name is TIME.

Every morning, it credits you with 86,400 seconds. Every night it writes off, as lost, whatever of this you have failed to invest to good purpose.

It carries over no balance. It allows no overdraft. Each day it opens a new account for you. Each night it burns the remains of the day.

If you fail to use the day's deposits, the loss is yours. There is no going back. There is no drawing against the 'tomorrow.' You must live in the present on today's deposits.

Invest it so as to get from it the utmost in health, happiness, and success! The clock is running. Make the most of today.

To realise the value of ONE YEAR, ask a student who failed a grade.

To realise the value of ONE MONTH, ask a mother who gave birth to a premature baby.

To realise the value of ONE WEEK, ask the editor of a weekly newspaper.

To realise the ! value of ONE HOUR, ask the lovers who are waiting to meet.

To realise the value of ONE MINUTE, ask a person who missed the train.

To realise the value of ONE-SECOND, ask a person who just avoided an accident.

To realise the value of ONE MILLISECOND, ask the person who won a silver medal in the Olympics.

Treasure every moment that you have! And treasure it more because you shared it with someone special, special enough to spend your time.

Author Unknown

Key Points

- All adolescents are at risk. Without support and education adolescents are at enormous risk of becoming first disengaged and then possibly delinquent.

- Parents and lighthouses need to help adolescents to overcome major setbacks.

- Adolescents can be very resistant to positive change.

- There are three dimensions to explain good and bad events:

    1. Permanence

    2. Pervasiveness

    3. Personal

- Optimism can be developed in children and adolescents.

- Helping adolescents gain perspective of their experiences helps them to learn and grow.

- Adolescents need help to decatastrophise.

- There are many ways to help adolescents change negative thinking and behaviour that uses the unconscious mind.

- Feedback needs to be offered in specific way or it will seem like criticism to an adolescent's sensitive emotional barometer.

- Adolescents experience emotional hijacking in their brain very easily when they sense criticism

- Positive, caring communication is a powerful ally in an adolescents' confused world.

Chapter 15

Adolescence: The **hero's journey**

To dare is to lose one's footing momentarily. Not to dare is to lose oneself.

Sören Kierkegaard, Danish philosopher, theologian and psychologist.

This chapter explores adolescence from a transpersonal place that may defy both logic and intelligence. I have been fascinated by the journeys that have been chosen consciously, or unconsciously, by adolescents and then to have seen the person they become later in life. Often the individuals who took the risks and were burnt by fire, who journeyed to the darkest place within their psyche were the ones to emerge years later to live fulfilling lives. The notion of 'being lost' often came to mean being released from predictable, logical expectations that they and their family had for themselves. It often involved unpredictable change and physical hardship and challenge. Joseph Campbell in his book, *The Hero with a Thousand Faces* explored the notion that we all live a hero's journey.

> *The basic story of the hero journey involves giving up where you are, going into the realm of adventure, coming to some kind of symbolically rendered realization, and then returning to the field of normal life.*
>
> Campbell, J., *Pathways to Bliss: Mythology and Personal Transformation*, (2004).

We can explore Campbell's hero journey in a simple way by seeing it as seven circles. The Seven Circles is a simplified version of the significant journeys people make throughout their lives. The different stages in the journey are ever widening circles, like the ripples that appear on the water's surface when you throw a stone. Each ripple widens and leads you to the next, and each ripple is inclusive of the previous ones. There must be a merging and a flowing, an absence of predictability and rigidity; life is always moving.

Campbell called it a hero's journey because it happens when life asks you to rise to a challenging situation, an awakening or a call and brings the best of you to face it. If it was easy then it wouldn't be a hero's journey. This journey is about healing wounds, as well as sharing and developing your gifts. Adolescence is the beginning of such a journey.

Traditional Indigenous communities have always seen the transition to adulthood through the lens of the hero's journey where individuals must be challenged to grow. This growth or expansion is one that is strongly mentored and also acknowledged and honoured by ceremony.

The Seven Circles are:

1. FIRST CIRCLE: The calling.
2. SECOND CIRCLE: Accepting the call.
3. THIRD CIRCLE: Crossing the threshold.
4. FOURTH CIRCLE: Finding your guardians.
5. FIFTH CIRCLE: Facing your dragons and challenges.
6. SIXTH CIRCLE: Transformation and development of the inner self.
7. SEVENTH CIRCLE: The return home.

The first circle is the invitation to embark on your adventure. For adolescents, hormones signal that things are changing and, like it or not, you have begun the bumpy ride of change. Any individual can recognise it as a calling because it marks a transition stage in your life. It is a challenging call that invites you to step out of our comfort zone and to expand your identity into something more significant. Sometimes there is no invitation and you're suddenly thrown into an unexpected life challenge like a death, job loss, relationship breakdown or a global financial crisis—you have started a hero journey. Your comfort zone will be stretched and often completely dismantled.

The second circle is accepting the call. Post-adolescent people can refuse the hero journey call, ignore the urgings and resist the invitation. Many young people want to resist the call out of fear of the unknown, however, the unique biological and physical changes of adolescence means refusal is not an option. Older adults who refuse can become lost in life and lose themselves; T.S. Elliot calls them the 'hollow men'. They can die, or live mundane and meaningless lives as shells of their former selves; lives of quiet desperation often numbed by addictions or abuse. Campbell claimed that 'to refuse the call means stagnation. What you don't experience positively you will experience negatively.'

The third circle is called crossing the threshold. It's when you begin to evolve and start travelling your path to transformation. Campbell defined this stage as a point of no return, because once you have crossed the threshold there is no return to the previous situation. This is where adolescents step back from parents and join the hunt to belong with friends and the need to fight for autonomy and independence. This is the beginning of risk-taking behaviours, and experimenting with alcohol, drugs and sex. This is when many adolescents get hurt, wounded or embarrassed. It symbolises the death of the child within and the beginning of adulthood.

The fourth circle is where you find guardians and allies that will help you navigate your way through the chaos and the turmoil. Having significant adult allies as lighthouses is so important on the bumpy road to adulthood. Guardians are people, elements, or forces you lean on in order to keep going forward. They are normally people who trust and have confidence in you, and who offer the support you need to trust in your capabilities and possibilities. Guardians act as coaches rather than parents. They often come from unexpected sources or environments, which means it's important to keep a receptive state and attitude throughout your journey—things are not always as they seem.

Adolescents also benefit from reliable positive friendships that can support the unfolding of their journey. Some adolescents are finding guardians online who have websites with helpful information that they can access invisibly. Without this circle many adolescents get very lost and some never return with any sense of expansion. Many disappear into mental illness or hopeless cycles of violence or criminality.

> *Adolescents of all ages need ecstatic experience to become adult, and if the culture will not provide it they will seek it in any case, often in ways which do them harm.*
>
> Neville, B. *Educating the Psyche*, (2005).

The fifth circle is facing your dragons and challenges. This is one adolescents know well where temptations, lust, gluttony, greed, and illegal and unsocial forces appear. There are many challenges they must face (this is where my suicide attempt appeared as something to overcome and conquer).

A dragon is a metaphor for some kind of opposition, resistance or refusal, and it is not necessarily bad. A dragon is an energy that needs to be acknowledged and redirected. It can be your own resistance, fear or weakness that causes you to make a dangerous choice; or a person or circumstance in whose presence you lose your centre, or who seems to diminish your self-confidence, self-worth or well-being. It can also be something or someone who awakens doubt and unease in you. Facing these dragons means developing your resources, acknowledging your own negative forces, or those of the people you consider significant in your life. The adolescent hero journey has a wide window when they can meet dragons or forces that peel away any illusions they may have about themselves, others and our world. This is a time when social consciences can be born due to a struggle with a situation that has shown blatant injustice. Every painful experience has great potential for growth and this is why adolescents need caring, empowering support to enable them to learn that they are more than a body and a mind.

The sixth circle is transformation and development of the inner self. This is where the growing occurs and an adolescent is able to transform their dragons into allies and overcome uncertainty, chaos and suffering. The hero's journey, above all, is a journey of personal development and learning. Other important resources appear in themselves, which allow them to cross the threshold wiser and stronger. When they transform their dragons they create a new roadmap, with new beliefs, behaviours and capabilities. This new map will allow them to face and overcome self-doubt, uncertainty, fear and resistance. As they begin to develop and use their resources, they will develop a new and renewed map of the world. Their maps are in a process of continuous transformation and restoration. They can never be who they were before.

> *The whole idea is that you've got to bring out again that which you went to recover, the unrealized, unutilized potential in yourself. You are to bring the treasure of understanding back and integrate it in a rational life.*
>
> Campbell, J., *Pathways to Bliss: Mythology and Personal Transformation*, (2004).

The seventh circle is the return home. By this stage of the hero's journey they have become transformed and they share their knowledge and wisdom with other people who might be on similar journeys or experiencing similar situations. This journey has sacred and maturation purposes. In this journey individuals taste their life purpose, the invisible sacred contract with which they already have all the natural talents to do, and do well. This final stage is best marked by a ceremony or a rite of passage that shows a new beginning has started. This is something our modern world has abandoned.

> *Your Soul has a goal that serves and guides you to your highest good and also that of others. Written in its depths is a memory of the purpose you came into this world to fulfil. It may not be what you think you are here to learn and experience. If you stray from its plan, uncomfortable events may occur to get you back on track. If you follow its messages your life can flow. Like a river that naturally moves towards the sea you are moved towards what is best for you.*
>
> Hobbs, A. *Getting Real About Growing Up*, (2003).

Without acknowledging the 'whole' child in many of our schools and homes, children are raised with a profound disconnection from the most important sources of life sustenance that comes from deep connectedness. Rachel Kessler writes:

> *When schools systematically exclude heart and soul, students in growing numbers become depressed, attempt suicide, or succumb to eating disorders and substance abuse.*
>
> Kessler, R, *The Soul of Education*, (2000).

Dr Michael Resnick from the Adolescent Health Program at the University of Minnesota, Minneapolis conducted a study of 12,000 adolescents from 80 high schools across the United States and found:

> *Young people who have a feeling of connectedness with parents, family and school have lower levels of smoking, drinking, other drug use, suicidal thinking, risky sexual behaviour and exposure to violence.*
>
> Resnick, Dr M. et al, *Reducing The Risk: Connections that Make a Difference in the Lives of Youth*, (1997).

Deep connection comes in many ways. Kessler explores the following forms of deep connection: These have been mentioned before and are so important, I am listing them again. Adolescents need to have at least two to ensure their health and well-being:

- Deep connection to self.
- Deep connection to another.
- Deep connection to community.
- Deep connection to lineage.
- Deep connection to nature.
- Deep Connection to a higher power.

Humans are social beings with a deep inner world that influences the essence of their reality in the physical and spiritual worlds. The increasing illnesses afflicting our children and adolescents shouts loudly that something needs changing. They are hungering for deep connections and a sense of soul; but in our busy consumer-driven world it seems acknowledgement and celebration is given to our wealthiest, most famous and most athletically gifted. It's no wonder so many adolescents are killing themselves. Do they want any part of a world that cares more for actors than for children, more for pharmaceutical companies than curing illnesses, and more about keeping food prices high than feeding the starving? The injustices based on religion, the irrational fear of diversity, the absence of compassion for those in need and the disrespect that many have for our natural world disillusion today's young people.

> *Human connectedness is the key to resilience, authentic happiness and a sense of well being. This can only be achieved through the recognition, honouring and nurturing of the human spirit that exists within every child ever born.*
>
> Dent, M. *Saving Our Children in our Chaotic World* 2nd Edition (2010)

The human spirit has a unique power and presence of its own and when it's nurtured it can save lives and transform communities. The opportunity for today's adolescents to have a voice that celebrates the mysterious in life and allows for the querying of the big questions—that often have no logical answers—may encourage our adolescents on their hero's journey to stay here and work with us. With unconditional support we can all learn from an adolescent and their journey.

When the physical body is challenged it is often the strength of the human spirit that brings us to safety. Lincoln Hall, the mountaineer who survived a night high on Mt Everest without protective gear willed himself to survive, his body could not do that alone. The power of the whole mind, conscious, unconscious and super conscious, when united with a loving intention, has seen miracles happen.

Dr Larry Dossey in his book, *Healing Words: The Power of Prayer and the Practice of Medicine* (1994), explored many stories of amazing miracles. He pondered the concepts of love, empathy and connectedness:

> Empathy, compassion and love seem to form a literal bond between living things.

To help adolescents hear the whisperings of their spirit or inner source of wisdom I often use Indigenous forms of guidance. There are many such divination systems that use Mother Nature as a source for hearing the silent voice. The Medicine Cards created by Jamie Sams and David Carson use animals as messengers from the Great Mystery, God or the Source of All. Each animal has a message about life; how to acknowledge your place in the great unfolding of life and to honour every living thing as a teacher. The cards allow the logical rational mind to be silenced and ponder with the wisdom of spirit. Each animal card has a powerful message and because it uses symbols and metaphors to teach respectful living, the unconscious hears and understands. If a horse has caught your immediate attention or you have chosen the horse card this is the message if the card is the correct way up:

> True power is wisdom found in remembering your total journey. Wisdom comes from remembering pathways you have walked in another's moccasins. Compassion, caring, teaching, loving and sharing your gifts, talents and abilities are the gateways to power.

If you had chosen the card upside down the message is:

> If your ego has gotten in the way, you may have failed to notice the lack of respect you have been receiving from others. You may on the other hand be struggling with others who are abusing their power.

The Sacred Path Cards: The Discovery of Self through Native American Teachings is another excellent set to use with anyone who feels lost and uncertain of choices to make in life. Jamie Sams writes in the introduction:

> The Sacred Path Cards are self-oriented in order for each individual to reflect upon the roles, gifts and self-reliant abilities that can be gained on this Earth Walk. This growth process is limitless and like each spirit is eternal.

The ancient knowledge that is present in these packs of cards is universal and honours respecting self, others and our world. They take individuals out of their heads, away from the chatter of the inner critic and the logical voice of reason. I am concerned that much of our focus in life coaching and psychological counselling, especially for young people, is problem focused, labelling, or looking for rosier futures without honouring the journey that allows a young person to explore themself deeply. This exploration helps find where they are on the hero journey and helps them create their own new map of how to return or recover. I have met many counsellors who want to fix, rescue or explain in great depth how an adolescent got to where they are. Even with the best intentions this can invalidate the transpersonal learning that can occur with an approach that helps individuals find their own solutions from deep within.

Another beautiful pack of guidance cards called Wisdom of the Four Winds. These are based on Maori wisdom, designed by Barry Brailsford and illustrated by Cecilie Okada .

> *To the ancestors who kept the dream of peace alive and carried it forward to this day. To all who walk the path of the gentle way.*
>
> Dedication Wisdom of the Four Winds.

There is the same sense of profound knowledge in these cards as inf the Native American cards. The role of archetypes and how they underpin and support the messages of wisdom is amazing. There is a profound connection to human wisdom and mysteries like the stars and numerology. In the Brailsford cards the wind songs of each of the four directions all have wisdom buried into them, and that is how ancient knowledge was passed down over the centuries without being distorted. This is the poem that ends the message from Tuatara, the 200 million-year-old lizard still found in New Zealand:

Trust the gentle voice
That echoes out of space and time
Trust your knowing
Truth moving beyond the mime
Trust the inner eye
That clearly sees the child at play
Trust your song
The uniqueness of your chosen way
Trust who you are
And who you were born to be
Trust, and in that trusting
Be forever free.

There are some profound similarities among Indigenous knowledge the world over, which shows that the knowledge learned from millions of lives has created a base of knowledge that's still appropriate today. It won't matter how much science and technology we have, humanity will still never know some big secrets that are beyond knowing. How did they build those pyramids in Egypt so precisely, how did the Easter Island statues get to the island, what knowledge was used to construct Stonehenge with such precision in terms of where the sun shines on certain key days of the year?

In my research I have found that at the core of every major religion in the world lies the same core truths that exist in Indigenous wisdom: love and respect for self, others and our natural world, and a deep acceptance of the

state of grace. This is only available to those who have faith in the truths and of living for the highest expression of oneself for the greater good of all.

There are also sets of cards based on Christian angels and saints that adolescents can use for guidance. They help them hear the whisperings of their spirit, or the God essence within—maybe it's just a means to hear their conscience which is often drowned by their inner chatter and confused minds.

Rachel Kessler in her 'passages' work includes a step she calls 'the mysteries question process'. This is another term to describe mindfulness where individuals are asked to ponder big and interesting questions not normally explored in schools or homes.

> *If we allowed children more silence and stillness in our homes and schools, they would ponder more, think more and question more—for themselves. When we tell them how to see the world, what to do and how to do, we are inhibiting the growth of their unique self and denying them the opportunity to realise their own potential. Mindfulness can only happen in an environment that values the space for silence and stillness. Mindfulness for children can only occur in the presence of people who genuinely respect others, themselves and our world.*
>
> Shaun Kerry MD, American Board of Psychiatry and Neurology.

We've been going through the life cycle of both living and dying for thousands of years without modern medicine or science. Indigenous people honoured the invisible world, and their intuitive and ancient knowledge. They knew what 'spirit' was and it was indelibly linked to their relationship to the Earth and all who walked, hopped, flew or swam on her.

Sometimes to help an adolescent reconsider who they are I analyse their numerology. I take their date of birth and plot it on a grid (see below). It stretches the young person's often inaccurate view of themselves and they are often surprised what comes up from such a simple exercise. Let's plot the date of birth of an adolescent boy born on 2 March 1989[2*].

3		99
2		8
1		

For this boy he has spaces down the central row. The Arrow of Frustration means he will tend to struggle with his will and confidence. He can be very sensitive and get frustrated easily over small things. Often these children come from a dysfunctional home life, but when they learn compassion and empathy they can overcome these weaknesses. He has the Arrow of the Planner, where all the numbers are filled on left hand side. He likes to be ordered and organised. The other rows have incomplete numbers. If you overlap their name chart over the top, often weaknesses can be resolved and strengths can appear as you have more numbers.

Once again this is another way to stretch the thinking of an adolescent who may need some guidance and direction. A full numerology chart can be incredibly revealing and I recommend you have them done for the whole family.

'To know thyself' is essentially the first building block to personal growth and development for anyone. This need to search for self-awareness is why I use

---

2   * I use the book, *Discovering the Inner Self: The Complete Book of Numerology* by Dr David A Phillips. The birth chart helps identify the overall pattern of strengths and weaknesses a person has. This technique is another form of ancient knowledge that has been known for centuries as the Pythagorean Birth Chart.

creative visualisation CDs when working with adolescents. With regular use new cognitive maps are formed that support calmness and stillness. Some tracks guide individuals to explore themselves from a deeply reflective place. In my Flight Fantasy[3*] track individuals are asked to search deep within themselves to find and acknowledge their strength and natural talents. The Dare to Dream track from the Kitbag helps them create expanded visions of possibility. The modern world steals dreams from children and adolescents so they need all the help they can get to dream positively. These guided visualisations give adolescents time out from their negative critic and their self-doubting thoughts in a positive way without chocolate, alcohol or drugs. Many adolescents tell me they have these calming tracks on their mp3 players and play them before tests and exams. When they feel frustrated and angry, no one knows what they are listening to so they have privacy in a public domain.

Many others who work with adolescents have been questioning the inadequate way we've been supporting today's adolescents on the bumpy road to adulthood. The original creator of the Pathways Program, Arne Rubenstein based his programs on the need for a rite of passage first for boys and later for girls. Amrita Hobbs has been taking girls on journeys to womanhood for many years. Andrew Lines in his Rite Journey programs for adolescents has based his work on Joseph Campbell's hero journey.

> *In seeking to understand traditions of ceremony including initiation and rites of passage I spent time in conversation with local indigenous elders as well as exploring other traditional rites and initiations. What became clear through these discussions and research was that it would be best to create a contemporary version of this life process.*
>
> Lines, A., *The 'rite' Way to Raise Teens*, [online] http://www.thenexgengroup.com/page/downloads.

Andrew's work is expanding rapidly because it makes a profound difference in the lives of young people. It supplies all the elements of the Seven Circles that adolescents need to journey down before returning 'home' to themselves in their 20s. If we are to seriously address the increases in mental illness, self-harm, homelessness and suicide we must provide the supports adolescents need. We need to honour their search for meaning and purpose, deep connectedness, creativity, silence and solitude while they still participate in their chaotic and rapidly changing world.

---

3   * From *Just a Little Time, Your Stairway to Better Choices.*

> *The absence of rites of passage leads to a serious breakdown in the process of maturing as a person. Young people are unable to participate in society in a creative manner because societal structures no longer consider it their responsibility to intentionally establish the necessary marks of passing from one age-related social role to another, such as: child to youth, youth to adult, adult to elder. The result is that society has no clear expectation of how people should participate in these roles and therefore individuals do not know what is required by society.*
>
> The Encyclopaedia of World Problems and Human Potential, Union of International Associations.

An essential part of the journey for adolescents needs to be a retreat from the world to allow time and space to explore themselves without distractions.

> *21st Century children are growing up in a world of risks and threats, one which even the adults of today struggle to comprehend and respond to. With the help of connection, guidance, celebration, ceremony and a school- based rite of passage the children and adolescents of today will gain skills, experience and values to assist them in navigating their way through their transition into adulthood and indeed, life beyond.*
>
> Lines, A., *The 'rite' Way to Raise Teens*, [online] http://www.thenexgengroup.com/page/downloads.

As I write this, 16-year-old Jessica Watson has just rounded Cape Horn, the half way point of her solo yacht trip around the world. This is a wonderful example of an adolescent on a hero's journey; symbolically Jessica is an excellent example of a healthy adolescent who has chosen to follow her inner urges. Many questioned Jessica's family and supporters because of the massive dangers and risks that her expedition held. Jessica has pursued her natural abilities and talents and she knows how to sail. She has been mentored by experienced sailors and is a sensible and capable young lady who believes in her ability to complete her dream.

Adolescents can be incredibly capable and wise if they have been allowed to develop their natural skills and have been guided to trust their inner selves to manage life's adversities. This 16-year-old is a credit to herself, her family and her community of lighthouses and mentors. The 'allowing' is a metaphor of the need for adults to let go of adolescents when they are ready to stand on their own. Some, like Jessica, are ready quite early and others may not be ready until the mid 20s, or even later. The age difference is due to the opportunities for growth that each has been given. Facing hardship and adversity comes in many forms, and for Jessica facing big waves and storms is no different to other adolescents who struggle with the potential dangers of sexual predators, drug overdose, car accidents and violence in our streets.

> You are here for a purpose
> There is no duplicate of you
> In the whole wide world
> There never has been
> There never will be.
> You were brought here now
> To fill a certain need.
> Take time to think that over.
>
> *Lou Austin*

During traditional rites of passage and preparation for adulthood, adolescents sometimes lost their life. To be confronted with your own mortality and to grasp the value of life is part of the journey. I have worked with many adolescents who almost died or killed themselves and many of them were different after the event. Some forgot about the danger and needed to be reminded again with another life-threatening experience; such is the nature of the hero journey where we need to be awakened from our mind- numbing living. To stay asleep and never be challenged may simply be a form of 'living death'.

One of the saddest consequences the modern world has done to today's adolescents is the threat of litigation that's seen schools, community groups and sometimes families stop creating opportunities of high risk for adolescents. Long treks, whitewater rafting, rock climbing, diving and abseiling have all but disappeared from schools and communities. Maybe that is why so many are hurting themselves, binge drinking, being violent, being 'jack asses', taking more dangerous drugs like ice and veterinary drugs, having aggressive sexual encounters and driving dangerously. This need to be frightened and to overcome that fear is a key transpersonal form of growth and it resonates on all levels of an individual—mind, body, heart and soul.

As an authorised marriage celebrant I have had the honour and privilege to conduct weddings, baby naming ceremonies and funerals for over 12 years, and I am still staggered by the power of a meaningful ceremony. The emotional intensity of a ceremony that honours life transitions can be memorable and transformative. May I suggest you consider a ceremony for your child's 21st birthday—if you think they are ready to step into adulthood—and honour the good, the bad and a bit of the ugly. Thank everyone who has been part of their journey, then celebrate respectfully and safely.

> *The challenge faced by modern humanity [...] is to passionately gather up the scattered fragments of our lives and channel them into the creative realm where, with insight or revelation, we will be able to become more than ourselves.*
>
> Pearce, J. C., *Spiritual Initiation and the Breakthrough of Consciousness: The Bond of Power*, (2003).

Key Points

- Adolescence is a hero's journey of growth.

- Adolescents need to be allowed to journey and to be guided and supported.

- The deeper adolescent connectedness is the healthier they will be on all levels.

- Being able to go on a 'journey' in nature with wise elders can be a powerful tool of transformation.

- Overcoming challenge and adversity is an important part of the adolescent hero journey.

- Ceremony is a significant way of marking growth and maturity.

- The modern world needs to offer more opportunities for adolescents to journey to adulthood purposefully instead of accidently.

IT CAN BE DAUNTING.

Cartoon by William Main

Chapter 16

Adolescents *in* today's **schools** and possible **innovations** in education

A soulful education embraces diverse ways to satisfy the spiritual hunger of today's youth. When guided to find constructive ways to express their spiritual longings, young people can find purpose in life, do better in school, strengthen ties to family and friends, and approach adult life with vitality and vision.

Kessler, R. The Soul of Education (2000)

Let's start with an accurate picture of youth disengagement in Australia so we can see how well our education system is doing in reality. It is completely inaccurate to focus on the scores and marks of the best students in our high school because about 30 per cent of students will do well enough to qualify for university. But what's happening to the other 70 per cent? Perhaps we are failing these students badly.

Some sobering statistics

Education, training and employment

- There have been no changes in school completion rates in the last 20 years—32 per cent of young people do not complete Year 12.
- Young people who leave school early are less likely to find a job.
- 50 per cent of young people who complete or finish school prior to Year 10 and 40 per cent of young people who complete Year 11 are not fully

engaged in study or work compared to 10 per cent of young people who complete Year 12.

- In 2006, 526,000 15–24-year-olds were not in full-time education, training or work (8 per cent of 15–19-year-olds and 12 per cent of 20–24-year-olds).
- The youth unemployment rate is higher than the national average—In 2006 the rate for 15–19-year-olds was 12.5 per cent, for 20–24-year-olds 6.3 per cent and the national rate was 4.4 per cent (Much worse since the global financial crisis).

The prison system

- Young people are over-represented in the prison population, accounting for 20 per cent of the total prison population whilst only 10 per cent of overall population.
- In 2003-04, 9,000 12–17-year-olds were under juvenile justice supervision (549 per 100,000), and in 2006 5,000 18–24-year-olds were in prison (251 per 100,000).
- Males are more likely to be in prison than females (458 per 100,000 versus 31.1 per 100,000).
- Young Indigenous people are over-represented in the prison population accounting for over a third of all 18–24-year-olds in prison, but only 3.3 per cent of the total population of young people

Statistics: Burns J. et al., *Preventing Youth Disengagement and Promoting Engagement*, ARACY (2008).

High schools have an enormous influence on how adolescents navigate the bumpy road to adulthood. The statistics above do not reflect the psychological well-being or otherwise of today's adolescents, with reports indicating that they are sicker on all levels, not just those for whom the schooling system fails. There has been an increase in the need for the school's role as being a safe and supportive place for adolescents to spend time. Our youth are highly susceptible to being influenced either positively or negatively.

The legacy of a teacher lasts a lifetime.
Anon.

Unfortunately, the legacy of a teacher can be positive or negative. Students are quite universal in the qualities they value in teachers. In a large study in the USA they interviewed thousands of students who determined that the three most important attributes they value in a teacher are:

1. Fairness.
2. Sense of humour.
3. Passion and competence for subject.

The schools that are doing well are those that have staff with the above attributes who are well trained to meet the needs of the Millennial adolescent, and are enthusiastic and passionate about making a huge difference in the lives of young people. Some schools have massive youth engagement and adolescents, even those who are not academically capable, are attending school. In terms of importance and value, there is nothing more important. Disengaged students who are wagging school are at high risk of walking pathways that lead to drug addiction, criminality and delinquency. We must create school environments where adolescents want to attend and offer education for life as well as for work.

For too long we have focused on the upper end of the spectrum of academic achievement, but now it is time we reviewed the role of schooling. Education must attend to the critical needs of adolescents by providing them with opportunities—especially in the window of sensitivity—that build their need to belong, feel connected, build autonomy, feel safe and be supported.

> *Because teenagers so frequently think with their amygdala, misinterpret emotional signs and signals and generally think everyone is looking at them, the socio-emotional environment must receive special attention from secondary teachers.*
>
> Corbin, B. *Unleashing The Potential of the Teenage Brain: 10 Powerful Ideas*, (2008.)

Dr Sheryl Feinstein connects the need for safety and a sense of belonging for adolescents with the need to capture student attention. This links well with my first step to being an exceptional teacher—capture student attention.

> *The three best brain-compatible ways to attract and keep a teenage student's attention are to introduce novelty, tap into emotion and present a meaningful curriculum.*
>
> Feinstein, S., *Teaching the At-Risk Teenage Brain*, (2007).

Adolescents value these three things even more today than 10 or 20 years ago when life was blander and school was filled with more interesting opportunities. The WIIFM (What's In It For Me) factor is stronger today partly because adolescents are exposed to much more, easily accessible information. They are asking: *'What can you teach me and why is it important?'*

Feinstein gives many examples of how to capture interest. You have to trigger a spark of interest in a sleepy, hormone-driven adolescent brain that would rather be asleep or online. You have about 7–8 minutes of student attention to work with in high school, and about 5–6 minutes in middle school before their brain turns off—unless you are providing interesting learning or interaction. This is not the student's fault; their brain will turn off involuntarily.

> *Such factors as motivation, emotional engagement with the learning task, learning style of the learner, relevance to the learning and even the physical environment can affect the brain's attention to learning.*
>
> Corbin, B. *Unleashing The Potential of the Teenage Brain: 10 Powerful Ideas*, Corwin Press, USA, 2008.

The second key concern in teaching adolescents is the need to find a balance between paying attention and processing information because the brain can only do one thing at a time. The brain processes information unconsciously for much longer than we are aware. Some processing activities include:

- Encourage students to keep a journal.
- Have students pick the most important thing they learned.
- Have class discussions.
- Have a think-pair-share for 2-3 minutes.
- Design a concept-web or a mind-map.
- Have 1–2 minutes of reflection time.
- Individually find examples to show learning.
- Create some key questions for a mini quiz activity.
- Role-play a situation that will use the information.
- Use circle work to build EQ

Jenny Mosley has some excellent techniques to build trust with adolescents that allow the circle process to become a powerful tool in classrooms. Students can learn to listen, think and speak with concern and compassion – and they can then learn to problem solve with the help of others their age. This also gives them a voice— and this is very important for them. *Education Review* (March 2008) published an excellent story about Redcliffe Primary School. It's an excellent example of an approach that met the needs of at-risk students in a school with high levels of disengagement. Although this is a primary school, we know that adolescence is starting earlier, often by 10 years of age, and for many girls by 11 (many of the most disengaged students were in the adolescent aged category).

This was a 'tired, little inner-city school' in Perth with a high truancy rate and massive student disengagement. The first step to change is to *decide* to change; so the school decided to do a warts and all survey of what the kids, parents and staff wanted to have happen in the school. At that time an innovative course began where a teacher and 10 children started a catering course with the canteen. Serendipitously, at the same time, a student won a competition where the prize was for a Melbourne boy band to come to the school. The band asked the students to put on a dance performance for them before they played.

The two events of the catering course and the dance performance ignited the whole school community and school attendance and participation improved radically. So, the next step *had* to happen: 'Let's make a new curriculum!' the school community worked together to give students a voice, as well as parents and staff. The new curriculum began with regular classes in the morning followed by diverse interesting programs in the afternoon. Afternoon programs include drama, catering, horticulture, art, specialised sport, specialised sciences, history, dance, computing, music, storybook workshop, Japanese and Italian. Students choose their own afternoon program which is brilliantly simple! Students choose the things that interest them, or just use it like a smorgasbord and sample a different program every term. This innovative integrated curriculum-driven school has created an environment that engages learning and cooperation among the multi-aged students.

This Integrated Curriculum model is needed in the lower years of secondary schools. It will improve school attendance much better than the punitive measures currently being touted in New South Wales, where parents are penalised for not getting their kids to school. Students *will* attend when there's something more interesting happening than what they do away from school. The Integrated Curriculum model gives students a voice and a choice, and in turn helps autonomy. It will also keep them engaged in learning and provide opportunities to build resilience. It gives a bored student the chance to open up a potential that may be lying dormant during those vital years of early adolescence. It also gives more opportunities for adolescents to find lighthouses, and to learn some life skills. The curriculum could include surfing, fishing, car maintenance or first aid; but it works only if they are presented by someone who is passionate about the topic.

I congratulate all schools that, like Redcliffe, have not given up when things got tough; where instead they listened to students and parents and created a school that makes learning on all levels a priority. A lot of poor behaviour stems from boredom and apathy about what we are teaching, how we are teaching it and an ignorance of how to reach today's students. It is time to fix that

Education is still the best doorway for students from troubled backgrounds to break the pattern of welfare and victimhood.

In my Year 9 class in a country government high school, a savvy principal identified our class of social studies students as being disengaged. He created a 'history of our town' project that allowed the class to find out about the real history of their local town. They spent a term visiting elderly citizens and conducting interviews and researching in the library. When they discovered the town was named after a spring, they located it and helped with a community project to build a rock wall around the original site of the spring to honour its importance. It made history come alive and they all became very passionate about the project.

There is nothing like <u>real</u> experience with <u>real</u> people and things, to make learning interesting.

Barry Corbin writes about the enormous potential of teaching adolescents with the understanding of how their brain works, and how the great doorways to possibility that open during this time of critical development need to be used:

- doorways for more highly refined and productive social and emotional skills
- doorways for the development and acquisition of languages, for increased facility in appreciation of music and artistic expression
- doorways for the development of advanced cognitive abilities in reasoning, decision making and problem solving.

Corbin, B. *Unleashing The Potential of the Teenage Brain: 10 Powerful Ideas*, (2008.)

Students spend more time at school than with their parents for nearly 40 weeks each year, so we need to have an invisible curriculum that is teaching Emotional Quality (EQ) and Social Quality (SQ)—whether we like it or not[4]*.

An excellent resource for working in this area is the *Chicken Soup for the Soul in the Classroom* text which uses true stories as a basis for self-reflection and personal growth. There is a transformative power of real-life stories that has been lost in our modern world. Indigenous peoples use stories and songs to teach everything of value. Yet, we have an over-reliance on logic and intellectual rigour, and maybe this is why so many students are disengaged. The unconscious responds to metaphors and stories in a very powerful way.

Adolescence is a time of significant brain development and adults or lighthouses who are positively involved in a teen's life hold the keys to their future success on all levels. Even for adolescents who have had challenging childhoods of abuse and deprivation, this time also has potential to reshape their brains and themselves. The lighthouses in our high schools need to be aware of this potential to take advantage of the plasticity of the brain especially during early adolescence. Eric Jensen writes about the following factors that contribute to brain enrichment:

- Physical activity versus passivity.
- Novel, challenging and meaningful learning versus doing what is already known.
- Coherent complexity versus boredom or chaos.
- Managed stress levels versus stressful conditions.
- Social support versus isolation.
- Good nutrition versus poor quality food.
- Sufficient time versus one shot experiences.

Jensen, E. Enriching the Brain (2006)

---

4   * For more information about building resilience and self-esteem in our children visit my webpage at: www.maggident.com/books.html.

Physical activity versus passivity.

Each of these can be achieved in our high schools. The physical passivity of many adolescents is negatively impacting on their brain development. Mind-numbing inactivity that often takes place in rooms with peeling paint and vomit-coloured carpet has a lot to do with adolescent disengagement and disillusionment.

> *In today's technology driven, plasma-screened world it's easy to forget that we are born movers—animals, in fact—because we've engineered movement right out of our lives. Ironically, the human capacity to dream and plan and create the very society that shields us from our biological imperative to move is rooted in the area of the brain that governs movement.*
>
> Ratey, Dr J. J. and Hagerman, E., *Spark! How exercise will improve the performance of your brain*, (2009).

Dr Ratey and his colleagues discovered that exercise not only increases the important neurotransmitters serotonin, norepinephrine and dopamine, they also discovered that vigorous exercise not only burns fat, it creates brain cells. As Zientarski, a PE teacher at Naperville High says: 'In our department we create brain cells, it's up to the other teachers to fill them'.

Studies on rats found that rats that run, massively increase neurogenesis—they grow more brain cells. Dr Ratey has a video on his web site at www.johnratey. com that shows students who were struggling and disengaged were not only getting fitter after exercise, their grades were improving too. When students get the required physical activity by playing games that build human connectedness, emotional and social competence and improve grades, high schools need to rethink their physical education programs.

Another study involving 163 overweight children in Augusta, Georgia, USA found that the cognitive and academic benefits of exercise seemed to increase with the size of the dose of exercise. For this study, a cross-disciplinary research team randomly assigned children to one of three groups. One group received 20 minutes of physical activity every day after school. Another group got a 40-minute daily workout, and the third group got no special exercise sessions.

After 14 weeks, the children who made the greatest improvement, as measured by both a standardised academic test and a test that measured their level of executive function (thinking processes) involving planning, organising, abstract thought, or self control, were those who spent 40 minutes a day playing tag and taking part in other active games. The cognitive and academic gains for the 20 minutes a day group were half as large.

Debra Viadero, 'Exercise Seen as Priming Pump for Students' Academic Strides (2008), *Education Week*, [online] http://www.edweek.org/ew/index.html.

One of the key findings from Dr John Rately's research was that vigorous exercise appeared to 'prepare' normally disengaged students for learning. He believed exercise stimulated the growth of cells in the pre-frontal cortex that controlled impulses. For normally engaged students it helped grow more brain cells, so everyone was a winner. (For adults who do the same, it will delay mental decay and could prevent dementia). Dr Rately also found that learning improved faster the closer it occurred to the exercise. Students needed to exercise immediately before they put focused attention into learning. A huge motivator in the program was the use of heart monitors so that students were able to gauge their own fitness improvement and were not in competition with anyone else but themselves. One of the classes in Rately's study worked with Indigenous Canadian students who were performing poorly. The class brought treadmills into the classroom to ensure the students were combining exercise and learning with immediacy. The increase in reading ages, behaviour and school performance was significant.

Perhaps we could look at the valuable life skills that students learn while growing new brain cells:

- How to create your own fitness program?
- What foods help grow muscle and not fat?
- How to monitor your own fitness?

The process of bringing real play, fun, laughter and human interaction into schools, at the same time as making more brain cells and improving grades, can be one of the answers high schools have been looking for—it's much cheaper than new laptops for everyone.

The window of fast learning in adolescence can be used fully if they are able to increase their emotional and social intelligences at the same time as their physical and intellectual abilities. The huge spin-offs are improved moods, emotional stability, stronger sense of belonging and better health and well-being—all important in an adolescent's tumultuous world.

Novel, challenging and meaningful learning versus doing what is already known

The brain can only change with focused attention and I believe that classrooms with too many bells and whistles can be too distracting for many students. Yes, they will be entertained, but positive brain changes can only occur when there is learning that has a high degree of relevance (WIIFM), is novel and interesting, and engages focused attention followed by a sense of reward or encouragement. Too much stress or tension will shut the brain down into survival mode; safe, calm environments are crucial to supporting brain growth.

> *Nothing speeds brain atrophy more than being immobilized in the same environment: the monotony undermines our dopamine and attentional systems crucial to maintaining brain plasticity.*
>
> Doidge, N. *The Brain that Changes Itself,* (2007).

We must not forget that this generation of digital natives are hardwired to being visually entertained, so their boredom button is more sensitive that previous generations. This does not mean we need more IT, screens and sources of entertainment, today's students still need what they are biologically programmed to experience:

- Human connectedness.
- Opportunities for autonomy and independence.
- Novel hands-on, real experiences that build competences across a range of areas.
- Plenty of physical movement.
- Positive involvement that creates neurotransmitters thatcreate feelings of well-being.
- Building a sense of belonging.
- Plenty of time with adults who can act as mentors and coaches.
- Environments that are conducive to feeling safe and valued.

Things have to change in our classrooms because too much class time is spent in brain antagonistic states of disinterest and lethargy during a vital window of possibility. Between 13 and 15 years of age is when most students become disillusioned with traditional classroom learning; it is not meeting Jensen's description for meaningful learning that allows for enrichment of brains. Much of what is in the curriculum has already been covered in primary school, and instead of challenging learners with novel new information that has a high relevance, it tends to be 'same old, same old'.

High school is the place where the greatest change needs to take place because it's where the hunger for meaningful learning of life skills by experts from the community can be met. Students need to experience more time outside the classroom being exposed to as many different life learnings as possible. Suggested opportunities for learning include:

- Going to the local fire station to learn about different types of fire, and what to do if caught in a house fire or a bushfire.
- Going to local the ambulance centre and learning how to do CPR, what to do if you come across a car accident and what to do if a friend passes out from excessive alcohol.
- Visiting a local mechanic to learn about how to take care of your car, including how to change tyres, oil and water.
- Experiencing law courts to see due process of the law.

- Dropping in to the police station to check out the cells and what processes take place if you are arrested.
- Visiting preschool and primary schools to help with classroom activities.
- Helping maintain gardens at local elderly homes.
- Helping with community programs like Meals on Wheels, soup kitchens, hospital visitations, op' shops and fund raising for local causes.
- Volunteering at the SES and learning about rescue and emergency procedures.
- Adopting a community park or garden to maintain and keep clean.
- Adopting a playground to help keep free of rubbish and things dangerous to children, like syringes and broken glass.
- Volunteering in the local library.
- Having professional artists, potters and photographers run mini classes.
- Doing a local history of community by interviewing elderly members.
- Creating a DVD promoting the local community.
- Helping at the tourist bureau.
- Creating a school mosaic or mural that celebrates diversity.
- Volunteering at the local wildlife rescue.
- Creating a school beautification project like a sensory playground for preschool, new seating for high school students and putting up shade areas.
- Creating a school play/performance evening to showcase the artistic talent in the school and raise money for a worthwhile project
- Having a sleepover during the school week to study astronomy.
- Creating a school vegetable garden.
- Creating a school café where students learn to cook, serve, design menus and manage a small business.
- Designing and creating picture books for children that teach important messages.
- Having a speed reading or memory improvement programs
- Having special arts programs where students are coached by professionals acting, dancing and set design.
- Having opportunities for students to do martial arts, yoga classes and mediation classes during school hours.
- Creating a T-towel or T-shirt design that celebrates youth week or raises money for a specific charity.
- Having a medieval festival or other festival.

These activities allow students to get out of the classroom to actively participate in projects that build their competence and knowledge in a wide variety of areas. Some are practical, while others are about building a stronger sense of community awareness and involvement. Exposing students to a wide variety of activities gives them a taste of many possible life pathways and careers. These special learning opportunities can occur in an integrated curriculum where the morning is for core subjects and afternoons are for students to choose other options.

Using this model, students can combine physical activities that have an element of risk, ensuring that another driver for adolescence—particularly boys— would be met in the relative safety of the school environment. Skateboarding, rollerblading, kayaking, mountain bike riding, water polo, martial arts and personal training provide students with fun, risk and massive engagement.

Peter L Benson of the Search Institute in America has discovered what he calls the key to help adolescents achieve well, find a clearer path and be healthier. He calls it the SPARKS. Within every adolescent there lays dormancy, smoldering and waiting to be ignited by an experience, a relationship, finding a talent or having a moment of profound insight that changes them.

> *We need to help our kids find their sparks. We need to listen closely to what genuinely excites our teenagers. It may start with a passion for the electric guitar, tinkering with a car, shooting hoops or another choice that we might never on our own thought about as a way to ignite our child's inner flame.*
>
> Benson, P. L. PhD, *Sparks: How Parents Can Help Ignite the Hidden Strengths of Teenagers*, (2008).

Dr Benson argues that every teenager has a spark, something inside that is good, beautiful and useful to the world. In a way it's just another way of saying that every child ever born has come with gifts and talents that they need to find and nurture and use in some way to make the world a better place.

Stanford psychologist William Damon believes that one of the most prominent trends of our times is a feeling of emptiness among adolescents and young adults. Maybe this inner spark is attached to our hidden life purpose and it only activates like a beacon when we connect with it. You can tell when an adolescent is connected to their spark because they have lots of energy, enthusiasm and feel driven from within to follow wherever that spark takes them.

I can think of students who were serious long-distance runners, surfers, dancers, painters, footballers and environmental warriors who never needed to be told to go to training or go and do what they loved. I remember one girl who often was caught wagging school to go surfing or skating; she became a world champion surfer. I remember the boy who never had a football out of his hands; he later played in the AFL. I recall a very talented long-distance runner who used to run 12 kilometres to school every morning; he became a national cross country champion and world champion tri-athlete. These former students found their spark while still at school. We have an obligation as parents and teachers to help our confused and unpredictable adolescents find a spark to help them locate a pathway that holds some sense of purpose and meaning for them.

An article written by experienced teachers, Jeanne Shaw and David Bott, links beautifully with Dr Benson's philosophies. They comment on the innovative program 'Teach for Australia', and how to give teachers more expertise to be even more exceptional. They write:

> *The Teach for Australia scheme will have a legitimate place in teacher selection, recruitment and training if it introduces into our schools real teachers who satisfy what we call the 'Seven Rules of Spark'.*
>
> Bott, D. and Shaw, J. 'Bright Spark: The Secret to Great Learning—Teachers with Spark', *Professional Educator*, Vol 8, (2009).

Their Seven Rules of Spark are:

1. It's your job to make the lesson fun—novelty.
2. Think like a kid, not a teacher—relevance.
3. Be friends with your students—relationship.
4. Have a barrier but let kids in—be professional and yet kind.
5. Break rules sometimes—safe responsible connections.
6. Never reprimand a student in front of their friends—respect.
7. Work harder than your student—be committed.

These rules apply to the specialist teachers who work with students in special behavior schools. They also have to have a much higher staff-student ratio so that at-risk students can develop much healthier relationships; the teachers are not only teaching school subjects, they are teaching vital social and emotional skills as well.

In an article in *The West Australian* (Dec 17 2009), the success of a program for behaviourally challenged students was shown by both teachers and students. These special teachers become lighthouses and they change lives positively on so many levels. One student, Connor, said of his teacher: *'She's helped me heaps. She's just like a guardian'.*

Another excellent example of a school that meets the unique needs of it's student *before* meeting the needs of the curriculum are the Toogoolawa schools that have been created by John Fitzgerald. He wanted to do something for the 'lost boys' who somehow cannot manage main stream schooling due to serious behavioural problems. With the help of a passionate clinical psychologist Dr Ron Farmer and his wife Su, they have created a program that allows these lost boys to reclaim themselves. They help them find their own voice of inner knowing by slowing down their worlds and by building genuine caring relationships. They create 'lighthouses' who are their teachers and the ratio of around 1 teacher to 3 boys allows this essential bonding to occur. If only main stream schooling could take notice of two things from John's work. The devastating damage large uncaring schools can do to some students and the potential for healing and true mentorship when relationship is valued and supported. I salute every lighthouse who works with our troubled adolescents – they are more than redeemable! They still have a potential to be exceptional human beings if they want – they just need adults who can see behind those masks and allow them to be heard without judgement and criticism, and then to guide or mentor them to a smoother part opf the bumpy ride to adulthood.

Academic success is not always a true indicator of life success. In my seminar for adolescents I share the following:

What do the following people have in common?

- Ludwig van Beethoven
- Richard Branson
- Kerry Packer
- Winston Churchill
- Charles Darwin
- Thomas Edison
- Albert Einstein
- Isaac Newton
- Louis Pasteur
- Auguste Rodin
- Leo Tolstoy

They were considered failures or having very little ability while at school.

Ludwig Beethoven: Famous German composer whose teacher said he was hopeless.

Richard Branson: Entrepreneur who set up Virgin Blue, and is now a multimillionaire. He is dyslexic and never passed an exam.

Kerry Packer: He became the richest man in Australia. He was dyslexic and saw himself as a 'dodo' at school.

Winston Churchill: Prime Minister of England. He failed his 11+ year.

Charles Darwin: The famous scientist who proposed the theory of natural selection. He was considered to be below the common standard in intellect.

Thomas Edison: He invented many things, including light bulb. His teacher said he was too stupid to learn anything.

Albert Einstein: Nobel Prize winner and discoverer of the Theory of Relativity. He didn't speak until he was four years old, didn't read until he was seven and his teacher described him as 'mentally slow, unsociable, and adrift forever in his foolish dreams'.

Isaac Newton: A mathematician and physicist who discovered the law of gravity. He did very poorly at school.

Louis Pasteur: The famous microbiologist who discovered penicillin, vaccines and the process of pasteurisation. He was a mediocre student rated 15th out of 22 for chemistry.

Auguste Rodin: A famous sculptor who was described as uneducable.

Leo Tolstoy: A famous Russian author who dropped out of college and was described as 'both unable and unwilling to learn.'

School is not always an accurate indicator of success in life or future academic success. If it allows a wide range of experiences and learning on all levels— mind, body, heart and soul—then maybe we can improve on school failure and disengagement.

> *Encoded in our genetic code, just as surely as the colour of our eyes or hair, is a call to greatness, an impulse to experience that part of us which lifts us above the mundane and touches upon the divine.*
>
> Auw, A. PhD, *The Gift of Wounding: Finding Hope and Heart in Challenging Circumstances*, (1999).

In his research, Peter Benson discovered that teenagers found that very few adults outside their families affirmed and nourished their sparks. This is something that exceptional teachers do naturally. They value the three essential ingredients to exceptional teaching: relationship, relationship and relationship.

Violence in our Schools

As I write this chapter a 12 year old student has died from a stabbing in a Brisbane school. Terribly sad and tragic to everyone concerned. This is a media release I wrote in 2009 following the death of a student in a Mullumbimby High School.

Schoolyard death reminder of heat of adolescence

Recent reports of schoolyard violence are a sign that modern adults have in many ways abandoned adolescents, according to parenting author Maggie Dent.

Dent says that while the death of 15-year-old student Jai Morcom in a schoolyard fight was something that could have happened in any school 30 years ago, it is more likely to happen today.

'The chance of violent incidents occurring at school both between students and between staff and students has increased frighteningly," Dent

"We must sit up and take notice of some of the toxic influences of the modern world that are creating serious challenges for our children and adolescents.

"Today's adolescents in our school grounds are more stressed than previous generations. They are often wired by high energy drinks, chronic lack of sleep, self medication, and on top of that feel pressured to look cool, own cool stuff and be forever connected via mobile, email or social networking sites."

Dent says many adults are failing the adolescents in their lives by not monitoring them and protecting them sufficiently from stress and other dangers.

"Many children have both a computer and TV in their bedrooms and that gap in human connectedness is very hard to rebuild when the bumpy ride of adolescence starts," Dent says.

"We can only learn how to be a human being with emotional, social and physical competence through real experiences.

"Young people today are exposed to so much screen life, with increasingly violent TV shows and movies, and competitive games focused on killing and maiming others to win at all costs."

Dent says this 'saturation' can be highly detrimental to the developing brain.

"The brain changes with focused attention, especially in the window of sensitivity of early adolescence, and that is why these forms of aggression and violence can become 'normalised'," she says.

"As a community, we all need to step forward and be present in our children and adolescents' lives knowing that they live with more stress, threats, chaotic change and fewer significant adult allies to walk beside them.

"We need to more closely monitor and guide our adolescents to stress less, eat well, sleep more and avoid energy drinks.

After all, adults are supposed to have a fully functioning brain capable of making mature decisions and protecting those most vulnerable."

The more alienated and disconnected an adolescent feels in any community the higher the chances of violence and destructive behaviour. We must build relationships that are based on genuine caring – and teachers who do this may be reducing the risk of abusive and violent behaviour in their school grounds. Also adolescents need to learn about the patterns of vulnerability that exist while they are adolescents.

> *Research supports the conclusion that if we feel safe, confident, accepted, valued and interested we will learn more rapidly and effectively.*
>
> Jensen, E. *Enriching the Brain,* (2006).

The secret to teaching today's students is to value and respect them as people who matter. We need to turn around our shame-based punitive behaviour management policies because they create havoc in the developing adolescent by adding to their stress and crushing self-doubt and low self-esteem. Creating smaller classes to improve relationship building is a good starting point. As is investing heavily in the student support team by having more youth workers and chaplains who can support struggling students to find safer and healthier ways of navigating the bumpy road to adulthood. A subtle shift towards an inclusive caring culture that recognises the unique risks, especially emotional, social and psychological, of all students would build an environment that feels safer and more caring for students. We need specially trained and enthusiastic support staff who work closely with Indigenous students and those from other cultures to keep them engaged in learning and interacting. Every student has a potential that can be realised if they get the support and encouragement they need during the chaotic years of adolescence.

> *Teach every child with passion, energy, creativity as if he/she would one day become a Mother Theresa, Thomas Edison, Madame Curie, William Shakespeare, Mahatma Ghandi, Nelson Mandela, Sir Edmund Hillary or The Dali Lama.*
>
> Adapted from Prof Kapinski P Frugenburger.

'Educare' is the verb that education comes from; it means to bring forth from within. Modern high-school teaching can do this better, but it needs teachers who are better trained to embrace the digital natives in our classrooms and to unashamedly nurture all levels of the students—not just the brain.

> *We do not believe in ourselves until someone reveals that deep inside of us there's something valuable, worth listening to, worthy of our touch, sacred to our touch. Once we believe in ourselves, we can risk curiosity, wonder, spontaneous delight, or any experience that reveals the human spirit.*
>
> *e. e. cummings*

If we accept that any individual student's development is about the interplay between the person and the environment that nurtures or blocks his or her development, then we must acknowledge that high school is blocking the optimal development of the majority of today's adolescents. To help students thrive and not just survive, they need the 'dynamic interplay of a young person—animated and energised—and others who ensure they discover his or her specialness and the developmental contexts (people, places) that know, affirm, celebrate, encourage and guide its expression' (Benson).

Every single student matters and they have equal worth, even when that may be hard to see. The potential to make the world a better place while living a life of worth and value needs to be our primary aim as educators in today's affluent and soulless world. It is not just about high grades and school rankings, especially if we keep losing more and more students to suicide and mental illness. We must stop kneeling at the altar of high grades over everything else. That means the primary aim of schools negates the collective, cooperative honouring of all: the greater good over the individual competitive good of some. This must change.

Six keys to exceptional teaching by Maggie Dent

1. *Be interesting*

Put yourself in their shoes. Would you be able to stay engaged in your class? Be passionate about your subject; enthusiasm is just as infectious as apathy.

2. *Help students to find their gifts and talents*

Everyone has an innate ability and talents that are waiting to be tapped. Keep looking and use the multiple intelligences as a guide. Support students and strengthen their weaknesses because no one is perfect, no experience is perfect. Teach students there is no such thing as failure and just feedback on what else is needed to be successful, then encourage them to have another go. The only failure is giving up.

3. *Teach them how the brain works*

Knowing what helps their brains to work best and how to 'turn it on' is essential for every student. Explore the power of the unconscious mind and how to 'turn it on' to support learning and growth on all levels.

4. *Practise 'kaizen'*

This is the Japanese art of constant improvement. It's an excellent practice for all exceptional teachers. Keep learning more and specialise in it so you become an 'expert'.

5. *Have the courage to care and connect*

Connectedness is the main key to successful teaching because it is a two-way process. This courage will help you create safe, interesting learning environments so students can take learning risks, as well as learn emotional and social competencies that they need for life. Don't be afraid to use the Five Cs of care, concern, compassion, connection and k(c)indness. Relationship is essential to successfully engage today's adolescents.

6. *Believe in the highest potential for yourself and your students*

Holding high, positive expectations for all students gives them the best chance to realise a potential higher than they can perceive. The power of hope and enthusiasm are as infectious as apathy and negativity. When high intentionality and concentrated focus combine in classrooms, amazingly positive things happen. Know that you exist within a 'morphogenic' field of teachers globally, and that one teacher's success will impact positively on you, and vice versa.

Dare to be Exceptional: Lighting The Flame of Possibility and Keeping it Burning.pdf [online] http://www.maggiedent.com.

Simply choose *exceptional* as your goal as a teacher

When someone asks what you do, rather than reply, 'I am a teacher,' try one of these responses and watch their faces:

- I am a highly skilled social engineer working in the field of human potential ensuring the world becomes a better place.
- I work in the second most important calling on earth: the art of people making.
- I am a global human specialist working with a team of millions, so that humanity can achieve its full capacity on all levels.
- I am a guardian and protector of the most important humanitarian principles, working beside children to ensure they will become healthy, happy and worthwhile members of tomorrow's world.
- I am an advocate and visionary who works alongside today's children ensuring that tomorrow's future will be as wonderful as possible.

It is also time we opened our classrooms for more innovative learning that uses the unconscious mind. Paul Scheele of Learning Strategies Corporation and others who work in the area of peak performance, have much to offer today's educators in terms of ticking the boxes of novel, challenging meaningful learning. Paul revealed a study that showed how an hour lecture, when condensed into 20 minutes, could give similar results of information retention as the full lecture even though the conscious mind could not recognise a single word. He has devised an innovative photo reading process that uses the unconscious and pre-conscious processing abilities of the mind. These cutting-edge learning techniques need to be in our classrooms because they accelerate learning and cognition.

If we could combine these new highly cognitive processes with the transpersonal explored in the hero's journey, I believe we could significantly improve the statistics of student disengagement, and adolescent wounding and emptiness.

Peter Ellyard (2004) in *Learning for success in an emerging planetary society* suggests that elements from 'A Preparation for Adulthood' (a school program) would be excellent to implement. The key elements he believes need to be present are:

- Nurture their own self-esteem.
- Respect others, including parents and elders.
- Initiate, nurture and maintain successful relationships.

- Develop healthy and sustainable lifestyles.
- Become enterprising self-actualising individuals.
- Become leaders of self and then of others.
- Become lifelong, learner-driven learners.
- Create career paths that bring economic and social security.
- Understand that individual rights should be balanced by reciprocal responsibilities and service to others and the community.
- Respect and know how to nurture the environment and other species.
- Respect and tolerate other cultures and religions, particularly Indigenous cultures.

Andrew Lines and his Rite Journey program uses the above as guidelines with which to identify the following five outcomes:

1. Consciousness
2. Connection
3. Communication
4. Challenge
5. Celebration.

The Pathways Foundation also runs programs that embrace similar guidelines and they are making profoundly positive shifts in the lives of adolescents. The list of possible interactive learning opportunities noted earlier in the chapter embrace these same five areas of human growth. So, for those who are unable to attend a program like the ones mentioned above, staff can still offer meaningful experiences that build strengths cognitively, socially, emotionally, physically and spiritually. As adult guardians we must offer more than we currently do and we must not do it in a half-hearted way. Rachel Kessler and her Passageways programs, and the Search Institute in Minneapolis also offer excellent holistic programs that support students while they are still at school.

> *People say that what we're all seeking is meaning in life. I don't think that's what we're really seeking. I think what we're seeking is an experience of being alive, so that our life experiences on the purely physical plane will have resonance within our own innermost being and reality, so that we actually feel the rapture of being alive.*
>
> Joseph Campbell

In my travels, I have seen some fabulous, innovative and exciting things happening in schools, and I have met many committed and dedicated teachers who make a difference everyday. To all of those who turn up to our schools with their hearts on their sleeves and enthusiasm, knowledge and skills in their back pocket: Thank you! So many students tell me: 'If it wasn't for a certain teacher, I don't know what would have happened to me'. *Some of the brightest lighthouses shine from within our school grounds and in our classrooms.*

They Didn't Tell Me

When I arrived at my first school
full of missionary zeal, enthusiasm and
lots of facts and theories about education
I felt I was ready.

Ready to start teaching
to touch the lives of my students
to fill those little sponges with knowledge
to help begin to make a positive
difference in this world.

I was ready to work with my peers
To share ideas, lessons and laughter
Plan the curriculum and help where I could.

But they didn't tell me
I would have students who couldn't read or write
in all my classes,
Students who wouldn't listen or care,
who would swear, spit and be ugly.

They didn't tell me
that parents would confront me,
question my training and my skills,
and tell me how I should teach.

They didn't tell me
Xerox machines could break down
before they became outdated,
that fax machines, computers and iPods would be sent
just to try me and give me stress.

They didn't tell me
that administration tasks would
confuse and frustrate me
that paperwork would swamp me,
that deadlines would overwhelm me.

They didn't tell me
that most of what I had learned at Uni
would be outdated, irrelevant and useless in 10 years
and that I would need to study more to get back
to where I thought I had already been.

They didn't tell me

That 50% of my students would experience divorce,
40% would drink alcohol daily,
25% would be sexually assaulted and
over 40% would consider suicide as a way to solve problems.

They didn't tell me
about PD days that would bore me to bits,
meetings that achieved nothing could takes hours,
and that meetings at night could happen as often as they did.

They didn't tell me
that there would be long hours of marking
that would keep me from my family,
and even longer hours report writing
 at the end of long tiring terms.

They didn't tell me
that there would be times
I would absolutely hate feeling stressed and tired,
and not sure that teaching was what I needed
to be doing anymore.

But I guess it's a good thing they didn't tell me
because maybe I would not have followed my heart,
maybe I would have walked away from one of the most
challenging, rewarding, and wonderful careers
that exists in the world today.

Maggie Dent, 1999.

In my view, teaching is the second most important job in the world after parenting. We need to value it as such and offer remuneration to match the importance that it has in the lives of our children, and especially in our vulnerable adolescents. Adolescents are yearning for teachers who build relationships and, above all else, who genuinely care. Then they want to learn from teachers who have a sense of humour, who are fair and who know their stuff and are passionate about what they teach. That's not too much to ask. Are all these qualities being addressed in our current teacher training? This key bench mark needs to be high to ensure today's adolescents stay at school and get as much education as possible.

Chapter 17

Letting *go:*
The greatest act
of love

The act of leaving home is very symbolic for young adults. It's a time of great excitement and plenty of confusion. Often, the pre-frontal lobe has not yet finished maturing, which means that impulse control is still developing—especially around novelty seeking behaviours, decision making, motivation and delayed gratification. Yet, adolescents are anxious to live independently and pursue their dreams.

When my oldest three sons completed their studies and started working as independent young men, I breathed a sigh of relief. It was a very deep breath in the knowledge that boys are 75 per cent more likely to die from accidents, trauma and suicide than girls.

There were many challenges in their bumpy ride after the safety of home: failed exams, crashed cars, funerals for mates, deaths of cousins, cars vandalised, sporting injuries, knee reconstructions and frequent mismanagement of money. These were life-enhancing experiences because my young men gained wisdom and learned skills, and discovered how to walk through the dark nights of the soul and reclaim life in the sun. There have been many brilliant moments such as shared surfing holidays, endless games of backyard cricket, golf, parties—lots of parties—new friends, falling in love, concerts, football games and graduations.

Each of my boys had to work out their own unique way of managing their lives. My extrovert sons were often pushing the edges of life and had weeks eating boring sandwiches because they spent too much on beer over the weekend. My introvert son needed extra support and encouragement through exam time when he lacked self-confidence; however, he never ate boring sandwiches and never ran out of money. These lessons helped develop their characters and the appreciation of a good salary and a worthwhile job to allow them to enjoy a good life.

The 18–25 years age range is a risky time, if not the riskiest time in a person's life. If your adolescent gets to 25 you can largely breathe a sigh of relief because their chances at survival and success have risen dramatically—this is sad but true.

Letting go of your adolescent happens in two ways. First, we have to let go of each of our children as they cross the threshold to adolescence and start that bumpy ride to adulthood. At this time we wish they could stay children in the sanctuary of our homes away from the harsh reality of the world and that they would keep listening to our good advice. Then, we have to let them go again as they leave home to follow their own path to wherever it may take them.

> *Remember, our children are meant to leave home. Sometimes they boomerang back, and they can sometimes pack you to the rafters.*
>
> Dent M., *Black Duck Wisdom*, (2004).

Allow your offspring to go and live their own lives, not live your lives through their lives

I am the proud Mum of four sons and over the last 28 years I have cooked, cleaned, run around after, laughed with, cried with and worried about these wonderful boys in every permutation possible. When it came time to let them go as they moved to the city to study, my head had told me this would be easy, but my heart did not listen. Every son was hard to let go, and each time it upset me. I pretended to them at times I was fine, and other times I told them I missed them. I saw them and knew they needed space to stand on their own. It was hard. I knew they had to work out how to manage money, food and the rigours of university study without me beside them. It was hard. I wanted to call them so often just to remind them of things or to check how they were going, and I resisted. It was hard. Instead, I looked forward to *their* calls and *their* visits back home.

Letting go is difficult, yet it is the greatest act of love we can give our adolescents. When we let them go as adolescents, at some point we meet them again in a totally different way as adults.

Being a mother—whether biological, step or surrogate—always has its moments and I am sharing this with you to remind you to be grateful for every moment in your child's life while they are still in the family home. Don't waste time nagging and growling, instead, let go and love them more often. Laugh with them and stand beside them as they discover who they are independent of you. Above all, when they choose to leave let them go no matter how much you want to hang on and keep them. It may very well be the hardest and kindest thing you will ever do for them.

Conclusion

In a recent paper published by the National Centre for Vocational Educational Research Professor Richard Sweet wrote of his concerns about the 'lost' 15- to 19-year-old Australian adolescents who leave our schools ill and untrained or prepared for work:

> *'Tens of thousands of teenagers are leaving school ill-equipped for the future, and facing a jobs environment that is hostile to the young.'*

For some reason Australia has always had a high proportion of 'lost' 15- to 19-year-olds compared to other rich countries, high school drop-outs or post Year-12 drifters whose idea of further training is a three-week bar course. Not only have they few skills and academic depth, they have poor personal and social skills which mean they are largely unemployable. This is simply not acceptable in a country of Australia's affluence. These adolescents who leave school for so many reasons—some that I explored in chapter 16, are abandoned in the cracks of our society. Many decide that future education would be a waste of time (based on their previous school experiences) and as they struggle with motivation and ambition due to the biological changes of adolescence, they are at risk on so many levels. This is the by-product of an education system that is only interested in the top 30 per cent the academic strugglers are essentially set up to fail life as well as school. We need to address this urgently. As a nation we need to hang out head in shame—Australia has around 78 per cent of its 15- to 19-year-olds engaged in education or training or apprenticeships. This figure is well below the OECD average of 85 per cent and that 22 per cent represents an unsatisfactorily high number of our sons and daughters.

> *Extended or successive periods without work is not good for young people. It teaches bad habits, induces depression and alienation. Yet Australia tolerates an education system that is unkind and unsuited to low academic achievers.*
>
> Professor Richard Sweet

As the book comes to a close I hope I have been able to give you the reader an improved understanding of the unique concerns and demands of the bumpy road from child to adult. No adolescent is completely safe and competent until that brain finishes its vital growth and development—and even then as adults we still have times when we bugger up and fail, get hurt and make mistakes. We have lost adolescents to accidents and suicide who did have loving families, friends and even lighthouses. The additional stressors and challenges of the Millennial adolescent are real and they need parents first and foremost to do what parents need to do—offer protection and guidance knowing that the dance will be one they will master some days and muck up on other days. Then every adolescent needs lighthouses—significant adults who offer essential support, more guidance and lots of encouragement. Positive relationships are profoundly important to our adolescents–every step along the bumpy road to adulthood and even beyond. Resilience is enhanced by human connectedness that is based on unconditional love, acceptance and respect–and re-building pathways to this emotional, social and biological need is the main challenge of adults today.

Please search for that 'spark' that lies waiting inside every single adolescent–and encourage it and gently nudge it until it can burst into flame. Be mindful of noticing strengths instead of faults as most adolescents are consumed by their flaws and faults and daily battle with a crushing sense of worthlessness. Also remember the hunger and yearning for intimacy, making a worthwhile difference in the world and hope. So much of what they really need cannot be purchased with money or credit or on eBay. It only comes from positive human interaction.

My wish and my prayer is that this book gives adults–parents, teachers and lighthouses–permission to follow their instincts to show **they do care**, and to know that they can change adolescent lives by just the smallest acts of kindness and compassion. If families work together within their communities to create pathways that honour the hero's journey that adolescents must journey to adulthood, we would have less death, depression and despair among our young. We must begin by having the courage to care about our confused adolescents and to know that continuing to abandon them to the impact of the rapidly changing modern world is no longer acceptable.

Finally, we must celebrate the enormous potential of this fascinating stage of life–and enjoy the bumps and bruises–with a good dose of patience, laughter, hugs and very good coffee with other parents who are also dancing the bumpy waltz we called 'adolescence.'

Maggie Dent ©2010

Appendix A

A letter to someone special in my life

I am writing this to show you how valuable you are in my life. Firstly I'm going to list five things I love about you:

1. _____

2. _____

3. _____

4. _____

5. _____

Now I want to tell you about something I'll always remember about you. This is a memory I want you to know that I keep with special memories deep in my heart:

_____

_____

I also want to thank you for:

_____

_____

You really matter in my life and I want you to know that if you ever need a safe person to be a friend or share a heavy load, then think of me—no matter what! There is nothing you can do that will stop me loving you.

Thank you for choosing me as your Mum/Dad/best friend/

And finally:

_____

_____

Yours:

_____

Date:

_____

Appendix B

Draft Letter to Re-Build Connection to Your Adolescent

Dear.....................................

We are writing this letter to open a doorway to re-connect to you in as positive way as possible. We know that, in many ways we have been the worst parents during the last...........months. For this we are sorry.

We weren't prepared for the huge changes that occur as you walk down this bumpy ride to adulthood—you are changing on so many levels to become an adult in the future and we now realise we haven't been helping with that massive, biologically driven change.

We simply did not understand what happens to the brain and the way you see the world and that these changes happen without even you knowing about them! How confusing that must be for you at times.

We can now see how our attempts to help you and protect you have probably made you angry and resentful towards us. We can also see that some of our attempts to help, especially some of our verbal fights, have probably hurt you deeply. We are both really sorry. We were simply doing the best we could—which wasn't much good at all!

We also need you to know how frightened we are. We both worry that you will make more poor choices that may stop you from realising your full potential as a person. We now have more information than we had before and would like you to know that we are going to do some things differently. (You are on a manhood journey and young men often make dumb mistakes—it's what they do afterwards that turns them into good men).

We want you to know that we will do anything to support you as you grow—and that you mean the world to us—regardless of what has happened, or what you think we feel. Yes we have said words that we regret—and if we could take them back we would. For these we are both sorry.

All we want is to walk beside you on this bumpy road—helping you to learn from all your experiences—the good, the bad and the ugly. We will also learn from you at times. As you grow in maturity you will need less of our support and guidance, and hopefully we can just have more good times as a family.

Please remember we have mucked up—and we are both sorry. We were doing the best we could with what we knew and we now have more knowledge and hopefully a better understanding about how life is for you. However, we will do whatever we can to support you, and to make our home a place you always want to come back to. We love you with every fibre of our being and only one day when you are a Dad/Mum will these words make any sense.

We love you.

Mum and Dad

Appendix C

Truth letter

Sometimes we can resolve issues with people by writing an honest letter to them....sometimes we do not even need to give them the letter, but the mere process of acknowledging what troubles you is enough to resolve it inside yourself. It is often better to burn the letter.

Dear.............

I am writing this letter to release my resentment and negative emotions and to discover and express any positive feelings that I might have towards you.

Anger
I don't like...
I feel angry... I hate it when...
I can't stand... I resent...

Hurt
It hurt me when...
I feel hurt that... I feel sad when...
I feel awful about... I feel disappointed about...

Fear
I'm afraid that ... I feel scared when...
I'm afraid ... I get afraid of you when...

Remorse, Regret, Accountability
I'm sorry that ... I didn't mean to...
Please forgive me for... I'm sorry for...

Wants
All I ever wanted... I want...
I want you to... I deserve...

Love, Compassion, Forgiveness, Appreciation
I understand that ... Thank you for...
I appreciate... I forgive you for...
I love you because ... I love you when...

Adapted from 1997 Self Esteem Seminars, Santa Barbara, US with permission from Jack Canfield

Appendix D

Letter when you are worried

Dear……………………….

Please take a few moments to read this letter. I know you think I am always worrying, and I try too hard or I am a try-hard (?) but I am your Mum/Dad and that's part of what parents are meant to do.

Just lately something is different about you and yes I am worried. You haven't smiled for weeks, and you are struggling to get good sleep. You are spending much more time than usual in your bedroom and your friends haven't been around for ages. You really seem down and I am worried.

I have been online and checked out some youth websites and some of these things are listed as being a sign that you may be struggling. There is just so much pressure on you kids these days—and too much stress can make you sick. I also know that you won't want to worry me—and that you might think you will be OK soon—and yet my Mum radar is ringing loud bells.

Can we have a chat? If not me my love, can you please have a chat with some other adult?? If you want to chat to Dr………..I am happy and I will let you go without me if that's what you want. I really want you to let someone listen to you and see if there's anything we can do to help you ride out this bumpy bit.

I have printed off some of the fact sheets and would love it if you could glance through them.

If you really are OK maybe we could just go for coffee, window shopping or a walk on the beach. Massage? Hot bath with bubbles? Swim with dolphins? Holiday in Monaco or Italy?

I am happy if you just write me a note—that will be a great start.

I guess I just want to know—how can I help? Can you please give me three clues on how I can help you at this time?

Remember that adolescence is a time of intense turmoil and confusion and it will one day get better when your brain finishes growing.

I love you with every fibre in my being.

Mum/Dad

Appendix E

Letter to Bring Up the 'S' Topic

Dear...

This is one of those things that parents find really hard to talk about to their kids, especially when you are an adolescent.

I need you to know that at times you get told things by your friends about sex and stuff—and just like when I was an adolescent, not all of it is true. I remember being told that all the girls in our high school had been having sex! I thought this was a fact and I felt a bit like a loser. I spent ages working out who I could have sex with so I wasn't a loser anymore. Luckily my cousins came for a visit and when I told them what had been said—they laughed and said, 'that was rubbish!'

I was so relieved! But I often wonder what would have happened if they hadn't come for a visit.

I am giving you a book about puberty and the physical changes that are happening soon if not now—and I want you to check it out. Then if you have any questions—I hope you will come and ask me and not ask your friends.

We could do it in the dark if it would be easier?

Please remember that having sex is a big step that needs much thought and preparation. I want you to leave it until you are **much older**, and for you to make sure that when it happens it is with someone you have strong feelings for. No not everyone is doing it and don't believe what people tell you! Telling fibs around the topic of sex is common.

Please also remember that alcohol and drugs can make it easy to be taken advantage of—and they can make you do things you may regret.

And always always remember that I will come and collect you from anywhere anytime you don't feel safe—NO MATTER WHAT. And I will do that for any one of your friends as well. No lecture – no cold shoulder—just safety!

Hope this is not too 'cringy' and uncool—this is important stuff and I would like you to know that we CAN have conversations about sex and stuff anytime you want.

Love you heaps, always, Mum/Dad

Appendix F

What is depression?

So how do you distinguish between clinical, 'capital D' depression and the common old blues? For some people, the symptoms are obvious. But others manage to keep up their daily routine, not really knowing what's wrong.

To get a doctor's diagnosis of clinical depression you have to have at least five of the following symptoms, including number one or number two, for at least two weeks:

- Depressed mood (feeling sad or low).

- Loss of interest or pleasure (in activities you normally enjoy).

- Significant appetite or weight loss or gain.

- Insomnia or hypersomnia (sleeping too little or too much).

- Psychomotor agitation or retardation (being restless and jittery, or alternatively, slower than usual).

- Fatigue or loss of energy.

- Feelings of worthlessness or excessive guilt.

- Impaired thinking or concentration; indecisiveness.

- Suicidal thoughts/thoughts of death.

From the Diagnostic and Statistical Manual of mental disorders, 4th ed. (DSM-IV)

Types of depression

Depression affects different people very differently. As a result, many psychiatrists now argue that it is helpful to understand depression not as a whole but as different sub-types. These sub-types can affect not only the symptoms a person has, but the type of treatment that is most likely to be effective. Common sub-types of depression include:

Non-melancholic depression

This is the most common type of depression and is also called 'reactive' depression. It can occur in response to specific life events or it can be the consequence of ongoing life events that may affect someone's self-esteem. Individuals with this type of depression are less likely to report psychotic symptoms—such as hallucinations—and don't tend to suffer symptoms of melancholia—such as extreme lethargy and a complete inability to be cheered up.

Melancholia

This kind of depression is primarily caused by biological factors, although episodes can be triggered by life events. Those suffering this type can display a profound lack of energy along with a significant mood disturbance, psychomotor changes (effecting concentration and movement), extreme lethargy—that is distinctly worse in the morning—and an inability to be cheered up or to respond to positive events.

Psychotic depression

Another type of depression caused by biological factors, this type is dominated by profound mood and movement disturbance together with delusions and hallucinations.

Depressive symptoms can also occur along with other mental disorders, especially bipolar disorder (which involves extreme 'up' moods as well as downs), anxiety and schizophrenia.

Appendix G

EVERYONE NEEDS ...

 Love

 To be heard

 To be understood

 To belong

 Empowerment–choices

 Respect

 Survival Skills

 Fun and laughter...

 Connection to heart and soul

Appendix H

Help for Parents

Lifeline 131 114
www.lifelone.org.au

24 hour telephone services are:
www.moodgym.anu.edu.au
www.beyondblue.org.au

Reach Out website
www.reachout.com.au

www.blackdoginstitue.org.au
www.bluepages.anu.edu.au
www.blueboard.anu.edu.au
www.ecouch.anu.edu.au
www.familiesmatter.org.au
www.headroom.net.au
www.parenthelpline.com.au

For Adolescents

Kids Help Line 1800 55 1800
www.kidshelp.com.au

www.reachout.com.au
www.headspace.org.au
www.reachoutcentral.com.au
www.youthbeyondblue.com
www.moodgym.anu.edu.au
www.oyh.org.au

24 hour telephone services are:
www.moodgym.anu.edu.au
www.resiliencedoughnut.com.au

Bibliography

Aldort, N., *Raising Our Children Raising Ourselves: Transforming parent-child relationships from reaction and struggle to freedom, power and joy: For parents of babies to teens*, Book Publishers Network, USA, 2005.

Auw, A., *The Gift of Wounding: Finding Hope and Heart in Challenging Circumstances*, Aslan Publishing, 1999.

Bahr, N. & Pendergast, D., *The Millennial Adolescent*, ACER Press, Victoria, 2007.

Bainbridge, D., *Teenagers: A Natural History,* Portobello Books, London, UK, 2009.

Bartlett B., Bryer F. & Roebuck D. (eds), Queensland, Griffith University, School of Cognition, Language and Special Education, 2004.

Benson, P., *Sparks: How Parents Can Help Ignite the Hidden Strengths of Teenagers*, Jossey-Bass, USA, 2008.

Bloom, W., *The Endorphin Effect: A breakthrough strategy for holistic health and spiritual wellbeing*, Judy Piatkus Publishers, London, 2001.

Bott, D. and Shaw, J. *'Bright Spark: The Secret to Great Learning—Teachers with Spark', Professional Educator*, Vol 8, (2009).

Borawski, E.A., Levers-Landis, C.E., Lovegreen, L.D. & Trapl, E.S. *'Parental monitoring, negotiated unsupervised time, and parental trust: The role of perceived parenting practices in adolescent health risk behaviors.'* Journal of Adolescent Health, 33, 60-70. (2003).

Brendtro, L., Brokenleg, M & Van Bockern, S. *Reclaiming Youth at Risk: Our Hope for the Future.* Bloomington, IN: National Education Service. (1990) Brooks, K., *Consuming Innocence: Popular Culture and Our Children,* UQP, Queensland, 2008.

Caine, RN and G., *Education on the Edge of Possibility. USA*, Association for Supervision and Curriculum Development. (1997)

Canfield, J., Hansen, M. V. & Unkovich, A., *Chicken Soup for the Soul in the Classroom*, HCI, USA, 2007.

Carr-Gregg, M., *Real Wired Child: What Parents Need to Know About Kids Online*, Penguin, Australia, 2007.

Carr-Gregg, M., *When to Really Worry: Mental health problems in teenagers and what to do about them*, Penguin Books, Australia, 2010.

Corbin, B., *Unleashing The Potential of the Teenage Brain: 10 Powerful Ideas*, Corwin Press, USA, 2008.

Covey, Stephen M.R, *'The Speed of Trust'* USA, (2006)

Currie, M., *Doing Anger Differently: Helping Adolescent Boys*, Melbourne University Press, Australia, 2008.

Dahl, R. E. MD, University of Pittsburgh Medical Center, *Adolescent Brain Development: A Framework for Understanding Unique Vulnerabilities and Opportunities*, [online] www.wccf.org/pdf/dahl/pdf.

Dent, M., *Nurturing Kids' Hearts and Souls: Building Emotional, Social and Spiritual Competence*, Dunsborough, Western Australia, Pennington Publications, 2005.

Dent, M., *Saving Our Children from Our Chaotic World: Teaching Children the Magic of Silence and Stillness,* Pennington Publications, Albany, WA, 2003.

Doidge, Norman, *The Brain that Changes Itself: Stories of Personal Triumph from the Frontiers of Science*, Penguin, USA, 2007.

Donnison, S., 'The Digital Generation, Technology, and Educational Change: An Uncommon Vision', *Education: Weaving research into practice*, vol. 2, pp.22–31.

Durston,S, Hulshoff-Pol, H.E.& Casey, B.J. (2001) *'Anatomical MRI of the Developing Human Brain: What Have We Learned?'* Journal of the American Academy of Child and Adolescent Psychiatry, 40, 1012-1020

Faulder, C., & Graham, C., *Leaving Home: Ready, Set, Go*, Australia, 2008.

Feinstein, S., *Parenting the Teenage Brain: Understanding a Work in Progress*, Rowman & Littlefield Publishers, Maryland, USA, 2007.

Grant, I., Growing Great Boys: 100s of practical strategies for bringing out the best in your son, Random House New Zealand, 2006.

Grille, R., Heart to Heart Parenting: Nurturing your child's emotional intelligence from conception to school age, ABC Books, Aust, 2008.

Hamilton, M., *What's Happening to Our Girls: Too Much, Too Soon: How our kids are overstimulated, oversold and oversexed,* Penguin Group, Australia, 2008.

Hamilton, M., *What Men Don't Talk About*, Penguin Books, Australia, 2006.

Hartley-Brewer, Elizabeth, *Self Esteem for Boys: 100 Tips for Raising Happy, Confident Children,* Vermilion, London, 2000.

Hobbs, A., *Getting Real About Growing Up,* Getting Real Books, Mullumbimby, Australia, 2003.

Irvine, J. *Suicide Becomes Our No.1 Killer of Under 35's-Dr John Irvine Coping with Kids*, ABC Sydney Breakfast with Anne Delaney blog [online] http://blogs.abc.net.au/nsw/2009/11/suicide-becomes-our-no1-killerdr-john-irvine-coping-with-kids.html?program=riverina_breakfast, 2009.

James, M., Anderson, J. & Putt, J., *Missing Persons in Australia Report*, [online] www.aic.gov.au/publications/rpp/86/rpp86.pdf, 2008.

J. Burns (Dr), '*Cyberia or Cytopia*?', Mind Potential conference, Sydney, 2009.

Jensen, E., *Enriching the Brain: How to Maximize Every Learner's Potential*, USA, Jossey-Bass, 2006.

Kessler, R., T*he Soul of Education: Helping Students Find Connection, Compassion and Character at School*, ASCD Publications, USA, 2000.

Kirberger, K., *Teen Love: On Relationships,* Health Communications, Florida, USA, 1999.

Koutsoukis, D., *366 Fun Quotes and Observations on Life*, Funstar Publishing, Western Australia, 2005.

Lashlie, C., *He'll be OK: Growing Gorgeous Boys into Good Men*, Harper Collins, New Zealand, 2005.

Levine, J., *Know Your Parenting Personality: How to Use the Enneagram to Become the Best Parent You Can Be*, John Wiley & Sons, Canada, 2003.

Lipton, B. H. PhD., *The Biology of Belief: Unleashing the Power of Consciousness, Matter & Miracles*, Hay House Australia Pty Ltd, 2008.

McGiven, R. et al., 'Teen Angst Rooted in Busy Brain', *New Scientist: Brain and Cognition*, vol. 50 p. 73, [online] http://www.newscientist.com/article/dn2925-teen-angst-rooted-in-busy-brain.html, 2002.

M. Gradisar (Dr), 'The Lost Hour', *Weekend Australian Magazine*, 2007.

Miller, D., *The Butterfly Effect: A new positive approach to raising happy confident teen girls,* Doubleday, North Sydney, 2009.

Mitchell, M., *What Teenage Girls don't tell their parents*, Australian Acadamic Press, Qld, 2011

Mosley, J. & Tew, M., *Quality Circle Time in the Secondary School: A Handbook of Good Practice*, David Fulton Publishers, 1999.

National Youth Commission, *Australia's Homeless Youth: A Report of the National Youth Commission Inquiry into Youth Homelessness*, Victoria, 2008.

Neville, B., *Educating Psyche: Emotion, Imagination and the Unconscious in Learning*, Flat Chat Press, Melbourne, Vic 2005.

Palmer, H., *The Enneagram: Understanding Your Intimate and Business Relationships,* Harper Collins,1995.

Passmore, D, '*Lifelong Debt Only a Click Away*', *The Sunday Mail*, p.38, 2005.

Pearce, Herb & Brees, Karen, *The Power of the Enneagram: Use the Enneagram to Enrich and Understand Every Aspect of Your Life*, Alpha Books, 2007.

Reivich, K. & Shatte A., *The Resilience Factor: 7 Keys to Finding Your Inner Strength and Overcoming Life's Hurdles*, Broadway Books, USA, 2002.

Robinson, B., *Daughters and their Dads,* MACSIS Publishing, Perth, 2008.

Roy, J., *The 'S' Word: A Boys Guide to Sex, Puberty and Growing Up*, University of Queensland Press, Australia, 2007.

Shandler, S., *Ophelia Speaks: Adolescent Girls Write About Their Search for Self,* Doubleday, Sydney, 2000.

Schwartz, P. & Cappello, D., *Ten Talks Parents Must Have With Their Children about Sex and Character*, Hyperion, New York, 2000.

Ungar, M., *Turning the Me Generation into the We Generation: Raising Kids That Care*, Allen and Unwin, New Zealand

Wagele, E., *The Enneagram of Parenting: The 9 Types of Children and How to Raise them Successfully*, Harper Collins, USA, 1997.

Werner, E. & Smith, R., *Journeys from Childhood to Midlife: Risk, Resilience, and Recovery*, Broadway Books, USA, 2002.

Wilson, C.J., Rickwood, D., Ciarrochi, J. & Deane, F.P., *Adolescent barriers to seeking professional psychological help for personal, emotional and suicidal problems*, Conference Proceedings of the 9th Annual Conference for Suicide Prevention Australia, June 2002, Sydney.

Witt, S., *Teen Talk: Become a Teen with Passion and Purpose*, Collective Wisdom Publications, Australia, 2007.

Witt, S., *Teen Talk: Girl Talk*, Collective Wisdom Publications, Australia, 2008.

Worsley, L. & Alpha Counselling Services, *The Resilience Doughnut: The Secret of Strong Kids*, Lyn Worsley & Alpha Counselling Services, Eastwood, N.S.W., 2006.

Seminars

Maggie Dent offers a range of seminars about adolescence for young people, parents, schools and community groups.

Adolescence Unplugged: Supporting the Bumpy Ride to Adulthood (for Parents and Community Members)
From Maggie's extensive experience of working with adolescents for over more than 30 years she has created an innovative, dynamic seminar for families, schools and communities to build resilience and connectedness for 12-25-year-olds. Adolescents need adult allies to help them navigate the tricky waters of the teenage years–the art of guiding, encouraging empowerment while strengthening self esteem and personal autonomy is one that can be learned. This seminar explores the shift in raising children to raising adolescents, and what works and what won't. (2 hours)

Your Kitbag for Adolescence: Understanding the Bumpy Ride through to Adulthood (for Adolescents)
The journey from child to adult is a bumpy ride for every adolescent and it's pretty confusing. Maggie is committed to helping adolescents better understand what's happening and why, so that they do not end up thinking they are the only dumb, stupid complete failure on the planet. Maggie really knows how it is for adolescents plus she's a crack up at the same time. Often after this seminar adolescents tell their parents to come and listen to what Maggie has to share. This seminar really helps young people feel better about themselves and the bumpy ride. (1.5 or 3 hours) For any number of adolescents–special package offered that includes the Kit Bag CD for every student.

Adolescence Unplugged: Engaging Today's Adolescents in the Classroom (for Teachers)
From Maggie's extensive experience of working with adolescents for over more than 30 years she has created an innovative, dynamic seminar for teachers to show how to build resilience and connectedness for 12-25-year-olds. Adolescents are digital natives and can struggle with engagement. This seminar explores the biological changes and how this influences what happens in the classroom. Maggie will give you insights into innovative ways of keeping them engaged and getting the most out of the high school, TAFE and university years. (2 or 6 hours)

Bringing Out The Best In Adolescents: Innovative Communication and Connections That Support Optimal Growth and Development (for Professionals including teachers, juvenile justice, youth workers and counsellors)
In this seminar Maggie will explore cutting edge techniques that help anyone who works with adolescents. She will explore her lighthouse model in depth and teach many powerful ways of supporting adolescents make positive changes painlessly. This will take your work to an exciting new level of competence. (2 or 6 hours)

OMG! Adolescence is so epic! (for High School Teachers)
This seminar will show how to teach today's adolescents what they need to know about what's really going on in their freaky brains and their bodies. It helps them discover they are 'normal' when they feel confused, dumb, lost and stressed, and how to get a grip. It will include a copy of Maggie's Powerpoint presentation and an extensive guide to teaching this vital information in health in lower school and in upper school as well. (6 hour seminar plus CD with Powerpoint, plus handout)

Resources for Adolescents

Available from www.maggiedent.com

Posters

Available from www.maggiedent.com

Books

Available from www.maggiedent.com